Be(com)ing Human

Semiosis and the Myth of Reason

Andrew Stables
University of Bath, UK

SENSE PUBLISHERS
ROTTERDAM/BOSTON/TAIPEI

A C.I.P. record for this book is available from the Library of Congress.

ISBN: 978-94-6091-995-4 (paperback)
ISBN: 978-94-6091-996-1 (hardback)
ISBN: 978-94-6091-997-8 (e-book)

Published by: Sense Publishers,
P.O. Box 21858,
3001 AW Rotterdam,
The Netherlands
https://www.sensepublishers.com/

Printed on acid-free paper

TABLE OF CONTENTS

Preface vii

Chapter One. Theoretical Foundations: Semiotics, Process and the
  Language Game 1

 1.1 Peirce and the Development of American Semiotics 1
 1.2 Saussure and the Continental Tradition 16
 1.3 Wittgenstein and the Language Game as
  Bridging Concept 27
 1.4 Semiosis as Fundamental Process: Three Further
  Sets of Considerations 35

Chapter Two. Moving in Time: Consciousness and Reason 45

 2.1 Physical Transcendent Presence: The Now and
  Then Dimensions 45
 2.2 Semiosis and (the Myth of?) Reason 55

Chapter Three. Thens Within Now 65

 3.1 Humanity as Aspiration 65
 3.2 From Literacy to Semiosy: Learning as
  Semiosic Development 72
 3.3 What do Schools do? 84

Chapter Four. Be(com)ing Responsible: Humans,
  Others and Ethics 95

 4.1 Towards Human Response-Ability 95
 4.2 Post-Humanist Ethics: Response-Ability
  Beyond the Human 106

Chapter Five. Promoting Human Progress 113

 5.1 Relative Safety? Differing Conceptions of the Good 113
 5.2 On Human Progress: Knowledge, Numbers and Time 120

Notes 125

References 131

PREFACE

Philosophy has long been concerned with what it means to be human, 'being' implying a fixed state. Although Twentieth Century analytic philosophers tended to be uncomfortable with such general questions, works such as John McDowell's *Mind and World* (1996) have begun to bring the issue back into the philosophical mainstream, while in the Continental tradition it was never abandoned.[1] Meanwhile, educational theory is necessarily concerned with what it means to become human, 'becoming' implying a process of growth and change. In general, philosophy of education has married these emphases in a way that is basically Aristotelian, taking the view that childhood (defined as the period during which one is being educated) is preparation for a settled period as adult citizen, during which one's life and role in society is relatively stable, and during which one's human nature is given its full expression.[2] Traditionally, then, first we become human, then we are (fully) human, and, indeed, conceptions such as childhood and human rights are derived from this premise. (The problems this raises for the issue of old age, albeit important, can only be a peripheral concern of the present argument.)

However, the premise is unsound. Childhood is a time of being as well as becoming, and adulthood a time of change as well as stability. Children have relatively fixed identities while adults are relatively insecure in theirs. Of course, not everyone's experience is the same, but throughout life the same paradox emerges: a person retains a sense of who she is in terms of name, history, values and so on, and this changes slowly if at all while nothing ever stops changing, even her physical appearance and capacities.[3] She experiences life that is never still, as if from a point of stillness. There is always a sense of 'now'. This is so throughout life. Indeed, social theory indicates that some of the traditional characteristics of adulthood, such as the settled career and the fixity of judgment and preferences, have become ever less stable in the late modern or postmodern age. Adults are not even more skilled than children in every respect: for example, in terms of general computer literacy.[4] Aristotle's views on the matter remain highly influential but are by no means the last word. At whatever stage in life, human being is human becoming, though not always human improvement. Indeed, the perfect human state is always one of aspiration not present reality. When we speak of ourselves as human, we do so in these two senses: as a present species marker, and as an ideal. Most literature focuses on the former sense; the argument that follows will focus on the latter. What, therefore, should be the grounds for a theory of the individual in society and the world that can best underpin approaches to social policy and education on the assumption that the human animal is always aspiring to fully human status that can never be attained? The work that follows is intended to suggest what those grounds might be and to suggest some of the theoretical frameworks that might logically be inferred from them. Not all of these frameworks will be original: the focus of this book is on premises rather than conclusions, and its aim is to develop a coherent philosophical position from which can be derived criteria applicable to the task of adjudicating between often conflicting positions in educational and social theory.

What, then, should we take for granted about human living? In the chapters that follow, the following arguments will be developed:

- that Cartesian mind-body substance dualism, though generally explicitly rejected, still infects educational and social thinking to an unwarranted degree. It is untenable, so its legacies must be challenged;[5]
- that the world as 'is' cannot therefore be divorced from the world as it means to us as humans;[6]
- that in this process of meaning making, or semiotic engagement, the fundamental ontological state is that of moving process, not of fixed substance. Life is always Now, but is also always in motion. Processes, events and forces are fundamental; matter and substance are the result of processes and events, not *vice versa*. Thus both the human condition and the rest of the universe, as the object of human understanding, are in continuous process. The state of being fully human is always yet to be. Experience is thus our implication in events, none of which achieves our ultimate ends;
- Given such lack of fixities, even species barriers are open to question. The human animal lives as much in relation to non-human entities as to other humans. Even within the human family, the non-rational actor poses a problem to fixed conceptions of human nature. In important respects, the problem of the infant is the problem of the animal, the foetus, the criminal, the demented, and perhaps even the slave, the ignorant and the foreigner; some feminists might even add of the woman.[7] Legal, moral and political conceptions of human rights are both drawn from, and help to shape, our treatment of those who occupy this liminal state between the standard human and the non-, or not yet, or not quite human, and such conceptions serve to validate definitions of the human itself.

None of these positions is new in itself. However, the present argument is the most comprehensive attempt to date to ground educational and social theory in this set of assumptions. The first section of the book will be concerned with justification of the position; the remainder of the work will explore its implications: for social and educational philosophy (Chapter 2); for understanding human development in relation to learning theory and educational intervention (Ch. 3); for ethics in terms of human responsibility, for other humans and for non-humans (Ch.4), and for the regulative ideal of progress (Ch. 5). The arguments will overlap and cross-refer. *Inter alia*, their development draws on several philosophical schools that are often considered distinct: the Peircean and Continental schools of philosophical semiotics; the Wittgensteinian response to analytic philosophy; process philosophy; posthumanism and general philosophical pragmatism.

The argument draws on the author's recent work on living as semiotic engagement.[8] Semiotics, understood as philosophy and not merely as method, can provide a non-judgmental theory of the subject as active rather than passive, applied and pathologised. The semiotic subject is a continual meaning maker and interpreter, yet not the autonomous rational agent of classical liberalism, for the semiotic subject is always relational and simultaneously constrained and empowered by the availability of shared semiotic resources.[9] Human beings can thus be understood as discrete and creative while also connected and co-operative, not because they started as 'free' individuals who gave up part of their freedom under the terms of a social contract, but because, as perceiving agents, the part that each plays within the whole is distinct. At the same time, both part and whole are not fixed entities but rather ongoing processes so both individual experience and social context are continuously 'new', 'different' and interrelated.

The merging of American pragmatist and Continental influences (Peirce, Dewey; Saussure, Derrida) into a 'fully semiotic' nascent educational theory (using 'educational' in a very broad sense) continues a research programme that is still in process and that will inform the argument developed in these pages.[10] The latter entails both drawing on and critiquing Peirce as the father of modern semiotics, while engaging with other major philosophical figures, among them Whitehead (for his account of process), Derrida (for the conception of '*différance*'), Dewey (for his attempt to undermine mind-body dualism) and McDowell (for his attempt to reconcile the uniqueness of human rationality with law-driven 'first' nature). The aim is an account of 'what it means to be human' that has objective, or intersubjective value though is grounded in subjective experience, and that is able to account (in broad terms) for both human collectivity and individual difference in terms of overlapping phenomenal worlds. Equally importantly, it will offer new insights into the human-nonhuman distinction, with the attendant consequences for environmental ethics. In short, the argument to be developed will offer a new account of what it means to become (and thus to 'be') human in a more-than-human world, and this account will have clear ethical implications for our dealings with others and with the nonhuman world. The argument will seek to move explanations of human being and action (which in turn steer social and educational policies) from positing the individual as 'applied subject' (such as bearer of social class and alienation under Marxism, of upbringing and psychological repression under Freud, or of rational yet constrained choice under classical economics) to conceiving of the person as 'active subject': not as purely autonomous rational agent (as in pure classical liberalism) but as worthy of respect as always interpreting and uniquely contextually positioned while always relational. It will be possible to construe the argument as semiotic, given the broadest possible definition of the sign; at the same time, its scope will extend beyond that of the existing body of work on social and educational semiotics, where the sign is normally construed more narrowly. The major concern of the present work is to provide a philosophical sound framework for thinking about the person as aspirational human rather than to insist on that framework being construed as the development of one particular tradition.

A commitment to meaning making as semiosis does, however, suffuse the argument. The difference between citizen and criminal, or between perceived understanding and ignorance, lies in how people respond to situations and this is informed and constrained, but not determined, by historical and geographical context. The position taken will thus bridge the unhelpful divide between a view of people as freestanding rationalities and, on the other hand, as determined automata. It may well be that a 'God's-eye view' would allow us to see all human life as determined, as it would be able to account for all contexts and their effects on all preconceptions – but as such a view will always be beyond us, regarding people as determined may well be the very worst basis on which to promote social policy. The book will therefore propose a sort of posthumanist liberalism, arguing passionately for the upholding of the feeling or fiction of freedom in relation to human affairs while valorizing the interdependence of all life.

More specifically, the work will examine human experience as semiotic engagement in an eternal Now, in which meaning is always deferred, conceived as the Physical Transcendent Present (PTP). It will thus offer an account of human being that is at the same time an account of human growth, development and change, and consider the implications of this account for education and social policy. Life is not divided into two successive stages: 'becoming' as a child and 'being' as an adult. On dualist accounts, experiential presence (my feeling of being here now) coincides with metaphysical absence (the I that is here now is not material or observable). Such accounts set meaning against its referents. On a non-substance dualist account a more satisfactory paradox is that which pits stability against change. There are some 'certainties' that we have to hold on to amidst endless change. 'Who I am' is one such certainty; 'who we are' is another. Paradoxically, it is this 'knowledge' that both creates the possibility of new knowledge and simultaneously prevents or constrains it: that is, only by sticking to some of our assumptions, even prejudices, do we have a framework for making sense of new experiences. Such a realization of the limits of human understanding is often absent from educational theory, though it is a recurrent, if not universal, concern within the empiricist and liberal traditions, finding expression, *inter alia*, in Hume's 'sceptical doubts' in Section 4 of the *Enquiry Concerning Human Understanding* (Hume, 1975) and in the work of the economic philosopher Frederick von Hayek (Kukathas, 1989).

If an account of human living is to inform social practices, such as education, law and welfare, it must nevertheless not be reductive: that is, it must not only be able to work by over-simplifying the human condition, in terms either of individual experience or social context. Rather, such an account should be grounded in the richness of human experience rather than in partial theories about the human condition. Those offered by, for example, Marx, Freud and classical economics are all partial in this sense. The reductiveness of these models does not lie merely with their assumptions about the inflexibility of human nature and individual orientations, but also applies to the context in which human nature operates: that is, 'society', for particularly in a globalised, virtually networked world, there are no closed social systems, and each person's network of relationships is increasingly complex, overlapping with others' yet unique to themselves. It is certainly misleading simply to equate 'society' with the nation state. Rather than seeing each person as a stable representative of a stable society, to make sense of human living, we should start with where human living makes sense: with my (and your) sense of being alive, now.

One implication of this is that human beings may not be alone as perceiving agents. Such an explanation would be limited if it were to assume that the specialness of humanity renders people as entirely qualitatively distinct from other species. This is not to argue that educational theory should be applied to animals, but rather that, in a more general sense, human action is both instrumentally dependent on the non-human and morally bound to consider the interests of non-human perceiving agents. It will be argued that all sentient beings as having a 'then dimension' (Chapters 2.1, 4.2) that enables them to make sense of currently perceived events as somehow sequential and predictable; after all, this is a survival imperative. It is also a logical inference from pragmatism, though one little explored in the philosophical literature; the line to be taken is therefore also posthumanist and pragmatic in particular senses that will be articulated as the argument develops. It will be Cartesian insofar as it is grounded in subjective experience, but *contra* Descartes, it will not accept that one's account of oneself necessitates having a mind of different substance from the body and of a sort only found in humans; rather, as in the later traditions of Darwin and Dewey, the phenomenal world must be non-substance dualist, with a further acceptance of overlapping (though not complete coincidence) between the phenomenal worlds of people and, particularly, animals. Recent developments in neuroscience have made it easier to recognize human thought as physical. The question remains, however, as to whether it is viable to create an account of what it means to be human that is naturalistic but not reductive (for even some phenomenological accounts 'bracket out' significant aspects of human experience) and that amounts to any more than irrational, or arational subjectivism. After Descartes, it remains a significant challenge to combine idealist and empiricist ontologies, but philosophical semiotics does offer a real opportunity to do this. Peirce began such a journey (Chapter 1.1), and John Dewey continued it, in relation to educational and social theory, though it will be argued that Dewey did not go far enough in embracing semiosis as foundational (Chapter 1.1; Stables, 2008b).

Taking the elements together, therefore, the argument is developed that all life proceeds as response to signs and signals (though the specific signs to which humans respond are, generally, unique to humans). Such an account might be construed as post-humanist liberal pragmatism. It is post-humanist in that it extends respect for the phenomenal worlds of all people to at least a minimal respect for the phenomenal worlds of all sentient beings, as well as an appreciation of the dependence of the human on the non-human (and *vice versa*); animals, for example, are not the 'mere animals' of John McDowell's *Mind and World* any more than the brutish automata conceived by Descartes. It is liberal not in the classical sense of believing that persons have autonomous rational souls but in the more guarded belief that no individual can have a God's-eye view that justifies stipulating what is best for others, and thus that the fiction, or feeling, of freedom is an important fiction or feeling for social policy to recognize and maintain. It is pragmatic in that it fails to acknowledge a gap between what is and what is meant and thus recognizes the touchstone of all judgments to be their impacts on the phenomenal worlds of individuals; as things are their effects (after Peirce[11]), it is the 'then dimension' in each sentient being's perception that allows that being to survive and, through survival in ever-changing contexts, to adapt.[12] Each being lives in a physical transcendent present, in which a sense of 'now', stillness and identity effectively transcends, or rather affords continuity to, change. While the book thereby offers a philosophical investigation principally into what it means to be human, thus attempting to forge a non-reductive, naturalistic account that can inform social policy and practice in ways that are as democratic and empowering as possible, it also recognizes humans as players in a much larger experiential network.

THEORETICAL FOUNDATIONS: SEMIOTICS, PROCESS AND THE LANGUAGE GAME

1.1 PEIRCE AND THE DEVELOPMENT OF AMERICAN SEMIOTICS

The aim of this book is to develop a philosophically sound theory to explain human being as becoming, not just in childhood but throughout the lifespan. A key component in this is a philosophically sound understanding of living as *semiosis*, as perpetual interaction with signs and signals where the response to a sign or signal is also a sign or signal. The first three chapters are devoted to a critical exegesis of the philosophical resources available for the construction of such a theory. They are, in turn, C.S.Peirce and American pragmatism, Continental semiotics as derived from Saussurean linguistics and developed through structuralism and poststructuralism, and Wittgenstein's 'language game' critique of analytic philosophy (Wittgenstein, 1967). Chapter 1.4 introduces other contributing perspectives, including that of process metaphysics, which itself draws on Peircean semiotics and pragmatism.

Contemporary semiotics comes in many forms, each grounded in certain philosophical assumptions, though often tacitly. In film and media studies, semiotics offers a broader scope and range of critical resources than conventional art or literary criticism,[13] and workers in the fields of visual literacy and multi-modal text analysis have also deployed these critical resources in educational studies. For example, Günther Kress has looked at children's writing development and the semiotics of textbooks as part of a larger project concerning the relative roles of the visual and the verbal in young people's sense making, and how this has been changing (Kress, 1997, 2003; with van Leeuwen, 1996). Social semiotics as a form of sociolinguistics owes much to the work of Michael Halliday (1978) and has been given a more socially critical, political edge in the Critical Discourse Analysis of Norman Fairclough (1995).[14] European social semiotics is heavily influenced by the analytical strategies of Greimas (1989), which have been applied to issues of education and human development by, among others, Cortazzi (1993) and Pikkarainen (2010). Work in biosemiotics and ecosemiotics draws on the biologist Jacob van Uexküll and his concept of the *Umwelt* as the meaningful environment.[15] (For example: a blade of grass might be a food item to a cow but a pathway to an ant). Each of these employs but does not question certain philosophical assumptions.

Contemporary semioticians tend to be chiefly influenced by one of the first two traditions above, either the American or the Continental, though the history of semiotics since the early 1900s reveals many overlaps. For example, one of the most influential centres of semiotic studies is Tartu in Estonia, yet leading names in the field associated with developments at Tartu have roots in the American tradition. Thomas Sebeok (1920-2001), who did much to develop the branches of semiotics that deal with non-human life in semiotic terms (zoösemiotics, biosemiotics and, most recently, ecosemiotics) was a pupil of Charles Morris who, in turn studied under George Herbert Mead, a colleague of John Dewey, who effectively developed Peircean semiotics as educational theory, at Chicago. John Deely, whose *Basics of Semiotics* (1990) is a standard textbook for those interested in a truly philosophical account of semiosis and the sign, has close connections with Tartu yet is explicit in his embracing of Peirce and rejection of Saussure and the Continentals. Indeed, many serious philosophers working on semiotics are inclined towards embracing Peirce and rejecting Saussure and his followers.[16] There is a *prima facie* case for this insofar as Peirce was a philosopher while Saussure was not, and commentators in the American tradition are satisfied that Peirce's nascent semiotics offers the only philosophically sound basis on which to proceed. I shall argue, however, that while such extrapolations from Peirce are valid, Peirce's foundational thinking is not necessarily more philosophically convincing than that developed after Saussure, particularly in the poststructuralism of Derrida, and that each tradition has something to offer to a theory of being as becoming. Meanwhile, certain Continental poststructuralists, such as Deleuze, acknowledge influences from Peirce (Bogue, 1983).

My own view is that Peirce's conceptions of *semiosis* and of the sign amount to necessary but not sufficient conditions of the development of a fully convincing semiotic theory. Such a theory can benefit from the specifically Continental concerns with language and meaning as difference and from Wittgenstein's warnings against language as 'bewitchment' from the more sceptical analytic tradition (Wittgenstein, 1967: §109). While owing a great deal to Peirce, I shall point to a certain essentialism in his conception of the sign, a complacency in his conception of the object and a naïve assumption of progressivism as limiting factors. All this notwithstanding, however, Peirce's contribution to the development of philosophical semiotics has been very great.

Peirce is widely accepted as the first philosopher of modern times to engage with issues of semiosis and the sign. (Peirce, who called his own emerging theory *Semeiotic*, was often self-consciously idiosyncratic in his use of English. However, the same might be said of Jacques Derrida's use of French: see Chapter 1.2). The word 'semiotics' derives from the Greek *semeion* (sign) and thus *semeiotikos* (interpreter of signs). A general, if occasional, recognition of the importance of 'signs' of various sorts, and of their interpretation, permeates the history of Western philosophy; Plato warned against being misled by the evidence of one's senses. For example, in the Myth of the Cave (written c.390BCE), Plato likens people who trust what they see around them to prisoners trapped in a cave who mistake the shadows cast by the firelight on the cave wall for the reality that lies beyond.[17] Aristotle (384-322BCE), however, was an empiricist who regarded observed phenomena as signs of a deeper order. St. Augustine (354-430CE) considered the evidence of his senses as divine signs (Markus, 1957). In *An Essay Concerning Human*

Understanding (1690), Locke went as far as to describe the third branch of knowledge – that which enables the active linkage between the nature of things and human rationality and action - as the doctrine of signs, though Locke did not develop this branch of science in his own writing:

> All that can fall within the compass of human understanding, being either, first, the nature of things, as they are in themselves, their relations, and their manner of operation: or, secondly, that which man himself ought to do, as a rational and voluntary agent, for the attainment of any end, especially happiness: or, thirdly, the ways and means whereby the knowledge of both the one and the other of these is attained and communicated; I think science may be divided properly into these three sorts. (Locke, 1690: Bk.4, Ch.21, $1).

Aristotle's father was a physician, and it is with medicine that semiotics arguably shares its longest history, insofar as the medical conception of the 'symptom' is, literally, a conception of the sign. The *sym-* in the Greek *symptoma* may be connected to the *sem-* in *semeion*, either way, the symptom, like the sign generally, is something that stands for something else, and forms part of a system of such signs that reveals the truth of an underlying condition. On this basis both medical science and semiotics are built.

Modern developments in semiotics owe most to two strongly contrasting figures, Charles Sanders Peirce (1839-1914) and Ferdinand de Saussure (1857-1913). However, tracing the heritage of the discipline between the ancients and these modern figures is by no means easy. Locke, as we have seen, used the term 'sign' but did not develop his use of it. John Deely (1990) identifies a group of Iberian philosophers who can also be regarded as influential. Firstly, Dominicus Soto 'introduce[d] into the Iberian milieu (1529, 1554) an *ad hoc* series of distinctions effectively conveying the objection to the linkage of signs as such ... to the sensible vehicle of the sign.' (Deely, 1990: 111). In pursuing these issues, Deely identifies John Poinsot (1632) as the most progressive figure:

> Poinsot ... was able to provide semiotics with a unified object conveying the action of signs both in nature virtually and in experience actually, as at work at all three of the analytically distinguishable levels of conscious life (sensation, perception, intellection). By this same stroke he was able to reconcile in the univocity of the object signified the profound difference between what is or what is not either present in experience either here and now or present in physical nature at all. (Deely, 1990: 112-113).

Unfortunately, on Deely's account, Poinsot's work was marginalized under the dominant influence of Descartes' subjective rationalism, which separates thought from sense experience, partly because his writing about signs formed only a small part of a long work on Aristotle. Ironically, Poinsot published this major work in the year that Locke was born.

3

Charles Sanders Peirce was an American mathematician and philosopher of science, whose general run of interests places him at a far remove from most thinkers associated with the humanities, under which umbrella semiotics commonly appears as a discipline. The son of an eminent mathematician, Benjamin Peirce, Charles spent much of his professional life as a surveyor. Despite studying Schiller and Kant as a young man and being increasingly influenced by Hegel (and, indeed, by non-philosophical evolutionists such as Darwin), he refers little to other philosophers and was certainly detached from contemporary movements in European thought in the 1800s. He appeared, for example, to be uninfluenced by his contemporary, Nietzsche, who has been a great influence on Continental philosophy as it relates to semiotics. (See Chapter 1.2). Ferdinand de Saussure, another seminal figure in the Continental tradition who will also be discussed in the following chapter, was a linguist whose work has nevertheless exerted a significant influence on movements in philosophy and across the social sciences, including structuralism and poststructuralism. Though contrasting in approach, scope and style, and seemingly ignorant one of the other (though Peirce somewhat precedes Saussure), Peirce and Saussure are each critical influences on semiotics as philosophy. Peirce offered a comprehensive logical scheme which has been largely followed and interpreted by more recent figures including John Deely (1990). Conversely, Saussure was a linguist whose insights about language and, by extension, other human sign systems, were extended into the social sciences and philosophy by a range of important figures in first the structuralist, and then the poststructuralist schools. Jacques Derrida and Gilles Deleuze, for example, make philosophical claims arising from Saussure but beyond the scope of the latter's argument; Peirce's influence, meanwhile, is unquestionably philosophical, and commentators including Deely and Eco (1986) stress its philosophical comprehensiveness in contrast, on their accounts, to Saussure's dyadic conception of the sign.

Peirce started with logic and mathematics and strove to understand language, art and human interest generally as part of the same logical system as mathematics and science. The diffuse, and sometimes scrappy, nature of his published work, coupled with some idiosyncrasy and tortuousness of expression, render Peirce a difficult writer to come to terms with. It is not surprising that interpretations of his thought, and of its influence, are diverse and not always consistent. However, recent compendia of his output are beginning to make it easier for the newcomer to Peirce studies (Houser *et al*, 1998; Peirce, 2000). However, although Peirce began, and arguably remained, primarily a philosopher of science, there is strong evidence that, as his career developed, he became increasingly aware of the ubiquity of what might be understood as sense-making processes throughout nature. Although his own term *semeiotic* features only rarely (though the sign is a recurrent concern), there is a strong case for regarding his intellectual trajectory as leading towards a fully, or foundationally semiotic position. Houser, for example, is in no doubt of the importance of semiosis in Peirce's later thinking, arguing:

At least by 1907, Peirce would recognise that the end of semiosis of the highest kind is an intellectual habit, which realization may lead us to wonder whether the third basic element that is active in the universe, habit-taking, is a form of semiosis, and if that is what imparts the teleological current that Peirce finds in evolution. (Houser, in Peirce, 2000: lxxxiii-iv).

This is, indeed, an insight of the greatest importance to the development of semiotics as philosophy, since it both grounds meaning in physical activity and gives semiosis a role in influencing the physical, thus positing the semiotic as part of nature and not a gloss on it. There is much evidence in Peirce's writings of a grand ambition along these lines, though it was never to be fulfilled. In the final letter of a series to Lady Victoria Welby (herself a strong promoter of 'significs' as a related development: Petrilli and Deely, 2010), written at the end of his life when he had little money and no academic position, and which remained unfinished owing to his poor health, he states he 'will do my best to send you in two months – or better say three - the first part of the book I so want to write.' (Peirce, 1966: 431). There are good reasons to believe that this projected work would be ambitious. However, its failure to appear is symptomatic of the problem of evaluating Peirce. He set many hares running, but it has been left to subsequent commentators to chart their possible courses.

However, although Peirce's writings about semiosis may have been left undeveloped, he did write a great deal about the sign and, despite considerable variations on the theme, stuck through most of his career to a tripartite division of the components of the sign that has been taken as the basis of his semiotic thinking by subsequent semioticians up to Deely and his contemporaries. According to Atkin:

For Peirce, developing a thoroughgoing theory of signs was a central philosophical and intellectual preoccupation. The importance of semiotic for Peirce is wide ranging. As he himself said, "[...] it has never been in my power to study anything, — mathematics, ethics, metaphysics, gravitation thermodynamics, optics, chemistry, comparative anatomy, astronomy, psychology, phonetics, economics, the history of science, whist, men and women, wine, metrology, except as a study of semiotic". (Atkin, 2010: introduction).

Atkin offers an overview of Peirce's development in his thinking about the sign, showing how his thinking is based on a triadic conception of Sign as Representamen, Object and Interpretant, though his definitions of these varied somewhat and in his later work so many kinds of sign are proposed that the triadic scheme that continues to underpin the taxonomy appears to lose its prominence. A standard definition of the sign offered by Peirce himself is:

CHAPTER 1

> I define a sign as anything which is so determined by something else, called its Object, and so determines an effect upon a person, which effect I call its Interpretant, that the later is thereby mediately determined by the former. (Houser, 1998: 478).

This is about as clear as Peirce's definitions become. Note that both the Object (which may be construed as psychological, conceptual or physical, but which must be assumed to be actual) and the Interpretant (which is what the sign means, and not what a person means by it; it is not an interpreter) are logical abstractions insofar as neither is directly empirically verifiable; it is only the Sign as Representamen (e.g. the word 'fire') for which this can be claimed. One can be burnt, certainly, but this does not clarify the nature of the Object in Peircean terms. Note also that the Sign on this account can be 'anything': in the context of language, therefore, it could be a word, phrase, sentence, or whole argument. On this account, we can understand an Object as, for example, fire, its sign-as-representamen as smoke (or flame) and its interpretant as, for example, something hot and dangerous, such that we respond to fire with extreme caution and use it in certain highly constrained contexts, thus contributing to an endless process of semiosis, whereby actions are undertaken as responses to environmental stimuli that are themselves symptomatic of objective realities. Fire, sometimes humanly made, changes the world in terms of both its biochemistry and its significance. Peirce here moves beyond Kant's distinction between the *noumenon*, the thing in itself[18] prior to our understanding of it, and the *phenomenon*, the thing as humanly perceived and understood. Peirce's ontology here is simultaneously realist, progressive and interpretive. On Kant's account, there is no discernible connection between the perceived and the underlying actual; on Peirce's, there is: we react as we do to the smoke because it is a symptom of fire and our reactions help to move the world along.

An early account of the sign appears in 1867, when Peirce was in his late 20s (Peirce, 1868: particularly $9). Here, Peirce gives an account much similar to the above. A sign, or representation as it appears in this early essay, comprises a sign-vehicle, an object, and an interpretant. The interpretant will then function as a more developed sign of the object in question.

> And of course, as a further sign, it will also signify that object through some features, which again, we must interpret, and generate a further interpretant. As will be obvious, this leads to an infinite chain of signs. If any sign must generate an interpretant in order to be a sign, and any sign is itself the interpretant of some further sign, then clearly, there must be an infinity of signs both proceeding and preceding from any given instance of signification. Some scholars ... think that infinite semiosis is a characteristic only of Peirce's early account. Others ... treat infinite semiosis as present in all of Peirce's accounts. (Atkin, 2010:$2, retrieved from http://www.seop.leeds.ac.uk/entries/peirce-semiotics/, 22 November 2011).

Interpretants can relate to objects in, again, three ways. An *icon* or likeness shares a quality: a photograph is an iconic image, for example (though Peirce, as a logician, should not be held to mean that an icon is always visual). An *index* has a factual relation to the object, perhaps of cause and effect: Peirce cites the weathercock. A *symbol* manifests a merely conventional or general connection, such as between a flag and a country. While logically these concepts are distinct, at the level of exemplification they can be hard to disentangle. One consequence of this is a certain bifurcation among those who consider the sign as a means for learning, with some committed Perceians claiming that all learning is undertaken through icons[19] while other commentators remain committed to a belief in the foundational status of symbols in human learning.[20] Comparing these accounts, it is often possible to substitute 'icon' for 'symbol' and *vice versa*,[21] notwithstanding that any developed Peircean account must remain true to Peirce's overall schema.

As Peirce developed, his conception of the sign underwent certain modifications. In the earlier expressions, signs are often synonymous with thoughts. While this may lead rather to a narrowing than a broadening of semiosis (the latter being Peirce's subsequent direction), it is clear from the beginning that semiosis is potentially infinite: that is, that the triggering of further interpretants is potentially endless.

By 1903, when he gave a series of lectures on the matter at Harvard (Peirce, ed. Turrisi, 1997), Peirce had both refined and complicated his scheme, though without undermining its triadic foundation. Now a long series of signs could be defined under the general headings of *qualisigns* (signifying in virtue of qualities), *sinsigns* (signifying in terms of existential facts) and *legisigns* (signifying in terms of conventions and laws). The same qualitative, existential and physical, and conventional and law-like conditions define how objects generate their interpretants, so this more elaborate scheme can be understood as a development of the earlier triad of *icon, index* and *symbol.* However, he was beginning to acknowledge that these can overlap, with conventional features affecting icons, for example. Thus a larger set of subdivisions of the sign was generated. Finally, on this revised account, a new triad purported to explain how a sign generates an Interpretant with respect to its Object. Thus when we understand a sign in terms of qualities it suggests its object may have, we generate an interpretant that qualifies its sign as a *rheme.* An example could be 'dog'. If a sign determines an interpretant *via* the existential features it employs in signifying an object, then the sign is a *dicent.* Atkin (2010) uses the example of 'Fido is a dog', reminding us that Peirce's signs, as 'thoughts', need not be limited to single words. Lastly, if a sign determines an interpretant *via* conventional or law-like features, it is a *delome.* A sign is of this sort when it serves to help us see something in terms of a rational argument or rule-governed system. Throughout all this, the underlying commitment to Firstness, Secondness and Thirdness, to which we turn below, is maintained.

A matter of debate concerning Peirce is the degree to which his thinking should be seen as progressivist, and the implications of this. He certainly associated semiosis strongly to scientific development, particularly in his later writings, where the concept of infinite semiosis is superseded by a movement from the Immediate to the Dynamical Object. The dynamism here implied is towards more perfect understanding, with semiosis construed as evolution of understanding itself, as Peirce explained in a letter to William James in 1909:

> The [Dynamic] Interpretant is whatever interpretation any mind actually makes of a sign. [...] The Final Interpretant does not consist in the way in which any mind does act but in the way in which every mind would act. That is, it consists in a truth which might be expressed in a conditional proposition of this type: "If so and so were to happen to any mind this sign would determine that mind to such and such conduct." [...] The Immediate Interpretant consists in the Quality of the Impression that a sign is fit to produce, not to any actual reaction. [...] [I]f there be any fourth kind of Interpretant on the same footing as those three, there must be a dreadful rupture of my mental retina, for I can't see it at all. (Houser, 1998: 499-500).

This is one of several ways in which Peirce's thinking can be understood as building on Hegel's. Hegel has been taken up political thinkers from both Right and Left, including the extremes. The degree to which Peirce's conception of an evolving phenomenal world might be so used and abused remains a matter of debate.

Taken together, these innovations produce further extended taxonomy of sign types in a letter to Lady Welby in 1908.

Peirce's theory of the sign, and concomitantly of semiosis, is thus developed over many years. It is comprehensive, methodical and highly progressivist. It leads towards absolute and collective understanding and is thus quite at odds with the thoroughgoing relativism of, for example, the poststructuralists. (See Chapter 1.2). For example, in relation to Kuhn's theory of scientific revolutions (Kuhn, 1996), it takes no account of the possibility of theoretical misconceptions within normal science taking the world a considerable distance in what will come to be seen as the wrong direction before a scientific revolution radically revises the discourse (as happened with increasingly sophisticated models of the Earth-centred cosmos before Copernicus, for example) and it takes no account of cultural or individual interpretive variations. Applying Peirce's progressivism in a multicultural context could raise problems that he does not consider.

While Peirce's scheme was developed over the years, it nevertheless continued to depend on an underlying and largely unchanging set of foundational assumptions about Firstness, Secondness and Thirdness. As the critical commentator Burch has expressed it:

> Merely to say that Peirce was extremely fond of placing things into groups of three, of trichotomies, and of triadic relations, would fail miserably to do justice to the overwhelming obtrusiveness in his philosophy of the number three. Indeed, he made the most fundamental

categories of all "things" of any sort whatsoever the categories of "Firstness," "Secondness," and "Thirdness," and he often described "things" as being "firsts" or "seconds" or "thirds." For example, with regard to the trichotomy "possibility," "actuality," and "necessity," possibility he called a first, actuality he called a second, and necessity he called a third. Again: quality was a first, fact was a second, and habit (or rule or law) was a third. Again: entity was a first, relation was a second, and representation was a third. Again: rheme (by which Peirce meant a relation of arbitrary adicity or arity) was a first, proposition was a second, and argument was a third. The list goes on and on. Let us refer to Peirce's penchant for describing things in terms of trichotomies and triadic relations as Peirce's "triadism."

If Peirce had a general rationale for his triadism, Peirce scholars have not yet made it abundantly clear what this rationale might be. He seemed to base his triadism on what he called "phaneroscopy," by which word he meant the mere observation of phenomenal appearances. He regularly commented that the phenomena just *do* fall into three groups and that they just *do* display irreducibly triadic relations. (Burch, 2010: $9).

In the 1880s, Peirce wrote two pieces in which he began to extend his thinking to the operation of the universe as a whole. In *A Guess At The Riddle* (1887-8: in Peirce, 2000: 165-210) and in *Trichotomic* (1888: Peirce, 2000: 211-215), Peirce gives a metaphysical explanation of Firstness, Secondness and Thirdness, the triadic account underpinning that of the sign as Representamen, Object and Interpretant that he would revisit, sometimes with modifications, throughout the remainder of his career. In these two works, Peirce applies this to various forms of human enterprise, including psychology. In the first chapter of *A Guess At The Riddle*, he states his ambition (in a form not dissimilar to that used in the letter to Lady Welby two decades later) as: 'to outline a theory so comprehensive that, for a long time to come, the entire work of human reason ... shall appear as the filling up of its details ... [A theory that would offer] simple concepts applicable to each subject.' (Peirce, 2000: 168-169). It remains the case, however, that the theory, notwithstanding its ambition, is not testable[22]: it is an explanatory scheme that is at the same time the Peircean's article of faith. Burch expresses clearly why some commentators remain to be convinced.

Peirce's triadic scheme is not explained with total consistency, and is not empirically verifiable. Nevertheless, it has provided an analytical framework for much of modern semiotics. It can be summarised as follows: Firstness is that which is immediate, characterised by qualities (such as colour: the degree to which Peirce intended something much the same as Hume's or Locke's sense impressions is not entirely clear), Secondness that which is 'Another, Relation, Compulsion, Effect, Dependence, Independence' and the like (Peirce, 2000: 170-171), and Thirdness 'that which bridges over the chasm between the absolute first and last and brings them into relationship' (172) such that Thirdness is always contextual and never absolute. Now, whatever the ultimate validity of this scheme, it allows for Peirce to develop the view that what had been taken as universal physical laws might, in fact, be no more or less than 'habits', and that this habit-taking might explain all activity in the universe from the purely physical to the meaning-making activities of human beings. This is self-evidently an insight of great potential significance. Peirce, it could be argued, was remarkably prescient in foreseeing the subsequent switch in scientific emphasis from certainty to probability, a move to be prompted by early investigations into quantum physics and denied even by Einstein in his famous retort that 'God doesn't play dice'. While Peirce denied arbitrariness, he did foresee later scientists' acknowledgment that physical laws are not immutable (2000: 191), but that chance, and thereafter 'habit' must play their part, and thus that 'Approximation must be the fabric out of which our philosophy has to be built.' (2000: 205). The apparent discovery in September 2011 of particles that can travel slightly faster than light might have come as no surprise to Peirce, who may well have argued that the speed of light would prove to be approximate and not absolutely constant. However, on the Peircean account, approximation is not synonymous with arbitrariness.

Peirce, therefore, offers the genesis of a pansemiotic theory as a necessary corollary of his pragmatism (or 'pragmaticism', as he chose to term it). However, it remains one in which habits, or Interpretants (the meanings of signs) have an existence separate from the human beings who interpret them, are therefore fairly static over the short or medium term, and, furthermore, are progressing towards a state of ultimate understanding. Although Peirce acknowledged contextuality, he did not go as far as some more recent thinkers whose primary concern has been with language and other clearly communicative systems rather than with logical processes, and he effectively locates contextual difference within an overall project of unitary progression. Peirce's interest was in understanding signs rather than people, interpretants rather than interpreters, and he was not much interested in diversity among human meaning-making. Insofar as he was, he would see such diversity as, at best, separate paths towards the same end state. He resisted relativism. In effect, he not only reifies but teleologises the Interpretant: he sees interpretation strongly as working towards some final end. In the final decade of his life and work, he stated one of his interests as being 'the science of the essential conditions under which a sign may determine an interpretant sign of itself and of whatever it signifies, or may, as a sign, bring about a physical result' (Peirce, 1904: 326), as though such conditions might ever be identifiable as essential under any kind of universal scheme. Such a universalistic ambition was not shared by those in the Saussurean tradition, as will be illustrated in the next chapter.

Before moving on to that alternative semiotic tradition, however, some remarks are due about the effects of Peirce's work on the American pragmatic tradition generally, particularly as that tradition has been under renewed scrutiny in recent years following increased military activity in the Middle East. After all, as a pragmatist (or 'pragmaticist', as he called himself, possibly to make clear his differences with his contemporary William James), Peirce himself believed that 'things' (a word he himself was happy to use) could only be judged by their effects. Indeed, in his 1878 essay, *How To Make Our Ideas Clear*, he provides what is often used as the standard definition of pragmatism:

> Consider what effects, that might conceivably have practical bearings, we conceive the object of our conception to have. Then, our conception of these effects is the whole of our conception of the object. (Peirce, 1878, retrieved from http://www.peirce.org/writings/p119.html, 13 October 2011).

The connection between pragmatism and semiotics – the study of signs – is self-evident in Peirce's thinking here. Things are their effects upon us; we might rephrase this as 'things are what they mean to us'. In Peirce's strongly realist pragmaticism, however 'what they mean to us' arises from innate qualities at the level of Firstness.

Historical evaluation of a philosopher's work is both inevitable and full of danger. It is, as Peirce would have acknowledged, a matter of interpretation. However, as this book is centrally concerned with human actions and policies, in education and other areas of social life, the perceived effects of Peirce's semiotics are the basis on which he must be judged. In terms of his immediate legacy, therefore, the next few paragraphs will consider the work of John Dewey in developing the pragmatic project, while the concluding paragraphs of this chapter will consider more broadly Peirce's legacy in relation to the American pragmatic influence in the contemporary world. The consequences of Peirce's extreme progressivism will be the focus of critique in this final section of the chapter.

Regarding theories of education and social and personal development, John Dewey is by far Peirce's most influential heir. To some extent, their work overlaps (as each overlaps with that of the other seminal American pragmatist, William James: 1842-1910). Dewey published his first significant work on learning theory, *The Reflex Arc Concept in Psychology* (hereafter, *RAC*) in 1896, the influential *My Pedagogic Creed* (*MPC*) in 1897 and other work on education before Peirce's death in 1910, including *The Child and The Curriculum* (*CC*: 1902, in Dewey, 1959). Dewey's first major extended philosophical statement, *Democracy and Education* (*DE*) was published in 1916. In many respects, Dewey can be seen as taking forward Peirce's progressive pragmatism.

Unlike Peirce, Dewey is not concerned primarily with semiosis and signs. It will be argued below that this is a potential weakness. Dewey's philosophy is nevertheless like Peirce's in being strongly naturalistic, evolutionary and avowedly non-dualist. That is, Dewey saw the human being as an integrated organism. In a later work, *Experience and EN Nature*, 1925, he coined the term 'body-mind' as an anti-Cartesian response to the mind-body dualism that has tended to bedevil learning theory by pitting cognitivist against behaviourist approaches. Cognitivist approaches focus on altering understanding as a means of altering action; behaviourist approaches consider the body to be a machine that responds in predictable manner to external stimuli so can be trained to respond positively if it receives positive feedback, such as rewards. In the context of tennis coaching, for example, a cognitivist approach might focus primarily on tennis as a 'mental game', and a behaviourist approach on reinforcement of technical skill through working on the dynamics of stroke-making. Dewey, though he did not write about tennis, may well have pointed out that effective coaching must involve playing the game against real opposition, since the most effective learning involves undertaking real-world tasks in social contexts and with significant consequences for the individuals involved. Dewey first developed this 'conative' approach in *RAC*, where he argues that a stimulus is never pure, or raw, but is always responded to by a creature that is habitual in its responses, and thus forms part of an ongoing feedback loop such that stimuli are to some extent responses and responses are stimuli. This has a strong resonance with Peirce's theory of initially infinite, then progressive semiosis:

> …what is wanted is that sensory stimulus, central connections and motor responses shall be viewed, not as separate and complete entities in themselves, but as divisions of labor, function factors, within the concrete whole, now designated as the reflex arc ... From this point of view the discovery of the stimulus is the "response" to possible movement as "stimulus". We must have an anticipatory sensation, an image of the movements that may occur, together with their respective values, before attention will go to the seeing ... (Dewey, 1896: 2,7).

Much unlike Peirce, Dewey was a man of the world, and his thinking had a direct and enduring effect on education and the social science emerging from the Chicago school at the turn of the Twentieth Century. He was a significant voice in the debates around ensuring social progress in the unique racial melting pots of cities such as Chicago and New York. As a professor of education as well as philosophy, and as head of the first education department in a major university, Dewey would have a major influence on US schooling, even running his own experimental school in Chicago from 1896 to 1904. Given this, it is noteworthy how strident and confident some of his initial pronouncements about education now sound:

> Through education, society can formulate its own purposes [and] organize its own means and resources and can thus shape itself with definiteness and economy. (*PC*:V).

This is not to accuse Dewey of a general naivety in his philosophy of education, but of an initial overenthusiasm for the potential of schooling which, though moderated by Dewey himself in other, particularly later writings, may well have been partly responsible for the partial perceived failures of both his own experimental school and the progressive education movement which, though inspired by him, he eschewed for much of his later career. By the time he published *The School and Society* (*SS*, 1915), he is much less committed to the distinctiveness of the formal learning context ('Learning? – certainly, but living primarily, and learning through and in relation to this living.'). (Dewey, 1915/1944: 36) and *DE*, arguably the most influential of all his works, is a densely argued development of the idea that social democratic development and education are inseparable concepts:

> ... all communication, and hence all social life, is educative (Dewey, 1916: 5).

There are obvious connections between Dewey's progressive pragmatism and Peirce's semiotic pragmaticism. Although Dewey soon realised that his early educational vision may have been Utopian, he is as wedded as the later Peirce to the belief that communicative social action (as Dewey construed it; semiosis for Peirce) was socially evolutionary. While Peirce emphasised semiosis, Dewey emphasised democratic action as rational social progression. For both, mutual problem solving creates not merely difference and diversity but progression towards an absolutely and objectively better world.

It could be argued, however, that Dewey's relative failure to consider semiosis directly prevented him from realising just how arbitrary interpretation can seem, given that the concatenation of circumstances that helps to determine a particular contextualised response to a sign can never be fully anticipated (Stables, 2008). It can also be argued that both Dewey and Peirce were blinded by the progressivist and positivist inclinations towards the limitations of their own positions, and that in both cases this is due in part to a lack of concern with language and other semiotic systems as meaning-making engines in practice: a concern that was beginning to be addressed in European thought by, among others, Ferdinand de Saussure, who is one of the major concerns of the following chapter.

Peirce's lack of inclination towards issues of language and human interaction is revealed in a comment to Lady Welby, in a letter to whom in 1908 he used the term 'person' in stating that a sign '... determines an effect upon a person', adding, 'My insertion of "upon a person" is a sop to Cerberus, because I despair of making my broader conception understood' (Peirce, 1966: 404). To Peirce interpretation can and should be studied somewhat abstractly from persons: arguably as with many philosophers in the Platonic tradition, considerations of humanity are subsumed within considerations of rationality according to Peirce, on whose account deduction, induction and abduction become forces of nature. (Many philosophers in this tradition would shy at speaking on behalf of the universe as Peirce begins to do: Hegel may have been happy to do this, but Kant would not, for example.) Of course, Peirce's thinking could not have developed as it did if he had been tied to issues of human interaction; furthermore, this orientation does not commit Peirce to a Cartesian or Newtonian view of the universe as mechanical and purely law-driven. However, Peirce showed little interest in, and may have been as little impressed as some of his followers, by the emerging Continental tradition in thinking about the sign as an extension of thinking about language. It is clear that Peirce retained his mathematical, as opposed to linguistic, bias to the end, writing in his last, unfinished letter to Lady Welby, that he 'will do [his] best to send you in two months – or better say three - the first part of the book I so want to write.' Furthermore, 'This part deals with the kinds and degrees of assurance that the different kinds of reasoning afford....I mean strictly logical differences. For instance, in the theory of numbers...' (1966: 431)

Recent disciples of Peirce are justified in asserting that his contribution would have been impossible if he had been tied to language. However, I shall argue in the next chapter that this does not amount to an argument that his triadic metaphyics offers firmer ground for philosophically sound semiotics than the dyadic model derived from the non-philosopher Saussure.

In Dewey's case, there is a clear inconsistency in his thinking about language. Dewey rejects mind-body dualism more explicitly than Peirce, yet retains an unexamined view of humans as symbolic language users. Consider the following from *EN*:

> Animals respond to certain stimuli ... Let us call this class the signalling reflexes ... Sub-human animals thus behave in ways which have no direct consequences of utility to the behaving animal ... Signaling acts evidently form the basic material of language ... [but] ... The hen's activity is ego-centric; that of the human being is participative. The latter puts himself at the standpoint of a situation in which two parties share ... The characteristic thing about B's understanding of A's movement and sounds is that he responds to the thing from the standpoint of A ... To understand is to participate together, it is to make a cross-reference which, when acted upon, brings about a partaking in a common, inclusive undertaking ... The heart of language is not "expression" of something antecedent, much less expression of antecedent thought. It is communication; the establishment of co-operation in activity in which there are partners ... Primarily meaning is intent. (Dewey, 1925: 147-149).

Dewey views 'symbols' as 'condensed substitutes of actual things and events' (1925: 71). Note that this does not coincide with Peirce, who regarded Icons as directly sharing characteristics of their objects while symbols were determined by law or convention. Dewey does not therefore have communicative activity grounded all the way down in sign systems, as would, for example, poststructuralist perspectives (given considerable latitude in the use of 'systems'). Perhaps as a legacy of the mind-body dualism he sought to escape, Dewey's system relies on an absolute qualitative difference between humans and other species that allows the former to engage in meaningful action which, while a response to some underlying reality, exploits language and other communicative tools without being dependent upon them. In this, he appears to replace the classical liberal belief in autonomous rational agency with one of collective rational agency. Whence this agency originates, other than as some mysterious force of nature, remains unclear, though it can be understood as a basically Peircean position, notwithstanding their differences. To Dewey, action invests meaning in language, but language remains somehow secondary to action. This might be interpreted as consistent with Peirce's views of infinite, then progressive semiosis, or as stepping back a little to a position in which language is merely a means of action or vehicle for action rather than fully-fledged action in itself, albeit as part of a broader nexus of action. Consider also the following in this regard. On the one hand:

> ..the supposed original faculties of observation, recollection, willing, thinking etc. are purely mythological. There are no such ready-made powers waiting to be exercised and thereby trained. (Dewey, 1916: 62).

and in *URE*, at the very end of his career, he berates the progressive education movement (largely owing its existence to him) for confusing ideas with 'inherent essences' (In Dworkin, 1959: 133).

On the other:

> It is a reasonable belief that there would be no such thing as "consciousness" if events did not have a phase of brute and unconditioned "isness," of being just what they irreducibly are. (Dewey, 1925: 74).

To Dewey, therefore, as to Peirce, semiotic activity arises from pre-semiotic brute nature. This is indeed non-dualist on the Peircean account insofar as it prioritises the Interpretant, the evolving sign, over the Interpreter, the (rational) human being, thus potentially seeing all entities as subject to semiosis, and not *vice versa*. However, it retains a form of dualism, between innate qualities at the level of Firstness and signification at the level of Thirdness, *via* relation at the level of Secondness. Unlike Peirce, however, Dewey's primary concern is with the messy world of human communication, with Interpreters as much as Interpretants, and Dewey retains a belief in the specialness of human communication. Dewey's semiotics is, in effect, anthroposemiotics, not the emergent pansemiotics associated with Peirce.

I have argued elsewhere that it would have been a logical step for Dewey as philosopher of body-mind to have problematized the sign-signal distinction, as, on a dualist account, signs are generally taken as the consciously controlled responses and utterances of minded humans whereas signals can operate unconsciously in non-minded physical nature (at the level of Secondness merely, in Peirce's terms). Had he done so, his philosophy of education, and thus of social development, might have looked quite different.[23] The crux of the argument is as follows, however: both Peirce and Dewey are too one-dimensionally progressive in their thinking, and too optimistic about human meaning making tending towards ultimate solutions to social problems that are in everyone's best interests. Each was insufficiently sensitive to cultural and interpretative difference, and to the possibility that collectively, people and societies may follow blind alleys in their shared beliefs, as the late Medieval scientists did in their increasingly sophisticated attempts to shore up the model of the Earth-centred cosmos. The Interpretant is, after all, an abstraction; empirically verifiable interpretations require interpreters, whose interpretive frameworks overlap rather than coincide. At least, that is the more strongly relativist account to which we shall next turn in considering the Continental semiotic, or semiological tradition.[24] Is it merely fanciful to see a Peircean ghost haunting American attitudes to world affairs in more recent times: for example, in the belief that a recognisable path of social development resulting in Western-style democracy is not merely the only form of social development worth realising (cf. Dewey's *DE*), but that this is so strongly the certainly the case that it justifies military action and the destabilisation of states perceived as rogue to achieve it? This may be positivist thinking, but it has been construed by many as dangerously so. Just as interpretations of Hegel by Romantic German nationalists and revolutionary Marxists resulted in arrogant assumptions about progress and power that may well have appalled Hegel, so the evolving world spirit of Peirce's semiosis towards the Final Interpretant might be regarded as, at best, naïve, and at worst, dangerous, as a means of conducting world affairs. If the potential of semiotics to pursue world peace lies in the epistemological primacy of the sign over the referent (that is to say, in acknowledging the fundamental appreciation that the sign 'God' evokes different responses to be more important than assuming that the entity who determines such responses demands a certain kind of response), then that potential demands a more thoroughgoing relativism for its fulfilment than the Peircean tradition may offer. That, at least, is the argument associated with some in the Continental semiotic, or semiological tradition to which we now turn.

1.2 SAUSSURE AND THE CONTINENTAL TRADITION

There is often a tension between proponents of the Anglo-American and Continental philosophical traditions.[25] In terms of thinking about the sign, semiosis and semiotics, there is a clear divide between the direct heirs of Peirce and those whose semiotic roots lie in the Continental tradition.[26] This divide has two main features. First, while the Peircean conception of the sign is basically triadic (Chapter 1.1), the Saussurean sign is dyadic, while the poststructuralists reject even this dualism, with Derrida construing semiosis as the 'freeplay' of signifiers (Derrida, 1978). Secondly, in the Peircean tradition, signs have meanings in their own right as Interpretants, whereas in the Saussurean tradition (broadly, from Saussure to Derrida), the meaning of a sign depends solely on its relation to other signs and is thus, in Derrida's terms, always a matter of *différance* (Derrida, 1978). Peirce's metaphysics may therefore be described as logocentric and strongly realist, while Derrida's is a metaphysics of difference, or absence, and is strongly relativist, though not necessarily anti-realist. To committed Peirceans, however, poststructuralists such as Derrida are merely heirs to an unproblematized dualism that separates language from the rest of reality (e.g. Deely, 1990).

Philosophy of education is one of the philosophical domains where there is some tolerance of work crossing this inter-continental disciplinary divide. Where such a crossing is possible, it often draws on one of the key concepts in the later work of Ludwig Wittgenstein, that of the 'language game' (Wittgenstein, 1967). Most notably, the postmodern philosopher, Jean-François Lyotard, has drawn on the concept in works such as *Le Différend* (Lyotard, 1988). Chapter 1.3 will consider Wittgenstein's concept and Lyotard's appropriation of it in terms of its possible contribution to a fully semiotic theory for education, the humanities and the social sciences.

Modern Continental semiotics begins effectively with the work of the Swiss linguist, Ferdinand de Saussure (Saussure 1974).[27] Immediately an issue is raised for many: Saussure was not a philosopher. However, tolerance of the philosophical contributions of non-philosophers, in the strict sense, is a feature much more of the Continental than Anglo-American traditions: Freud is an important case of a theorist whose work has had significant influence on philosophers outside the Analytic tradition. Saussure's work has similarly influenced many who are, if sometimes grudgingly, accepted as philosophers. Philosophical rigour is not, however, dependent on job titles. The argument under development here rests on the case that there is no more, and arguably less, philosophical justification for Peirce's triadic conception of the sign than for the initially dyadic, but ultimately unquantifiable conception developed from Saussure through structuralism and poststructuralism. Peirce tacitly accepted, through characterising a sign as a thought, that the sign cannot validly be quantified; nor, by extension therefore, can its elements.

Saussure's defining work is his *Course in General Linguistics* (Saussure, 1974), effectively a collection of lecture notes.[28] Arguably as with Peirce, there is no succinct statement of his philosophy of language. However, unlike Peirce (for whom the job would be more difficult to undertake), there is an excellent standard summary of Saussure's thought written by Jonathan Culler (Culler, 1976).

The central features of Saussure's philosophy of language are his overall conception of language, his distinction between deep structure and surface utterance, his distinction between Signifier and Signified, and his concern with meaning as relational.

Intuitively, it is common to regard language as either a mirror or a vehicle: as either reflecting reality (words for things) or conveying it (as in the teacher conveying information through language). On both these unexamined accounts, language is merely parasitic on reality. Saussure, unlike Peirce, is not particularly interested in metaphysics, but he is clear that language is a socially constructed system of signs. Words, like other signs, convey meanings to people in cultural contexts that are culturally determined, and the relationship of a culture to any reality external to it is never callable if the only means of understanding that reality comprises sign systems such as language. Note that already clear water is being drawn between this tradition and Peirce's progressivism and pragmatic scientific realism. Linguistic variation for Saussure is not necessarily progressive; rather, the relationships between elements of a language system appear arbitrary.[29]

Saussure was not a thoroughgoing linguistic relativist, however. He did assume a hidden machinery, but its operations are limited to language; unlike Peirce, Saussure does not venture into speculations about how the universe operates as a whole. It is on this basis that commentators such as Deely draw a distinction between Peircean 'semiotics' and Saussurean 'semiology'. Ironically, given the Analytic-Continental divide, Saussure might be seen as more Kantian in this respect, Peirce as more Hegelian. Peirce assumes that processes of human meaning making can be extended to account for the workings of nature, at least potentially, whereas Saussure assumes that processes of human thought can only explain human life at the phenomenal and not the noumenal level: that any direct knowledge of things-in-themselves is therefore closed off. Saussure does assume, however, that the seemingly infinite variety of linguistic and, by extension, other communicative acts that we experience must constitute a surface manifestation of language, but that language must be driven at a deeper level by a set of operating instructions that are fixed and potentially understandable. Saussure referred to language at the surface level of utterance as *parole* and employed the terms *langue* and *langage* for languages and the concept of language itself in the abstract. This broad distinction would have significant effects on the development of linguistics and theories of language development if not on philosophy *per se*. Notably, Chomsky would develop his theory of universal grammar on a very similar set of assumptions about the deep and surface nature of language, even though Chomsky was critical of Saussure's *langue* in his later work (Chomsky, 1955, 1972). In the specifically Continental, largely Francophile tradition, this element of Saussure's thinking would influence the development of structuralism and then poststructuralism, as will be discussed below. However, Saussure's legacy is much broader than this. For an author who was not a philosopher, and who did not even publish the material in the *Course in General Linguistics* in his lifetime, Saussure had a remarkable influence on Twentieth Century thought. In contrast to Peirce, who developed his own conceptions of the sign and semiosis at great length, and in a highly individual, even idiosyncratic, and often quite difficult way, Saussure is a more accessible iconic figure around whom many debates have evolved. In short, his work is incomplete, easily refutable in certain respects from a number of expert perspectives, yet has proved immensely fruitful.

In general, Saussure was not at first regarded as an important a figure in the Anglophone world, where philosophers experimenting with logical positivism and the development of analytics more broadly were little interested in the musings of a linguist who had no interest in their debates, and who, in any case, was interested in language as prior rather than expressive of the world, and who controversially construed the relationship of signifier to signified as arbitrary (a view that even Derrida would later take issue with) and affirmed boldly that 'in a language there are only differences without positive terms' (Saussure, 1974: 120). In Britain, C. K. Ogden and I. A. Richards, who were interested in the psychology of meaning and literary response, did engage with Saussure to a limited degree, though only to dismiss him as an anti-realist:

> Unfortunately this [Saussurean] theory of signs, by neglecting entirely the things for which signs stand, was from the beginning cut off from any contact with scientific methods of verification. (Ogden and Richards, 1923: 8).

This brute and, frankly, anti-intellectual rejection of the relativism that Saussure implies has unfortunately been widespread in Anglophone culture and continues to the present day. The objection, though rarely considered by such detractors, could hardly be simpler or more obvious. How can one take account of 'the things for which signs stand' other than through signs? (Note that mathematics is a sign system, as are the forms of formal logic). Indeed, how can one do anything other than assume them? Peirce is unable to address these objections, though he does construct an explanation – and interpretation, in fact - of how semiosis might be implicated in objective physical reality, such that the distinction between signs and what they stand for is eliminated, although this account requires conceptions of Firstness and the Object that lie beyond direct empirical verification. Any evidence we could bring forth for Firstness or Secondness would be at the level of Thirdness; any evidence for Object or Interpretant is *via* the Representamen. Scientific methods of verification require empirical evidence, which is more easily available of a Signifier or a Signified (someone's interpretation of a Signifier) than it is of several of Peirce's key terms. The fact that Peirce's model purports to explain reality as a whole does not guarantee its verifiability. Saussure did not develop his thesis philosophically but he did raise a serious philosophical issue that surely deserves better than such rejection. Irrespective of the validity of Ogden and Richards' view, however, Saussure remained a generally insignificant figure in the largely English and American traditions of the past century, either disregarded or viewed with mild opprobrium as the instigator of 'Continental' anti-progressive relativism and postmodernism.

Saussure received rather more generous treatment in the early 1900s from linguists – though, again, not philosophers – in the United States. Leonard Bloomfield reviewed the *Course* favourably in 1924 and also praised Saussure in works published in 1921 and 1927 (Falk, in Sanders, 2004). However, Falk argues that American linguists had already become interested in descriptions of the current state of a language (Saussure's 'synchronic' analysis) before encountering Saussure, and that beyond Bloomfield's general approval, there was little American interest in Saussure prior to the Second World War.

That such interest increased thereafter is the result of European migration to the US: in this case, the arrival of the Russian Roman Jakobson, one of the co-founders of the Liguistic Circle of Prague, in New York in 1941. Although

Jakobson was critical of much of Saussure's work, including the construal of the sign as arbitrary and the Saussurean conception of *langue*, he referred to Saussure frequently throughout his professional life and gave an entire lecture series on Saussure's linguistic theory in New York in 1942 (Jakobson, 1971-1985). In general, the Russian formalists went further than Saussure in shifting the linguistic from the diachronic, historical and philological towards an enhanced model of the synchronic, descriptive and analytic that incorporates the historical. Hutchings (in Sanders, 2004: 150) cites Jakobson on what he regarded as Saussure's confusion of the synchronic with the static: for example, when we see things, we often see them in movement.

The critical interest in Saussure was maintained by those in the Russian school who wished to move beyond formalism, most notably by Bakhtin and his circle in 1920s Russia (e.g. Voloshinov, 1973. Note that the authorship here is disputed). Here again, Saussure is a central critical target, particularly in relation to his concept of *langue*, which is taken as representing a spurious objectivism. Bakhtin took the example of the novel and showed how it could be understood as a *heteroglossia*, a multiplicity of voices, without recourse to any hidden deep structure. Beyond the novel, Bakhtinian notions could explain ideologies and broader cultural movements in a more empirically satisfying way than Saussure, a way that accounted for the individual in the social context as Saussure's crude *langue-parole* distinction could not remotely achieve. Ultimately, Saussure's direct heirs, the poststructuralists, would also do away with this particular form of dualist account.

Perhaps unsurprisingly, it is in the Francophone tradition that Saussure has been most warmly received and most widely influential, and where he has been taken most seriously by philosophers as well as theorists of language. Saussure was an inspiration for the development of structuralism, and relatedly French semiotics as semiology (Saussure's original term). He also influenced French phenomenology and psychology. The poststructuralists, including Lyotard and Derrida,[30] would draw on all these influences in radicalising a philosophy of difference that Saussure inaugurated though he would presumably scarcely recognise. The discussion here will focus on the taking up of Saussure by those beyond linguistics.

It was in the 1940s that the anthropologist Claude Lévi-Strauss and the German philosopher Ernst Cassirer began using the term 'Structuralism' in a general sense, i.e. beyond structural linguistics. Lévi-Strauss lauded linguistics as a developed science that had much to teach the other social sciences, and found structural linguistics influential in his own studies of kinship systems (Lévi-Strauss, 1969). Put simply, Lévi-Strauss was in the vanguard of those who exploited Saussure's partly explicit realisation that semiology could deal with sign systems well beyond the narrowly linguistic, but that linguistics of itself had something to offer to the study of such systems.

The phenomenological philosopher Maurice Merleau-Ponty was interested in Saussure's work on the relationality as well as the structure of language. He found Saussure useful in developing his own understanding of the work of the pioneering phenomenolgist, Edmund Husserl. Merleau-Ponty wrote:

> Structure ... enables us to understand how we are in a sort of circuit with the socio-historical world ... the philosopher it interests is not the one who wants to explain or construct the world, but the one who seeks to deepen our insertion in being. (Merleau-Ponty, 1964: 123).

Given the trenchant rejections of Saussure's relativism from other quarters, it is interesting to note Merleau-Ponty's interest in him as potentially deepening understanding of lived reality.

The psycho-analyst Jacques Lacan is another important promoter of the broader application of Saussure's insights. From the 1950s, Lacan developed an elaborate and influential theoretical framework on the basis that language simultaneously reveals and conflicts with the unconscious, while the unconscious is somehow semiotic, or structured like a language, in its own right. For example, when I see myself in a mirror, this conflicts with what I know about myself, and both these conflict with my pre-conscious drives. Thus what I am is always in conflict (Lacan, 2006). Like many theories in the social sciences (Marx's, for example) Lacan's ideas may be scientifically verifiable but are not easily open to attempts at falsification, as the philosopher Karl Popper would wish a truly scientific theory to be (Popper, 1959). That is, if one accepts Lacan's account, evidence can be found for it, but acceptance is ultimately a matter of faith. However, this is equally true, *inter alia*, of Peirce's Firstness, and thus his triadic conception of the sign. It was equally true of Freud. Whatever the level of one's commitment to Lacan as psychologist, his work opened up two areas of extrapolation from Saussure, each of which would have profound implications for the development of Francophone philosophy. The first is that the signifier is of greater importance than the signified; the second is that meaning is always deferred: that is, identity is never fixed but always suggestive, elusive and conflicted.

The final important strand of French thought in the middle 1900s owing to Saussure is the semiology of Roland Barthes. Although some (e.g. Mounin, 1970) have criticised Barthes for taking from Saussure in a not very scholarly and even capricious way, there is no doubt of the former's debt to Saussure's semiology. A detailed account of this is provided by Ungar and McGraw (1989). In texts including *Mythology* (1972, first published 1957), Barthes dealt with certain contemporary French 'myths', including a strip-tease, a wrestling match and a car advertisement, in the manner of literary texts. In his well-known essay, *The Death of the Author*, he further problematized matters by fundamentally questioning the role of the author in creation of the text (Barthes, 1977). In short, Barthes, for all the potential weaknesses of his argument, seriously challenges assumptions about the scope and boundary of textuality, another issue that would be developed further in the writings of Derrida and the poststructuralists.

From the 1960s onwards, Continental philosophy took its most radical turn away from the Anglo-American tradition, resulting in the set of positions collectively referred to as poststructuralism:

> For the semiotic generation of the 1960s, the interface with Saussure's ideas was not in the form of textual erudition and exegesis. It was rather in the context of an overarching epistemological framework in which Saussure occupied the unquestioned position of the founding father to whom regular homage was rendered. (Bouissac, in Sanders, 2004: 247).

Key figures in this group, including Barthes and Greimas (Greimas, 1989), were Saussure's heirs rather than his direct progeny: Bouissac argues that each was more immediately influenced by Louis Hjelmslev (1899-1965) whose own work was a significant development of Saussure's. In the case of Julia Kristeva, the Paris-based Bulgarian philosopher, literary critic and psychologist, Saussure is more of an inspiration than a direct guide. Kristeva's work on poetics, signification and decentred identity is as much Lacanian as Saussurean, and she is a key figure on the borderline of structuralism and poststructuralism (Kristeva and Moi, 1986).

The most decisive move away from, or against, structuralism from within semiological ranks is marked by Jacques Derrida's 1966 essay, *Structure, Signification and Play in the Human Sciences* (reproduced in Derrida, 1978: 278-294), in which he argued against the viability of the very concept of centred structure:

> The center ... closes off the freeplay it opens up and makes possible ... From the basis of what we therefore call the center (and which, because it can be either inside or outside, is as readily called the origin as the end, as readily *arché* as *telos)*, the repetitions, the substitutions, the transformations, and the permutations are always *taken* from a history of meaning *[sens]-* that is, a history, period - whose origin may always be revealed or whose end may always be anticipated in the form of presence. This is why one could perhaps say that the movement of any archeology, like that of any eschatology, is an accomplice of this reduction of the structuralality of structure and always attempts to conceive of structure from the basis of a full presence which is out of play ... Totalization can be judged impossible in the classical style: one then refers to the empirical endeavor of a subject or of a finite discourse in a vain and breathless quest of an infinite richness which it can never master. There is too much, more than one can say. But nontotalization can also be determined in another way: not from the standpoint of the concept of finitude as assigning us to an empirical view, but from the standpoint of the concept of *freeplay.* If totalization no longer has any meaning, it is not because the infinity of a field cannot be covered by a finite glance or a finite discourse, but because the nature of the field - that is, language and a finite language -excludes totalization. This field is in fact that of *freeplay,* that is to say, a field of infinite substitutions in the

closure of a finite ensemble. This field permits these infinite substitutions only because it is finite, that is to say, because instead of being an inexhaustible field, as in the classical hypothesis, instead of being too large, there is something missing from it: a center which arrests and founds the freeplay of substitutions. Retrieved from http://hydra.humanities.uci.edu/derrida/sign-play.htm 13 October 2011.

Here we have a post-Saussurean undermining the concept at the heart of Saussure's structural linguistics: *langue* as an expression of *langage*. It might also be argued as, in effect, an attack on Peirce's 'submitting of the sign to thought' in the Classical tradition. Derrida's essay marks at least a symbolic boundary between structuralism and poststructuralism, though, as has been described, Saussure's conceptual framework had already been severely distorted by some of his followers. Derrida's key ideas, developed through a large body of work, can be summarised as follows.

Following Lacan and then Kristeva, it is the signifier, not the signified, which is the prime object of interest. Language is a 'freeplay' of signifiers. To give equal, or greater, weight to the signified is to acknowledge a surface-depth distinction that assumes that structures at the deep level drive expression at the surface level. With an intellectual honesty that should appeal to all philosophers, Analytic as much as Continental (and, indeed, that had already been employed by Wittgenstein: see Chapter 1.3), Derrida acknowledges that we are on certain ground in recognising signfiers but not signifieds, but must remember that all attempts to systematize sign systems will be undermined by the play of signs within those very systems. Peirce's model, by contrast, treats Signs effectively in isolation, as if they appear one by one, retain their identities for a while (for otherwise they could have no status separate from their interpreters) and then evolve.

Signifiers, as Saussure pointed out, take their meanings from context and relation to other signifiers. Derrida takes this relational view of meaning one stage further by rejecting the idea of fixed linguistic structures in which these relationships are played out. The relationships, and thus meanings, can never be fixed: a finite language can produce infinite relationships. Derrida, who often drew on word-play inherent in contemporary French, coined the term *différance* to indicate how meanings are both 'different' and 'deferred'. Again, this is an idea that can be credited to Lacan, though Derrida applies it to a broader canvas. In *The Post Card*, for example, Derrida illustrates *différance* by constructing a novel (or is it?) around the charred fragments of postcards following a fire (Derrida, 1987). All our meanings are, Derrida implies, tenuous, impermanent and ultimately uncertain; the recognition of uncertainty is of more value than the assumption of certainty; uncertainty should be sought where certainty seems to have taken hold. (In *Aporias*, 1993, for example, Derrida deconstructs assumptions around, *inter alia*, his own death. How can it be his death when he is not there to have experienced it?) Languages – sign systems – destabilize the explanations we are driven to create of sign systems. Semiology ultimately (but never ultimately) destabilises semiotics, perhaps.

Derrida also argues against assuming fixed roles for writing, speech, or, by extension, any form of life (to borrow a phrase from Wittgenstein: see Chapter 1.3). Writing is not just transcribed speech, and speech is not natural language upon which writing and other sign systems are parasitic. *The Post Card* is one of Derrida's most notable attempts to problematize writing conventions in order to problematize writing itself. Again, he is not totally original in this. Setting aside debates as to whether an Eighteenth Century novel such as Tobias Smollett's *Tristram Shandy* (1759) should be regarded as postmodern or poststructuralist, the use of the novel to convey philosophical ideas is part of the Francophone tradition as far back as Rousseau's *Émile* (1762) and had been very successfully taken up by Proust's *In Search of Lost Time* (Proust, 2003, originally published in volumes from 1913 to 1927) and Sartre's *Nausea* (1938) not long before Derrida. However, again, Derrida takes the issue further by rejecting the 'logocentric' assumptions of both philosophers and linguists that speech must be the prototypical sign system. After all, if not only words carry sign or signal value, how can it be assumed that speech takes precedence? Derrida, instead, proposes the notion of 'archi-writing' (*archi-écriture*: Derrida, 1978), not to suggest that some primordial form of writing can be found to replace speech, but rather to stress the primacy of the expressive act, be it mark or utterance, that precedes both speech and writing as we understand them.

Understanding, continuity, ideas of progression and communication therefore rely not on Peirce's relatively stable Interpretant or on the conveyance and perfection of whole packages of thought, but rather on the 'trace' (Derrida, 1978). Each expressive utterance and each response carries traces of previous responses. Meanings, though deferred and indefinite, rely on traces. In an interview, Derrida refers to the act of reading a text as 'counter-signing' (Derrida and Attridge, 1992: 71); other readers have been there before but each has read and responded to something a little different, mediated by her own context of reading and interpretation.

The act of textual analysis, therefore, and of meaning-making more generally, is one that should aim to avoid the fallacy of closure and completeness. Criticality should be an act of deconstruction rather than purely construction, of seeing how that which at first seems coherent and complete contains that which relies on, yet simultaneously belies, incompleteness and incoherence. Derrida refused to develop deconstruction as a method, for self-evident reasons, but his work exemplifies it. One very small example concerns his discussion of the Preface or Foreword, in Cixous, 1998. The Preface only makes any sense in the context of the work which follows it, which has to be assumed before it has been read, for example.

Finally, Derrida did not shy away from the overtly philosophical implications of this work. His fully relational view of meaning without fixed structures to explain it makes him a thoroughgoing relativist – indeed, more radical than a thoroughgoing relativist who believes that contextual relativity can always potentially be adequately explained – but not necessarily an anti-realist. To Derrida, the Other is ever-present. Again, this is not an idea unique to Derrida: Emmanual Lévinas, for example, more or less simultaneously developed an ethical theory based on respect for the never fully knowable Other: Lévinas, 1967). Derrida's epistemology is deconstructive: we should seek to unsettle certainty wherever we find it. Derrida's metaphysics and ethics both embrace the sense that what is at the heart of things is not substance, essence, innate qualities or even Being (in the sense of Heidegger's *dasein*) but rather difference and otherness. This non-logocentric, alogical metaphysics of absence sets Derrida against virtually the whole Western philosophical tradition from Plato, though it has antecedents at least as far back as the metaphysics of flux promoted by the Heraclitus (535-475 BCE) and the thoroughgoing relativism of the Sophists to whom Socrates and Plato are commonly seen as a response. Interestingly, albeit not conclusively, the quantum physics of the last century has similarly challenged the assumptions of centrism in the previous atomic accounts of matter.[31] Ethically, Derrida respects that decisions must be made but that they should always be made with reference to the ultimately unknowable Other. This an ethical position quite at odds with one derived from Peirce that assumes that progress in human understanding is, or at least can be, universal. Derrida, along with Lévinas and others of like mind, urges us to respect other viewpoints non-judgmentally while recognising the imperative for specific action. The implications of this difference will be explored more fully in future chapters.

Taking the Saussure-inspired tradition as a whole, Saussure's dyadic conception of the sign, as Signifier and Signified, generates the greatest philosophical difference between the American and Continental traditions, though Saussure himself may not have been fully aware of its philosophical consequences, and later writers, from Lacan through Derrida, have emphasised the unquantifiable nature of the sign as (merely) signifier. At face value, the Signifier-Signified distinction is intuitively common-sensical: on the one hand is the word 'dog' (or *chien* or *hund* or whatever); on the other, the mental image evoked by hearing or reading the word. However, the simplicity of the distinction masks a largely tacit philosophical claim. We can confidently understand a language is a socially constructed system of signs, at least if we do not require much clarification of 'social': languages evidently vary with cultures, and the elements within a language are interdependent. We cannot confidently assert, however, that signifiers are one-to-one representatives of *noumena*: that is, the signifier does not disclose the physical reality of the referent; at least, it cannot be assumed to disclose it, as we are unable to tell either way. Now, Peirce does not claim simple one-to-one representation either: on his triadic conception, both the Interpretant's and the Representamen's relationships with the Object are mediated by semiosis, and Peirce can be interpreted as doing away with the phenomenon/noumenon distinction altogether, as signs are both phenomena and physical reality.

However, Peirce never abandons the metaphysical premise that there is not only an enduring, but ultimately a logically explicable tie between the physical substrate and the world of human meaning, even though that tie may involve elements of chance and habit. Peirce is committed to the view that ultimately what the Kantian would regard as *phenomena* will affect *noumena*; perhaps even change them, depending on how we interpret the Dynamical Object. Peirce's theories of the Sign and of semiosis, at whatever level of sophistication and development, are predicated on this assumption. To Peirce semiosis, by changing the world of signs, changes or reveals the physical substrate and thus is objectively progressive. To Saussure, the relationship of the internally interdependent workings of a sign system to the physical substrate must remain permanently uncallable, not because there is no physical substrate (who can tell?) but because the Signified can no more be assumed to be a manifestation of the physical substrate than the Signifier's relationship with the Signified can seem anything more than arbitrary. Of course, one might argue that the relationship of Signifier and Signified is clearly not always arbitrary, for example, in the case of onomatopoeia ('buzz' for the sound of a bee, for example). However, this ignores the variation between even onomatopoeic Signifiers between languages and, in any case, applies to only a tiny percentage of the lexicon. It is always possible to speculate on the ultimate origin of words. Perhaps 'water' (*aqua, agua*) is originally onomatopoeic but this raises two unanswerable questions, concerning the validity of onomatopoeia as a conception (for things might sound to us a certain way because of language and culture, not *vice versa*) and the grounds for verifying such a claim. *Aqua* is not clearly definable as symbol, icon or index on Peirce's account, but rather has characteristics of all three, varying somewhat as to the context of its use, for nothing means quite the same thing all the time. According to Saussure, we are only safe when allowing language, and thus semiotic systems, to make sense on their own terms. This may grate with many philosophers, as it threatens to undermine centuries of debate around the competing claims of realists as against idealists and nominalists. (Peirce is strongly realist, and followers such as Deely and Stjernfeld are strongly anti-nominalist. Peirce can be understood as an idealist, however, at least towards the end of his career, depending on how Firstness is understood.) It may even seem to threaten an abandonment of the whole dominant Western philosophical tradition. Certainly, Derrida would later threaten that. However, such concerns do nothing to invalidate Saussure's position on the sign in this one key respect: the relationship of the sign in either of its forms to the physical referent is unclear, as is the nature of that referent, and the relationship of the Signifier to the Signified is uncallable, if not necessarily arbitrary. Thus there are no grounds for regarding semiosis as progressive, though it can be interpreted as such. Peirce's explanatory scheme remains, on this account, an explanatory scheme; it cannot assume ultimate legitimation.

Insofar as real-life practices and policies are understood as semiotic, this distinction between Peircean and Saussurean derived schemes is of very great importance. International politics, for example, may be conducted quite differently by those who are committed to semiosis as universally progressive from the way it will be conducted by those lacking such commitment. Derridean ethics, derived in part from Saussure, look quite different from those derived from the American pragmatism derived more directly from Peirce.

At the level of detail – of words, phrases, non-verbal signs; Signifiers, Signifieds and Interpretants – Saussure's scheme stresses more strongly than Peirce's the fundamental role of relationship and difference in constructing and validating the sign, at any level. While Peirce acknowledges that signs, in all their elements, stand in relation to each other, Saussure implies that that the sign is created by relation and difference. To take a very simple example, imagine you had never seen a fox. How might you recognise such a thing? It might be explained that it is rather like a certain kind of dog in appearance, but modify that image of 'dog' with, perhaps, certain elements of 'cat' or even 'ferret'. Then, and only then, when a fox is seen, it can be recognised as such. The fox as noumenon or as Firstness is not fox. Who knows what it is: a moving shadow? A cry? A rustle in the grass? A certain sharp odour? All these are no more than clues or elements, if that. They are traces, in Derridean terms. Without the frame of reference provided by languages and other semiotic systems, it is a something-and-nothing, not even a nothing. Is there an essence of fox? Only, as far as we can tell, in the context of a semiotic system, yet post-Saussureans such as Derrida deny the stability of such systems.

As with Peirce, Saussure did not call his semiotics always by that name, but rather *semiologie*. This term is sometimes employed by those in the Peircean tradition not as a description of Saussure's semiotics so much as a signifier of the fact, as they see it, that Saussure was not a fully semiotic thinker. The line to be developed in the present argument is that neither the Peircean nor the Saussurean account offers enough to construct a fully semiotic conceptual framework for understanding human being and becoming that is completely philosophically satisfying, but that each has important elements to contribute to such a theory.

Chapter 1.3 will consider work deriving from the Analytic tradition that can contribute to a fully semiotic perspective, as here developed, focusing on the contribution of Ludwig Wittgenstein.

1.3 WITTGENSTEIN AND THE LANGUAGE GAME AS BRIDGING CONCEPT

Analytic philosophy is the dominant philosophical tradition in the Anglophone world. Drawing ultimately on the Platonic rejection of Sophistry, it seeks conceptual clarity through the application of rigorous logical processes that owe much to the pioneering work of Gottlieb Frege (1848-1925). As an enterprise, it is strongly anti-relativist, and thus intensely skeptical of much of the work referred to in the two preceding chapters: most particularly of Continental language philosophy, especially in forms associated with postmodernism, which is often rejected as not philosophy at all. Ironically, however, the major Twentieth Century figure in this tradition of most interest to later Continental philosophers, and whose work most obviously bridges the considerable gaps between the traditions is the towering one of Ludwig Wittgenstein (1889-1951). For example, Richter writes:

> Similarities between Wittgenstein's work and that of Derrida are now generating interest among continental philosophers, and Wittgenstein may yet prove to be a driving force behind the emerging post-analytic school of philosophy. (Richter, 2010).

Wittgenstein's work also has resonances with that of C. S. Peirce. There is little evidence of direct reference; nevertheless, although, while in general, Wittgenstein makes little reference to any other philosopher, he does, interestingly, make several references to Peirce's most influential pragmatist peer, William James, in *Philosophical Investigations*, finding James's assumptions of interest though leaving philosophical questions unanswered (Wittgenstein, 1967, $342, 413, 610; p. 219). It is interesting to compare Peirce's interest in semiosis working through 'habit' rather than immutable natural laws with the following from Wittgenstein, bearing in mind that Wittgenstein eschewed metaphysical schemes whereas Peirce effectively invented one:

> The whole modern conception of the world is founded on the illusion that the so-called laws of nature are the explanations of natural phenomena. Thus people today stop at the laws of nature, treating them as something inviolable, just as God and Fate were treated in past ages. And in fact both were right and both wrong; though the view of the ancients is clearer insofar as they have an acknowledged terminus, while the modern system tries to make it look as if everything were explained. (Wittgenstein, 1953, 6: $371-2).

The purpose of this chapter is two-fold. First, Wittgenstein will be considered for his problematisation of the analytic tradition, particularly within the *Philosophical Investigations* (Wittgenstein, 1967, first published 1953). Secondly, the Wittgensteinian concept of the 'language game' will be considered for its potential relevance to semiotics, with reference to Jean-François Lyotard's taking up of the concept in *The Postmodern Condition* (Lyotard, 1986).

Throughout his work, Wittgenstein tests the limits of analytic philosophy, using it to cast doubts on what it can achieve. This concern dominates his two major works, the *Tractatus Logico-Philosophicus* (*TLP*. 2001, first published 1921) and the *Philosophical Investigations* (*PI*: 1967, first published 1953). *TLP* explores the idea that whatever can be thought can be made clear in language, and that whatever cannot be made clear in language cannot be thought. Although *TLP* begins with the confident assertion, 'The world is everything that is the case' (*TLP* $1), the work that follows all serves to problematize this assumption. Wittgenstein's work is open to multiple interpretations, and commentators cannot agree on even his most basic metaphysical assumptions, including whether he is best understood as a realist or anti-realist (Richter, 2004). It seems clear, however, that he is concerned to explore his opening proposition as critically as possible. Indeed, as *TLP* develops, Wittgenstein stresses how much philosophical thinking leads to 'nonsense'. Again, there is considerable debate about what Wittgenstein means by 'nonsense' here. Reid argues, drawing on work by, in particular, Cora Diamond[32] and James Conant,[33] that what is said (or written) can only be understood at face value; there is no possibility of understanding the author through the text, for example:

> (W)e do not understand the author of the *Tractatus* until we throw away the ladder, unless we discard any claim to have understood his text. (Reid, 1998: 100).

Whatever is implied, however, Wittgenstein has been concerned to expose fallacies and inconsistencies in assumptions about the world as neatly encapsulable in logical propositions.

In *PI*, Wittgenstein goes further than *TLP*, though how much further depends on readings of *TLP*. In *PI*, the concept of the 'language game' will be employed, but even in *TLP*, Wittgenstein is inclined to the view that the sense of a proposition, and the meaning of the objects that partly constitute it depend on contexts of use that are themselves not amenable to logical analysis. Consider the following:

> ...think of the following use of language: I send someone shopping. I give him a slip marked 'five red apples'. He takes the slip to the shopkeeper, who opens the drawer marked 'apples', then he looks up the word 'red' in a table and finds a colour sample opposite it; then he says the series of cardinal numbers—I assume that he knows them by heart—up to the word 'five' and for each number he takes an apple of the same colour as the sample out of the drawer.—It is in this and similar ways that one operates with words—"But how does he know where and how he is to look up the word 'red' and what he is to do with the word 'five'?" Well, I assume that he 'acts' as I have described. Explanations come to an end somewhere.—But what is the meaning of the word 'five'? No such thing was in question here, only how the word 'five' is used. (*TLP* $1).

We use a knowledge of red in, for example, shopping for apples. The word 'red' pictures something in the world, as does the phrase 'red apples'. It might be said that we know red is red from activities such as buying red apples. However, while the word 'red' (in the collocation 'red apples' for example) shows us something about the world, it does not logically disclose the meaning of 'red'; it does not tell us what red is, for we only assume that from our dealings with red things. Whether or not Plato might have been justified in assuming that the philosopher will come to an understanding of the ideal form of true redness, Frege's logic cannot do this; it is questionable whether a physicist's explanation of colour in terms of wavelengths could offer the true meaning of 'red' either. The same can be said of 'five'. Meaning then, at least in such cases, is meaning in use. Wittgenstein's use of red as illustrative is continued in *PI* (several references), much to the same end as in *TLP*.

From his starting point that 'the world is everything that is the case', *TLP* quickly moves to the acknowledgements that 'the limits of my language are the limits of my world' (*TLP* $5.6) and that 'whereof one cannot speak, thereof one must remain silent' ($7). As Pincock, for instance, notes, this position can be interpreted as realist or anti-realist; it does not necessarily imply the thoroughgoing relativism of Derrida's '*il ny'a pas de hors-texte*' (literally: there is nothing of outside-text, or nothing about a text or meaning that is not contextually dependent: Derrida, 1988:136 – itself not necessarily an assertion of anti-realism), though it does seem to confirm the inability of language to move beyond itself in accounting for what may lie outside itself. On Wittgenstein's account, language may be able only to show, or picture, what it often cannot say, though philosophical attempts to articulate what is beyond articulation will result in nonsense.

PI was published two years after Wittgenstein's death, in 1953, and contains work developed throughout the period of his return to Cambridge (1929) after several years during which he worked variously as a gardener and elementary school teacher, feeling that he had nothing to add to the philosophical contribution of *TLP* (Monk, 1991). While *PI* is widely regarded as a great work, commentators remain divided on how far it marks a radical departure from *TLP*. Ostrow (2002), for example, identifies an increasing linguistic turn within the earlier work:

> (W)hat begins as an attempt to specify the necessary features of the world ends with the recognition that these extend as far as our language itself, that the "specification" can be no more than an acknowledgement that we speak, sometimes with sense, sometimes nonsensically (p. 72). (Pincock 2003, quoting and reviewing Ostrow, 2002, retrieved from http://ndpr.nd.edu/review.cfm?id=1174, 29 November 2011).

In *PI*, the primacy of language seems to be stressed, in a way that can be seen as either reinforcement of or departure from the earlier work. *TLP* begins with an unconsidered proposition from logical analysis, whereas *PI* begins with a consideration of the nature of language, showing the untenability of the position articulated by St. Augustine that words simply picture objects. How far the argument here is developed from the 'five red apples' example above remains a matter of debate; however, it is certainly reinforced.

A key message of *PI* seems to be that concepts cannot be divorced from contexts. That is, what something means, linguistically, can only be understood in terms of the 'language game' being played, and each language game is itself part of a 'form of life'. Perhaps this expresses an even bolder move against logical atomism (the belief that there are core concepts or propositions that underpin all other propositions, as argued by members of the Vienna Circle with whom Wittgenstein was associated[34]) than its rejection in *TLP*, for here understanding is, and only is, an ability to proceed with a game according to its rules, when those rules themselves can only be shown, not explained. This has radical implications for the practice of philosophy itself, for epistemology and for education. For philosophers, language imposes the limits of what can be explained (cf. *TLP*); rather, philosophers should seek to clarify how language games work and concepts work within them, as concepts cannot be understood independent of context and only the 'that' and the 'how', and not the 'why', of a language game is potentially explicable. Furthermore, many traditional philosophical questions are unanswerable, merely the product of attempting to answer questions in one language game in the context of another. For example, it would be meaningless to ask, 'Is Maths fair?'[35] even though concepts such as 'beauty' and 'elegance' can be used in the context of mathematical discourse; perhaps it would be equally fruitless to attempt to prove whether beauty is logical, despite the long history of philosophers from Plato to Kant who have attempted to show that it is. We are frequently 'bewitched' by language in this way, to invoke a term from *TLP*. Rather, as philosophers, we should concentrate on explaining how concepts such as mathematics, fairness, beauty and elegance work in the language games in which they are played. On epistemology and education, the challenge from *PI* is similarly stark. Consider the following:

> Try not to think of understanding as a 'mental process' at all. – For *that* is the expression which confuses you. But ask yourself, in what sort of case, in what kind of circumstances, do we say, "Now I know how to go on" (*PI*§154).

Understanding, on this account, is knowing how to play specific language games. It comes from immersion in those games and not from a detached rational process of working out. Returning to mathematics, we might assume that Wittgenstein would have more sympathy with teaching approaches grounded in repetition of practices until they are mastered rather than those grounded in understanding maths in terms of its relevance to things beyond itself: in short, that he might be more sympathetic to the kinds of approach adopted at the time of writing in countries such as Taiwan rather than the UK. International league tables of children's mathematical competence would support Wittgenstein in any such view[36].

For the purposes of the present argument, Wittgenstein's key contribution can be seen as undermining the logical positivist position that the world is constructed of facts ('everything that is the case') and replacing it with the view that language games, and broader forms of life, are ultimately rule-dependent not fact-dependent, and that these rules demand utilisation such that meanings are always meanings-in-use and concepts are empty without contexts:

> Don't always think that you read off what you say from the facts; that you portray these in words according to rules. For even so you would have to apply the rule in the particular case without guidance (*PI*§292).

In Section 320 of *PI*, Wittgenstein offers a simple example:

> When, for example, I am given an algebraic function, I am CERTAIN
> [Wittgenstein's capitals] that I shall be able to work out its values for the
> arguments 1, 2, 3, ... up to 10. This certainly will be called 'well-founded',
> for I have learned to compute such functions, and so on. In other cases no
> reasons will be given for it – but it will be justified by success.

In short, you know things when you can do them: knowing-that is not easily
divorced from knowing-how. This move from rationalising to enacting
knowledge is pragmatic. However, it is important to stress that Wittgenstein is
not embracing thoroughgoing, 'anything goes' relativism or anti-realism.
Metaphysically, he suggests questions of realism and relativism may be
unanswerable, but in practice, he rejects solipsism entirely. In *PI*, two of the
examples he develops at length to make his case are those of the experience of
pain and the possibility of a private language. In $292-296, the two themes are
combined. When I talk of 'my pain', this does mean that I can only be sure of
pain because it is in my unique experience, any more than I can assume that
everyone else is experiencing pain when I am. It is more the case that I simply
know about pain; pain is an occasional part of my experience, as it is of others
who may from time to time speak of pain: i.e. everyone (though not, perhaps,
animals: a point Wittgenstein is not interested in, but which will feature later in
the present argument). Pain is, or is part of, a form of life, and that is how we
know it. It is, we might say, a sign and a signal.

> Suppose everyone does say about himself that he knows what pain is
> only from his own pain. – Not that people really say that, or are even
> prepared to say it. But *if* everybody said it – it might be a kind of
> Exclamation. And even if it gives no information, still it is a picture, and
> why should we not want to call up such a picture? Imagine an allegorical
> painting take the place of those words. (*PI* $295).

While Wittgenstein has been hugely influential on philosophers in the analytic
tradition, he has also, as indicated above, been an inspiration for some closer to
the Continental post-Saussurean tradition. Perhaps most notably, Jean-François
Lyotard embraced the concept of the language game in *The Postmodern
Condition* (*PC*: Lyotard, 1986). Lyotard argues that the modern (cf.
postmodern) condition has been characterised by universal acceptance of a
series of 'grand narrative[s]', 'such as the dialectics of spirit, the hermeneutics
of meaning, the emancipation of the rational or working subject, or the creation
of wealth.' (Lyotard, 1986: xxiii). One such grand narrative is that of science,
many of whose adherents deny its narrativity. This notwithstanding, it might
be noted that since Lyotard, cosmologists have continued to be happy to
construe the history of the universe as a narrative; they have no choice but to
frame their thinking within beginnings and ends. The postmodern condition,
however, is characterised by 'incredulity towards metanarratives' (*ibid.* xxiv)

on the grounds that not only are all activities recognisable as narratives, but also none can claim universal legitimation, including science, which only permits of certain sorts of knowledge and learning. 'Postmodern knowledge', therefore, is not simply a tool of the authorities; it refines our sensitivity to differences and reinforces our ability to tolerate the incommensurable.' (:xxv) On these grounds, Lyotard differentiates between the 'expert' and the 'philosopher' on the grounds that each is playing a very different 'language game' (:xxv). Lyotard goes on to describe the language game as his 'method' in *PC* (*ibid.* 9ff.). Lyotard makes clear his debt to Wittgenstein (*ibid.* 10), and adds three elements of his own:

> ..first ... rules do not carry within themselves their own legitimation, but are the object of a contract, explicit or not, between players (which is not to say that the players invent the rules). The second is that if there are no rules, there is no game, that even an infinitesimal modification of one rule alters the nature of the game ... The third remark is ... every utterance should be thought of as a "move' in a game. (Lyotard, 1986: 10).

Thus Lyotard is addressing some of Wittgenstein's unaddressed implications, in particular in relation to persons, communication and what Lyotard refers to as 'the social bond' (1986: e.g. 14). As for Wittgenstein, the language game has absolute priority for Lyotard: it is 'already the social bond' (:15), while the self exists in a 'fabric of relations' (*ibid.*). Also like Wittgenstein, Lyotard explicitly addresses issues of learning and understanding, arguing in the chapter 'The Pragmatics of Narrative Knowledge' (Chapter 6: 18ff.) that 'science is a subset of learning' (18) not its totality. Indeed, even science does not develop in the narrowly rational linear fashion that is sometimes claimed, but rather by 'paralogy' which 'is not under the command of the system' (:61). (This argument is reminiscent of Thomas Kuhn's theory of scientific revolutions, with its claim that scientific breakthrough does not come about through the routine progress of normal science: Kuhn, 1962). Science, which often seems to valorise only deductive inference, in fact relies on more than deduction itself to progress, according to Lyotard (as according to Kuhn). Note that Peirce stressed the importance of inductive and abductive reasoning in scientific enquiry,[37] but Peirce's reification of the Interpretant gives a certain stability and universal legitimacy to this changing scientific consciousness that is not present in Lyotard or Kuhn. There is a serious political implication here that goes far beyond the recognition that scientists sometimes 'think outside the box.' A society that offers narrow scientific logic as having universal legitimation will increasingly disregard the associative, paralogical capacities of human beings in favour of the purely 'performative' intelligence of the machine.[38] One implication, shared by many contemporary commentators, is that educational debate, starved of recognition of cultural difference and debate over aims and values, becomes constrained into a delivery model, whereby students and teachers are merely components in a grand social machine designed to produce results in relation to prespecified criteria. (For educational arguments specifically drawing on Lyotard, see, for example, Blake, Smeyers, Smith and Standish, 1998). Accepting the forthcoming ubiquity of computerised information systems, but writing before the Internet, Lyotard ends *PC* with a plea for an open information society: to 'give the public free access to the memory and data banks' (Lyotard, 1986: 67), for, if the acquisition of knowledge is easy and universal, space can then once again be made available for the kind of paralogical thinking that science has tried to suppress whilst being itself reliant upon it.

The development of a foundational semiotic theory can therefore draw important elements from both Wittgenstein and Lyotard. The development of a post-analytic philosophy, as signalled by Richter at the beginning of this chapter, may draw from the analytic tradition a rejection of speculative metaphysics and a concern with what we can be most sure of. Semiotics, whether developed through Peirce, Saussure or Derrida, echoes Wittgenstein in claiming that we must accept language and other semiotic systems for what they are: we cannot think outside our mechanisms for thinking (although Peirce does explain the processes in the context of what amounts to a metaphysical scheme). When we talk of 'beauty', for example, the thing we can be most sure of is that we are talking about a word, a sign. We can never be sure that beauty is an abstract truth, like a Platonic form, or of where it comes from. Fundamentally, 'beauty' is a word; signs are signs. As Wittgenstein showed, we can become clearer about how 'beauty' operates within language games, but not what the 'beauty' is that is being expressed through those games. The sign must remain epistemologically prior to its referent. To Wittgenstein, as to Saussure and his followers, conceptions are contextual and language can only show us what it can show us as language. It cannot fully explain what it shows. We are effectively trapped within, or enabled by, language games. Peirce is a particular case here, insofar as he develops his own speculative metaphysical scheme within in which his account of semiosis lies.

Lyotard takes from Wittgenstein that everything is progressed *via* language games, in the broadest sense. He effectively concurs with Wittgenstein in arguing that no language game can enjoy universal legitimation. However, Lyotard goes further: while 'knowing how to go on' is indeed a matter of rule following, it is not a matter of consensus, passivity or mere invention (in the sense of following the rules to make something new); rather, it is agonistic and paralogical, a matter of making moves that modify the games themselves. Lyotard thus addresses one gap in Wittgenstein's language philosophy: the issue of how language games change and, potentially, how they affect or infect one another. However, the biggest difference between the poststructuralist position and others lies in the lack of faith in ultimate consensus. This philosophy of difference is expressed variously: in Derrida's *différance* (discussed in Chapter 1.2), in Deleuze's assertion that philosophy is about the creation rather than the clarification of concepts (Deleuze and Guattari, 1996), and in Lyotard's 'dissensus' and his later concept of the *différend. Différends* are concepts or propositions that cannot be reconciled 'for lack of a rule of judgment applicable to both arguments' (Lyotard, 1988: xi.).

Despite these very considerable differences, however, Peirce, Wittgenstein and Lyotard unite in one important respect in terms of the present argument: in effect, it is more justifiable to think in terms of contingent rules rather than universal laws. The cultural practices that express human consciousness are certainly normatively driven, but we are on safer ground understanding them in terms of their internal rules, *vis-à-vis* the rules of others, than as the expressions of inviolable regularities in the world beyond consciousness. Such perceived contingent rules may point to universal truths, but we are bound to know no more or less than the manner of the pointing. The emphasis on habitual, rule-governed (and therefore mutable) rather than universal, law-governed (and therefore immutable) systems is an element that to a degree therefore reconciles Peirce, Wittgenstein and Lyotard to some extent. Wittgenstein's potential influence on a fully, or foundationally, semiotic and anti-dualist educational and social theory is therefore considerable.

The final part of Chapter 1 will briefly consider three other possible influences on such a theory: process philosophy, quantum mechanics and biological semiotics. Chapter 2 will then begin to construct a theory of understanding and meaning making on these foundations.

1.4 SEMIOSIS AS FUNDAMENTAL PROCESS: THREE FURTHER SETS OF CONSIDERATIONS

The major influences on the development of a fully semiotic, mind-body non-dualist, pragmatic perspective have been described in the previous chapters: Peirce, post-Saussureanism and Wittgensteinian language philosophy. In this chapter three final influences are acknowledged: process philosophy, quantum mechanics and biosemiotics.

The perspectives described in Chapters 1.1 to 1.3 cohere around certain key propositions. First, both thinking and behaviour (human certainly, and possibly non-human too) are best understood as governed by contingent rules rather than universal laws. While acknowledging that social life is highly normative, therefore, we must also acknowledge that norms are subject to change, that such change may not always be or seem rational, and that incredulity, or at least scepticism, towards both metanarratives and assumptions about essence are the inevitable consequences of the overlapping of norming systems in particular contexts. Secondly, the relationship of language and other sign systems to the physical substrate is at least problematic: we do not simply read off nature through language and culture, though we can alter nature through culture. However, not only is the relationship of signifier to signified beyond complete explanation but that of sign at every level to what is not sign. As one sign system, language can picture the world but not show it, on Wittgentstein's account; that is, it is one aspect of the world that does not directly express other aspects. We can never be sure of the nature of any noumenal world to show or picture beyond what is signified, though we are always confronted by Otherness.

A fully semiotic perspective as presently developed therefore construes experienced reality as characterised by impermanence, by probability rather than certainty and, from time to time, by inexplicable fundamental shifts. It offers a complete break from a world view based on substance metaphysics, whereby reality can be broken down into smaller and smaller particles: to the level of the atom, according to Leucippus and Democritus in Ancient Greece, the monad according to Leibniz around the turn of the Eighteenth Century, and sub-atomic particles according to modern physicists. Actually, one branch of Twentieth Century physics offers significant support for such a shift in perspective, as will be explained below. However, the issue to be considered first is the broader metaphysical one of whether it is more productive to consider the universe fundamentally as matter that moves or interacts or as processes that give the impression (sometimes) of solidity and permanence through duration.

This conflict between substance and process metaphysics predates Plato and was of considerable interest to the Ancient Greeks. Plato, like many Greek philosophers, sought to identify what might be considered permanent in a shifting world: his own answer comprised intellectual forms such as justice and beauty, which he took to have universal and unchanging universal value.[39] Others, as noted above, developed atomic theories to explain such permanence. (Note that on this account, the atom is the smallest building block: to speak of sub-atomic particles would be to commit a category mistake). This broad party, with its belief in identifiable universals, would form the basis of the rich philosophical and scientific tradition from which we benefit today. There is no doubt that substance metaphysics, taking a particular view of Plato's forms, largely won the battle of ideas within that tradition, sustaining Western culture through the Enlightenment and the scientific and industrial revolutions that followed by working on the basis that physical reality is fundamentally material. It proved, therefore, very useful. However, as we shall see below, science itself began to come unstuck in certain areas about a century ago by adhering to substance metaphysics.

It is not necessarily a betrayal of Plato and universalism more generally to construe certain processes rather than certain kinds of matter as fundamental. However, process philosophy has tended to be regarded as very much a minority commitment (Rescher, 2008). This may be in part because analysis works most easily on the basis of inert substance rather than on that which is in constant movement, and in part because process thought admits of the possibility that there are no universals beyond change and reaction and thus poses a fundamental threat to many philosophers and scientists. Indeed, Plato himself expressed such a mistrust in the work of Heraclitus, who is widely regarded as the seminal figure in process philosophy. Motivated strongly by distaste for the highly relativistic, and sometimes unprincipled Sophists, Plato was scornful of Heraclitus, for whom the prime element was fire, and the fundamental truth was change and impermanence. Only fragments remain of Heraclitus' writing, but enough to make clear his basic position: for example, 'This world-order... is... an ever living fire, kindling in measures and going out in measures', and (most famously) 'one cannot step twice into the same river' (Fragments 217, 215).[40]   As Rescher (2008) notes, this position was quite unconvincing to Plato.

Recent interest in process philosophy has largely been 'in and for American philosophy – especially owing to its increasingly close linkage to pragmatism in such thinkers as Peirce, James and Dewey' (Rescher, 2008: 9). A. N. Whitehead's *Process and Reality* (1929a) is a seminal text for the process philosophers of recent times.

Substance metaphysics, as explained above, assumes that the universe is material. People subjectively perceive this objective stuff. Change happens to material, as it interacts with other material. In terms of language and other semiotic systems, substance metaphysics tends to separate the sign from that which it represents, and the signal from that which sends it: the sign is generally taken to represent either a thing or an aspect of the relations between things or what might happen to a thing. On a process account, however, responding to signs and signals is living itself; signs and signals are not merely things that refer to other things; they are more than 'tools', for example, as semiotic engagement is often construed in sociocultural, post-Vygotskian educational theory (e.g. Daniels, 2010), even if they do not directly 'show' that which they are not.[41]

A fundamental tenet of process philosophy is that being is always a process of becoming. Whitehead states, 'How an actual entity becomes constitutes what that actual entity is.' (1929a: 31). By the same token, knowledge and understanding must always be understood as coming to know and understand. In *The Aims of Education* (1929b), Whitehead warns of the futility of teaching 'inert' knowledge;[42] that is, content or even knowledge of processes taught outside the context of meaningful experienced processes for students. Of course, what makes a student feel he or she is engaged in a meaningful process will vary from case to case - the process of studying towards a desired qualification may provide this continuity for some – but Whitehead is as firm as Dewey[43] in his rejection of the aridity of much formal instruction. This is not to claim that relevance to students' interests is enough. Meaningful experience must always draw on previous experience. 'In Whitehead's terms, apprehension - the grasping of immediate experience - in some sense precedes (though relies upon) prehension - our residual knowledge (for want of a better term) of what seems to be fixed and substantial (though in reality certain processes have duration, which creates this substantiality): the sequence is thus WE EXPERIENCE → WE REMEMBER → WE KNOW → WE EXPERIENCE AND RECOGNISE (i.e. have consciousness); we have consciousness as we recognise our experiences as particular selections from the infinite range of possible experiences.' (Stables, 2005: 49-50)

Whitehead's position has ethical as well as pedagogical implications. A person is not a detached observer, as assumed by positivism and by much of modern science, but rather an actor in the events he or she experiences. Human beings are part of the ongoing work of nature. We are not simply responsible for it as if we were alive and it were inert machinery (as suggested by Descartes, for example), but can only be responsible insofar as we are responsive. (Note that this is a position also shared by Buddhists, as in the work of the philosopher of education, Heesoon Bai: e.g. Bai and Cohen, 2007). To experience is to be implicated in a process (indeed, my experience is my implication in a process, or event[44]), and thus what happens to me is connected to what happens to the human and non-human entities around me. It is not, on this account, possible for us to create or destroy nature though we are implicated in its forms, processes and events. Whitehead wrote that 'A living society ... destroys ... its food ... life is robbery' (1929a: 146); by this I take him to mean not that we destroy nature, but that we appropriate it, and that the changes that happen to it and to us are inseparable. Substance metaphysics, therefore, creates a false separation with ethical as well as ontological and epistemological consequences. Insofar as humans are always part of a nexus of 'actual entities' in Whitehead's terms then (as for the process theologists who have been inspired by Whitehead, such as Charles Hartshorne[45]), freedom is inherent in *all* process and ethics operate relationally rather than instrumentally. Human interests are not separable form either other human or non-human interests, whatever our problems in identifying 'interests' among the non-human.

It should be noted at this point that not all process philosophers are persuaded by this religious or teleological view. The sense human beings have of freedom may or may not have metaphysical validity. The point is that we experience life as though we have ethical commitments, and the working out of those commitments cannot be effectively undertaken by regarding the individual as discrete stable substance, or by pretending that the human interest can be separated from the non-human world with which humans interact.

This strong sense of relationality has been inherent in all the philosophical positions so far considered. Semiosis implies a sharing of meanings and processes of meaning making. Language games are social practices. Saussurean linguistics posits all meanings as relative. Derrida's position is strongly relativistic.

Indeed, while at first glance, Derrida's position might seem a very long way from Whitehead's, there are significant points of connection. They are at odds on one level, for Whitehead assumes that we are always engaged in presence as process while Derrida rejects the metaphysics of presence and sees meaning as always deferred. However, on closer inspection the two positions are not so far apart. For Whitehead, individual context, memory and previous experience determine apprehension, while for Derrida each meaningful encounter draws on 'traces' of previous encounters. In *Acts of Literature*, for example, Derrida writes of each new reader 'countersigning' a text (Derrida, 1992: 72).

Similarly, while being part of a nexus of actual entities on Whitehead's terms has ethical implications, Derrida's sense of the ubiquity of the Other, as with Levinas's, also carries with it a sense of deference towards that which is not ourselves. (See also Chapter 1.2.)

An inevitable intellectual influence on Whitehead, given the time of his writing, was that of the new physics, both Einsteinian relativity and the emerging challenge to it from quantum mechanics. Whitehead had worked on mathematics with Bertrand Russell (Whitehead and Russell, 1910-1913) and would have been amazed at the scientific revolution happening around him. This took two forms. Einstein revolutionised physics on a big scale, reversing the ancient assumption (shared by Newton and Kant, for example) that space and time were separate to developing an account of space-time that offered the possibility of a theoretical framework for physics that was simultaneously relativist (in the sense that no two observers could have the same experience) and coherent (in that it explained the effects of physical forces on each other). (For a general introduction to relativity, see Geroch, 1981.)

Einstein's theories have been empirically verifiable at all but the smallest scales of operation. However, at the level of subatomic particles (if they are indeed particles), even Einstein's laws break down. Einstein himself caustically remarked that 'God doesn't play dice' when confronted with the claims of the new quantum physicists that at the subatomic level events can only be predicted according to rules of probability rather than immutable laws. This shift from certainty to probability is consistent with Peirce's later semiotics, however, and it remains the case a century later that physicists cannot fully square the circle between Einsteinian relativity, which continues to explain larger scale events, and quantum mechanics, which struggles to explain the mysterious world of elemental particles, waves, or strings – however they should best be described. (For an introductory history of quantum mechanics, see Rae, 2005.)

Although both strands of modern physics deal with the operation of forces, it is quantum mechanics which poses the greater threat to substance metaphysics. Atomic theory, as noted above, was predicated on the assumption that the atom was indivisible, was discrete, and that nothing could be smaller. This view did not hold long into the development of modern physics, however. Subatomic physics struggles to explain events recorded (not literally 'observed') at the subatomic level where things appear and disappear in bewildering ways, leading to a host of labels for 'particles' and even the theory that much of the universe must be constructed of 'dark matter' that is effectively unobservable. It may be that some of these problems are the result of trying to make a substance perspective work increasingly against the odds, and that a process view would remove them, for on a process view, there is no reason why events and experiences should be recognisably divisible or why particles should in any way be responsible for them. In philosophy, logical atomism had a short life at the beginning of the Twentieth Century. Wittgenstein appeared to embrace it at the beginning of the *Tractatus* but had wholeheartedly rejected it by the time of the *Philosophical Investigations* (Wittgentstein, 1967, 2001). Physical atomism, however, has a much longer and more stubborn history.

The final influential movement on the development of a fully semiotic theory comes from the development of semiotics itself, and particularly from the development of biosemiotics, grounded in the belief that non-human natural systems work semiotically.

A short and accessible introduction to biosemiotics is provided by Sharov (1998). It grows from the insight of Jacob van Uexküll (1957) that non-human organisms live, as do people, in environments loaded with significance. Uexküll's term for the semiotic environment was the *Umwelt*. (Biosemioticians distinguish between the surrounding *Umwelt* and the personal *Innenwelt*.) A blade of grass might be a tender morsel for a cow but a footpath for an ant. The degree to which cow and ant are conscious of such significances is by the way. The important point is that there would be no natural variation if every living thing were indiscriminate. Each creature 'reads' its environment in ways that are species specific, and perhaps sometimes individually distinctive; indeed what makes a species is the system of signs that constitutes its rule book of engagement with the rest of nature. Pattee (1982, 1995) has coined the term 'semantic closure' to describe the system of meanings that constitutes a species' set of resources for survival, thus bringing the language of evolutionary biology very close to Saussure's conception of a human language as a socially constructed, self-referential system of signs in which the meaning or value of a particular sign is always relative to others in the system and the system as a whole. Furthermore, these 'readings' (given that animals do not literally read) are passed on from old to young just as cultural conventions (or 'memes': Dawkins, 1976) are passed on through human generations; survival itself is a matter of the interpretation of signs. In recent years, broad interest in biosemiotics has begun to produce further specialisms, such as ecosemiotics (Maran, 2006). The development of the field as a whole probably owes more to Thomas Sebeok (e.g. Sebeok, 1992) than any other individual, though Sebeok began with the term 'zoosemiotics', building on van Uexküll.

To sum up, what will the characteristics of a fully semiotic perspective be that draws on all the influences outlined in Chapter 1?

1. Ubiquity of interpretation

The first is that interpretation and reinterpretation are ubiquitous, inevitable and often unconscious. Whether the sign is an actual entity independent of the interpreter (as for Peirce) or something much more contingent and elusive (as for Derrida), we know through signs and things are (as) signs, though full acceptance of this proposition depends on adoption of a non-dualist position that does not make a firm qualitative distinction between Signs, as the expressions of minded beings, and mere Signals, as the mechanical prompts delivered and reacted to by non-human entities.

The assumption of ubiquitous variation is not at odds with that of respect for cultural practices as the primary unit of analysis, as in Wittgentstein's Language Games and Forms of Life. While Wittgenstein's construal of understanding as 'knowing how to go on' (Chapter 1.3) appears to rule out interpretation, two points must be borne in mind. Firstly, Sign, particularly in Peirce, is very malleable, incorporating everything from a word to an extended thought. It is not inconceivable to regard a language game as a sign on this basis. Secondly, cultural practices, by definition, change. They are, in effect, reinterpreted. That this reinterpretation is not mostly conscious does not render it lacking in interpretation if the sign-signal distinction is problematized. We might go further and suggest that it is only when we are surprised by, or unfamiliar with certain aspects of a practice that we consciously reinterpret it in managing to 'go on'; most of the time, adaptation is pre-conscious, even though each new encounter with a practice is in a new context that will inevitably impact on the practice as well as the response to it (as a practice is kept alive by enactments of, and responses to it). This latter perspective can be taken as consonant with both Peirce and Derrida.

2. Belief in evolution: interpretation as adaptation

Where the sign-signal distinction is problematized, the distinction between mental interpretation and physical adaptation is also problematized. In a move that is also consonant with Peirce, interpretation can thus be associated with adaptation. The difference between Peirce and, most strongly, Derrida, concerns the degree to which such interpretation/adaptation should be seen as progressive. It is also debatable how far this matters, since whether something is seen as progressive can be regarded as a matter of post-hoc social judgment. On the other hand, as suggested earlier (1.1 and 1.2), there are potential political and practical consequences that emerge from following either Peirce or (to take the extreme opposite position) Derrida on this. By giving the Interpretant a life of its own as an actual, non-personal entity, Peirce posits semiosis as objective, universal progress. Derrida's conception of signifiers in 'freeplay', however, disrupts the perceived centredness of any structure, and thus the possibility of conceiving of universal progress as Peirce conceives it.

There is, of course, no necessary connection between such thinking and, for example, political action. Nevertheless, it does not seem fanciful to suggest that strong proponents of Peircean pragmatism might, for example, see the progress towards liberal democracy in the West as a sort of universal truth, leaving Americans and others of like mind with a moral duty to encourage it wherever it seems it may be beginning to flourish. A Derridean model, on the other hand, would be more likely to stress that other cultures will always remain Other, and that morality consists in recognising Otherness as Other and not in trying to mould it to what are perceived as progressive agendas. If accepted as valid, this distinction has very important consequences for the conduct of international relations, *inter alia.*

3. The rejection of Cartesian mind-body dualism

Peircean semeiotic dissolves the qualitative distinction between mind and matter that infected, according to Peirce, the Kantian tradition into which he was inducted. In Peirce, there is no gap between *phenomenon* (thing-as-experienced) and *noumenon* (thing-in-itself). On the other hand, a Kantian might respond that Peirce had no more idea than Kant about whether a form or reality might exist beyond any human access. Peircean scholars, such as Deely (1990) and Stjernfeld (2007) critique the French semiological tradition for tacitly accepting such dualism in its preoccupation with language and other cultural systems, yet Derrida, Levinas and others, though they insist on an ever-present Otherness that sits in opposition to all human knowledge and understanding, do not clearly think of this Otherness as matter in contrast to mind.[46]

Dewey, as partial heir to Peirce, and as applier of pragmatic ideas to the social and educational domains, rejects the mind-body distinction, yet retains faith in the qualitative distinctness of human language.[47] (In the Analytic tradition, McDowell's Second Nature similarly stresses such a difference while rejecting stronger forms of dualism: McDowell, 1996). It has been argued that problematising the sign-signal distinction potentially invites some revision of Dewey's educational and social philosophy.

Taken all in all, the above deliberations result in two conclusions. First, there is a strong consensus against naïve mind-body substance dualism, though its legacy can be found even where it is not explicitly accepted (as in cognitive and behaviourist learning theories, for example, or even, it could be argued, in Peirce's distinction between Interpretant and interpreter). Secondly, and as a result of this, there is scope for new or revised theoretical perspectives that continue the quest towards a further reappraisal of human experience and meaning-making with these considerations in mind.

4. Pragmatism as meaning in use

Semiotic perspectives stress the merging of the ontological and the epistemological insofar as meaning and objective nature cannot be divorced. This in no way implies that there can be no reality beyond human understanding. It does, however, imply that what meaning is cannot be divorced from the way that meaning works in, at least, human communication. This is the case whether or not one separates Peircean Interpretant from human interpreter. In this sense, there are strong consonances between the semiotic (/semiological) approaches here discussed and Wittgenstein's language philosophy, both in the context of the Analytic tradition and as reviewed through its co-option by Lyotard.[48] Overall, if we wish to understand what things mean to a culture, or as part of a tradition, or even in the context of a rational argument, overriding attention should be paid to usage. Ordinary language philosophy, therefore, may yet have unrealised potential in terms of understanding how key concepts work in their contexts, whether these be broadly cultural, or more specifically professional or academic-disciplinary.

5. Process: the primacy of events and experiences over essences and substances

Materialist and semiotic approaches are fundamentally at odds. Construing mind as manipulating and reacting to matter is dualistic in the way that is explicitly rejected above. By contrast, a view of human experience as implication in events entails recognising both relationality and contingency as constitutive of all branches of experience. This seems more fully recognised in Derridean poststucturalism than in Peircean semiotics, though there is scope for interpretation here. (It is not clear that Peirceans always acknowledge the scope of Peirce's work for multiple interpretation, perhaps because too much credence is awarded to the integrity, and therefore implied stability, of the Interpretant).

Taken together, the above have implications: for understanding individual human development, and the relationship of humans to other humans, to non-human animals and to non-sentient beings (therefore to ethics), for social understanding and for policy, and it is these concerns that the rest of this book will address.

The following sections will deal with these issues in turn. Chapter 2 will address the human condition as a whole, as 'fully semiotic', offering a non-dualist, pragmatic, process account of human conscious being as always becoming in a 'physical transcendent present'. Chapter 2.2 will consider the traditional role of reason in relation to such a view of human consciousness.

Chapter 3 will expand the ideas to examine specifically issues of human growth, nurture and education. Chapter 3.1 will consider humanity as aspiration rather than given state; Chapter 3.2 will consider the problem of the language of literacy and its inadequacy to express aspects of a fully semiotic perspective; Chapter 3.3 will reflect on the role of formal education under the conceptual framework so far developed.

Chapter 4 will consider the human relationship with the non-human, the limits of semiosis, and the ethical implications that flow from these. It will relate the (educational) problem of the child to the (ethical) problem of the animal, and will consider the possibilities of a post-humanist ethics based on these ideas more broadly.

Finally, Chapter 5 will examine how the conceptual framework might inform social policy at the broadest level. Chapter 5.1 will consider the connections between the overlapping concepts of morality, rights and preferences. The final chapter will use the arguments developed to reflect on understandings of time and progress and the inevitable constraints on human knowledge.

MOVING IN TIME: CONSCIOUSNESS AND REASON

2.1: PHYSICAL TRANSCENDENT PRESENCE: THE NOW AND THEN DIMENSIONS

Suppose that my phenomenal world, incorporating the sum total of my present experience, and involving my different awarenesses of past and future, can be referred to as my 'My Now' (MMN). This is a phenomenologically, or phenomenographically, or existentially derived definition, though as comprehensive as possible on those terms. It does not attempt, for example, to clarify the nature of 'now' beyond 'what I am experiencing'. It accepts as valid that I have experience. Furthermore, this experience carries with it traces of previous 'nows' and awareness of other experiencing persons. Again, it cannot be proved ultimately that 'Your My Now' (YMN) is real for you, but, on the basis that you are likely to respond that you do experience, I can safely posit that the world comprises not only My My Now but also as many Your My Nows as there are people in the world. At least, therefore, I can conclude that the totality of phenomenal experience comprises $MMN + YMN^n$. (Stables, 2008a.: 92).*

This chapter addresses the paradox of eternal Nowness: the sense that experience is present while it is always in flux. To find stillness in movement is effectively to problematize understandings of time, as well as to raise questions about the nature of meaning.

My experience of Now is always what Now means to me, for otherwise it is too diffuse to qualify as an experience. Nevertheless, it appears that meaning does not simply exist, or even come to be, at a precisely identifiable point in space-time. Note that we refer to critical incidents in the development of our experience in the past tense: 'I have decided/ chosen/realised....I decided, chose, realised' Decisions, choices and realisations are events that are always realised in retrospect, and in retrospect, certain points in the continuous stream of events are remembered as having been significant. Some may have become important signposts for future understanding. Some of these 'signposts' are shared or intersubjective, such as the Millennium, the fall of the Berlin Wall, or the 9/11 attacks, while others are more personal.

It is clear that time in relation to meaning, and thus to human identity, learning and personal growth, cannot be measured accurately using objective clock time. Insofar as the world around appears as a set of signs, or prompts human action through unconscious signals, each sign or signal cannot be precisely spatiotemporally located.[49] Even apparently mechanical prompts cannot be so located. If someone punches me in frustration with the present argument, there is still much scope for interpretation about when exactly the punch was thrown or felt. Even the most brute physical acts only make sense in terms of sequences, not identifiable moments.[50]

An individual's evolving world view, as process, therefore runs in relation to but not as subservient to the progress of clock time, but it is not necessary to infer from that this that mind and matter are of different orders. On a fully semiotic account, influenced particularly by Peirce, but also by Derrida's *différance*, this is not best understood as a conflict between realist and idealist commitments for it does not imply a clash between mental phenomena and physical reality. Rather, it is a recognition of the limitations of clock time as simply a mechanism designed to facilitate various instrumental functions associated with modernity. (Note Anthony Giddens' depiction of standardized time as the first 'abstract system' to define the modern age: Giddens, 1991). In this limited sense, therefore, present experience (MMN) is transcendent, but such transcendence does not require explanation in terms of mind-body dualism. Indeed, as this argument seeks to show, all sentient entities (at least) must experience Now in relation to sequence and (as Peirce suggested, or at least implied), the movement of the universe as a whole is best understood as changing, or evolving, process rather than as a collection of atomistic moments.

Adopting the terminology from the paper quoted at the head of this chapter, my 'My Now' (MMN) embraces much more than, for example, what my senses are aware of as I write this sentence – noting that there is no static point during this process. MMN comprises the sense I am making of incoming sense data (by 'data' I refer to that which makes the first, pre-articulated effect on the receiving organism and imply no more; I do not imply that 'data' are ontologically given and thus distinct from signs and signals) in the context of previous sense making. I bring myself to every party, as it were. If I am demented, with weak senses and poor brain functioning, I will only be able to make any sense of MMN by drawing on memories and patterns from long past, the sequencing of which will be confused. The dementia patient may therefore seem to be guessing rather than knowing. Knowledge is recognition of sequence prompted by immediate contextual signs and signals; the mentally and physically frail may both misremember aspects of sequences and (in the case of blindness, for example) have a relatively undifferentiated response to new sense data (such as colour and contrast).

In MMN therefore, if I am functioning normally, a stream of sense data is appropriated, or interpreted (responded to) with respect to habits of response[51]. In Stables, 2005 (:12), this was explained as follows: $O=(cd+cn)$, where O refers to outcomes or actual behaviour (including mental acts and emotions), cd refers to conditioning, habit or tradition (the diachronic dimension of context) and cn refers to environmental conditions, including the interpersonal (the synchronic dimension of context). As the context of my present reception is always distinct, both synchronically (as no two present contexts are ever fully identical) and diachronically (in terms of the habits at play), the following can be inferred about how any individual will respond to any new situation:

- This response will carry strong resonances ('traces' in Derrida's terms) of previous responses to identifiably similar situations;
- This response will never completely correspond to previous responses (so that history seems iterative yet never exactly repeats itself; it rather echoes), and
- As both 1. and 2. apply to all individuals, there will always be individual variations in responses, however slight, even within relatively highly cohesive social groups, as well as between groups.

That it is always Now is therefore both possibility and constraint. Nowness renders impossible unconstrained knowledge while enabling all knowledge. What we experience as the present is often the occasion for new realisation, when formerly disparate strands of thought or feeling are synchronised, for example in the case of a problem solved or an issue resolved. The feeling that an intractable problem is suddenly solved, or at least eased, at an unlikely moment that seems unrelated to it, is a common one, and illustrates how the distinction between conscious sign and unconscious signal is by no means clear or absolute. On the other hand, while personal history enables new understanding, it also constrains it, for without such history, there can be no response at all. It is an important truth little acknowledged in educational theory that that which makes knowledge and understanding possible – our interpretive frameworks including our assumptions and prejudices - is also that which limits them. However, this realization of the constraints on human understanding as well as its reliance on experience is a recurrent, if not dominant, motif in the empiricist tradition, evident in works as far apart as Hume's *Enquiry Concerning Human Understanding* in the Eighteenth Century and the political and economic philosophy of Hayek in the Twentieth. (Hayek was specifically opposed to the assumptions about society that informed, or misinformed, socialist rational planning). (Hume, 1748; Kukathas, 1989).

A simple way of conceptualizing the diachronic and synchronic dimensions is to assert that there is a (Just) Now dimension and a Then dimension to MMN. The Then dimension can be further divided into retrospective and prospective aspects manifested in turn as memory and as various sorts of anticipation or expectation (hope, ambition, vision, expectation, resignation and so on). That is, I can only make sense of the present by simultaneously being aware of who I am experiencing it, and of my experiences of like situations (the Then dimension), and by responding to the unique combination of sense data that determine the present context. Of course, it is not possible to be consciously aware of either everything from one's past or every aspect of one's present: one's response in each new moment is far too complex to be fully rationalisable even if, objectively, it may seem potentially fully rational were the entire personal history to be fully understood.

In effect, acknowledgment of the Then Dimension has always been a central tenet of pragmatism. As Peirce put it:

Consider what effects, which conceivably might have practical bearings, we conceive the object of our conception to have. Then our conception of these effects is the whole of our conception of the object. (Peirce, 1878, retrieved from http://www.peirce.org/writings/p119.html, 13 October 2011. See also Chapter 1.1.).

The capacity to respond to things in terms of how they behave and change must necessarily be shared by all sentient beings, even if the idea of non-humans having 'concepts' is unacceptable. The implications of this will be explored later, but at this point in the argument, it is necessary only to consider this as it applies to human beings.

MMN, therefore, is not strictly spatio-temporally locatable. However, MMN is, in the broadest sense, a physical reality, taking the mental as explicable in physical terms. That is, the 'how', if not the 'why', of Physical Transcendent Presence (PTP) is explicable in terms of biochemistry and neuroscience. (It is not clear that Why can ever be explained other than in terms of personal agency, invoking the languages of values and morality: as both Hume and Wittgenstein argued, not all belief can be fully rationally justified). In terms of clock time, therefore, I am both detached from, and of, the moment as physical entity, but this paradox can be explained as a weakness in understanding time. Hence the depiction of the sense of Nowness as PTP: MMN is characterised by a sense of PTP, of something ('me') that has stability and observes a stream of events from an apparently detached vantage point that allows for such events to make sense. The sense of the 'something ... me' comes from recognition of sequence but need not be understood as a mental act. It may be better construed, on a process account, as implication in events. To quote Wittgenstein:

Try not to think of understanding as a "mental process" at all. – For that is the expression which confuses you. But ask yourself: in what sort of case, in what kind of circumstances, do we say, 'Now I know how to go on...' (Wittgenstein, 1967: $154).

On the one hand, 'knowing how to go on' brings a settled sense to a restless process. On the other hand, and going beyond Wittgenstein here, each actor's involvement in an event or process is different in some way from each other actor's, thus 'knowing how to go on' does not imply that every participant has the same experience of an event or situation. Thus the present argument may seem strongly relativistic. This acknowledgment raises the issue of other minds, or rather experiencing bodies, and of answering the possible charge that the above account of the sign(al) is over-individualistic. For example, Russell critiqued Stables, 2008b. as, '... overly focused on individual rights and freedoms.' (Russell, 2009: 623). This charge is relatively easy to counter.

Consider events or processes as recognisable patterns arising from the 'white noise' of background energy, or life force. (As lying beyond or prior to our understanding, we can only experience and thus articulate this background energy in the vaguest way: classical examples include Kant's *noumenon* and conceptions of the Will, through Kant, Schopenhauer and Nietzsche. This background energy is prior to individual identification). As 'recognisable' patterns, they will not be experienced equally by all implicated entities. Thus what are traditionally conceived of as 'sense data' can be understood as intrusions into one's experiential world, either of aspects of an event in which one is implicated, or of events in which one is becoming implicated, the origins and development of which to varying extents lie outside it. On the fully semiotic account, events and processes are never closed systems, so there is inevitably ground for different interpretations of where individual events or processes begin, end, separate and merge. For example, when I hear a sound, either it is obvious what it is (in my view) or I am not sure what to make of it at first. In the first case, it does little to alter my Now (as in the case of a clock ticking that I was aware of before). In the second case, I have effectively been drawn into the process, or set of processes, in which that sound plays a part, the antecedents of which lay in events beyond my experience. Ongoing life is inevitably a mixture of recognized and unrecognized sense impressions, not least because events and processes overlap, are not discrete, and are always matters of interpretation, in the broadest sense. Experience can be understood as a sentient entity's implication in events and processes, where 'implicated in' includes 'affected by'. The event cannot occur without the involvement of that entity, and can only be understood from the perspective of understanding entities. Thus each individual experiences events in a somewhat distinct way, but this does not imply that she or he has made it up. Therefore the present argument is strongly relativist but also realist. It is not solipsistic.

It is self-evident that the resources that I bring to MMN are not unique to myself. They include words from a shared language,[52] and body parts that correspond to those of others and react in similar ways to environmental stimuli; if this were not so, medical science would not be possible, let alone organ transplantation. My 'My Now' is not possible without your 'My Now' (YMN) and, by extension, others' 'My Now' (OMN), including the 'Now' of entities that may not be conceived of as having any consciousness at all. However, just as organ transplantation is not simple or always effective, because bodies have the tendency to reject elements from other bodies (though they also sometimes welcome them, as in sexual activity, and even in the act of eating), so each individual is unique in the pattern of responses to which s/he is prone, and such patterning also modifies over time. YMN therefore overlaps, but does not coincide, with MMN. While we merge, we confront. It is likely that such phenomenal worlds overlap more closely in some cases than others, including within close family groups and very cohesive communities, but they can never overlap completely: truths about communities can never be guaranteed to apply fully to individuals, irrespective of the emphases put on social and cultural cohesion through education and other social institutions. Furthermore, nature as a whole demands the mixing of different, though not entirely distinct elements, rendering breeding impossible between species yet highly undesirable within close family groups. (It might be inferred from this that the racist's error is to confuse or conflate tribes and races with species, thus regarding those of different race as not worthy of respect as fully human, while the possibility, and arguably desirability, of at least occasional 'cross-breeding' of this sort, renders such conflation untenable.)

The sum total of all human experience is therefore $MMN + YMN/OMN^n$. This raises the question of where YMN ends and Other MN begins. On one level, there are human beings with whom I have no personal relation, but must all OMNs be human? If a foundationally semiotic account is strongly anti-substance dualist, there can be no absolute mind that humans possess and non-humans do not. Furthermore, a Now dimension must be complemented by a Then dimension for action and survival, thus animals (at least) must live in PTP. On this understanding, the experiential, or living universe comprises $MMN+YMN^n+OMN^n$. On a fully pansemiotic account, however, such as that towards which Peirce seemed to be tending, the whole universe is thus comprised: ie it is as much mind as it is matter insofar as the distinction is at all valid.[53]

For the time being, discussion will be limited to what we know to be sentient beings, and in the present chapter, to the human only. What does the argument so far imply about our ethical and practical commitments towards ourselves and others? This will first be considered purely within the context of human society, with the biosemiotic and pansemiotic emphases strengthened in subsequent chapters. The basic principles will be enunciated now, specific instantiations later.

Recognition of overlapping phenomenal worlds carries two clear epistemological and ethical implications. The first is that to know someone else fully is impossible. The second is that to know nothing about those whose phenomenal worlds overlap our own is also impossible. This partial recognition explains the human senses of both individual lack and attraction to others; in short, it explains the need for relationship. Sexual attraction, friendship and competitive team building, in business or sport, rely on a mixture of empathy and a sense of difference. Animist religious and cultural practices that involve the taking on of spirits, either of other people (including the dead) or of other animals express the same complex yearning. The animal-worshipper who wants to take on the spirit of the lion both recognizes himself in the lion and seeks to be transformed through an injection of its courage and strength, while other animals have different characteristics more strongly than human beings. The ancestor worshipper who seeks the blessing of one of the ancestors (sometimes characterized as a god in, for example, Chinese religious traditions) similarly seeks to imbibe something of a spirit that both shares what she has and can contribute something she lacks.

To what extent there is commonality among all phenomenal worlds remains unknown, as there is no one position from which all phenomena can be experienced, and no experience-transcendent reason. This exploration of overlapping phenomenal words therefore leaves open two questions: how much we can know of other people's phenomenal worlds, and how much overlap exists between the phenomenal worlds of human and non-human entities. The following general ethical considerations emerge from consideration of these.

First, all other people should be recognized as fully human, in the sense of aspiring to be fully human. (See Chapter 3.1 for a full discussion of this). There is, however, a conceptual difficulty in defining where humanity begins and ends. If this were not so, there would be no debate around abortion, for example, since there would be universal agreement concerning the point at which an organism becomes human. This notwithstanding, there are no justified grounds for selectivity in the attribution of full human rights in law to those logically accepted as human, except where these are temporarily withdrawn for reasons of personal protection: in the cases of children, criminals and the insane. (In practice, as opposed to law, no one may enjoy full human rights: see Chapter 3.1.) In these exceptional cases, the intention is that full legal human rights will be granted or restored as soon as possible. Selectivity cannot be justified because understandings of others' phenomenal worlds can never be full, but there is evidence of considerable overlap, including the powerful biological evidence provided by the ubiquity of racial interbreeding and more recent DNA analysis. If this seems uncontentious, it is salutary to recall both historical atrocities and academics' arguments to show that such a realisation has all to often been lacking. Indeed, according to Alain Finkielkraut (2000), historically people have scarcely if ever regarded all other people as fully human. Retrospectively, this seems self-evident in a number of 20th Century contexts including the Holocaust, Rwanda and former Yugoslavia. 'Ethnic cleansing' implies that contact with cultural others pollutes and corrodes, though the biological evidence may well suggest the contrary. Finkielkraut's argument, however, includes the proposition that the 'tourist' mentality prevalent at the Millennium represents only a thin toleration of others, and continues to veil an unwillingness or incapacity to engage fully with those of evidently different cultural background. While Finkielkraut's argument may lack full justification, it presents the possibility that the geographical mixing of people under globalisation may do little or nothing to challenge or repair the dangerous narrowmindedness of the recent past, a thesis for which it is depressingly easy to find supporting evidence.

Some blame Enlightenment rationalism for the failure to acknowledge full humanity in others, echoing the criticism of atomistic conceptions of time above. Hung (2009), for example, explores the implications of Richard Rorty's question:

> Why should I care about a stranger, a person who is no kin to me, a person whose habits I found disgusting? (Rorty, 1993, p. 133).

Hung argues that 'The building of a common and rational community seems to be a general *motif* implied in many civilisations' (2009: 2) and that such a community inevitably diminishes the outsider. Lingis (1994) refers to this as the 'rational community'. Drawing on a number of sources, including Lingis and Kafka's *Metamorphosis*, Hung argues 'The above description shows that emotional responses emerge prior to rational justification; human acts can be driven by taste to a greater degree than by reason. In this light, it can be questioned how far rational communication or the idea of duty can promote or raise human rights culture without taking taste into serious consideration.' (Hung, 2009: 5). Possible response to this unwarranted alienation is the development of what Lingis refers to as 'depth perception': the deliberate seeking out of the other's memories, assumptions and values. According to Lingis, the possibility for this lies with the realization that there is always a sense in which I am other to myself: I experience myself as myself and as other. Hung therefore concludes by responding to Rorty's question, 'Because I am the stranger and the stranger is I as we are in our mortality'. (Hung, 2009:9)

Furthermore, all sentient beings can be recognized as likely sharing some human characteristics. If phenomenal worlds overlap, there must be some overlap between human and, particularly, animal worlds. Again, biology offers clues though not a final answer. While humans cannot breed with non-human animals, there are strongly shared physical traits. Furthermore, there is increasing interest in the evident possibility of using animal genetic material in the treatment of human disease, continuing and developing a long tradition of using animals as test beds for human medicines[54]. The evident delight – on the human side, at least – derived from relationships with non-human companions, such as dogs, cats and dolphins, further suggests points of experiential contact. Given the inevitable uncertainty around experiential overlap within the human species, the boundaries between human and non-human living (and between the life experiences of other species) are less obvious and impermeable than is often assumed. This has ethical implications that will be explored later, though it is perhaps worthy of note at this point in the argument that an assumption that animals share aspects of human responsiveness does not necessarily imply that animals can be held responsible, though we often do, for example, hold dogs accountable in certain situations. Insofar as rights entail responsibilities, the rights due to non-humans will inevitably be less than those accorded to persons.

Secondly, therefore, there are no closed systems, however counterintuitive this may at first seem. Confusions about what constitutes humanity are evident in a number of areas, some of which have already been signalled: they include the status of the foetus, the brain-damaged, the insane and the criminal (the inhumane, in some cases). Opinions are fiercely divided about the point at which the infant becomes human, from the point of conception (when the newly fertilized egg is yet far from a foetus) to the moment of birth, while the law only grants full human rights at the end of childhood. Meanwhile, research shows that neonates' cries mirror the intonation patterns of the linguistic groups into which they are born[55], thus indicating that experiential life as understood in the present argument begins before birth. When those with brain damage are not deemed capable of looking after themselves, they are still regarded as worthy of treatment that reflects their status as fully human.

Meanwhile, criminals are forcibly deprived of some, though usually not all, their human rights, thus suggesting a further overlap between commonly accepted conceptions of the human and the humane.

Other systems sometimes treated as closed include those of gender, race, culture (or ethnicity) and social class. There is a tendency within so-called identity politics, for example, to see group membership as the dominant determinant of personal identity. This tendency can be challenged on at least two fronts. The first challenge is that an individual's group allegiances are never single, the second that there is arguably a psychological imperative to be distinct from the group as well as accepted by it. This tension, described by Rom Harré in terms of the need to balance personal and social identities (Harré 1983, 1998), explains, for example, the strong behavioural and attitudinal differences among otherwise close siblings: to be part of a group but not a person in your own right is as bad as to be isolated from all groups. Sociological analyses that focus on social class similarly run the risk of inferring from the general to the particular, in seeing an individual's actions as always both sympathetic to the aspirations of her class and largely determined by them. Again, it should be stressed that our backgrounds are things we rebel against, up to a point.

Thirdly, acknowledgement of overlapping phenomenal worlds problematizes both the nature and the outcome of communication. If we can never fully understand the other, yet never fully not understand her, then communicative activity can never provide complete understanding or resolution, nor does it ever function purely solipsistically. To employ the terms of a debate between Jean-François Lyotard and Jurgen Habermas, communication neither aims purely for dissensus nor for consensus (Lyotard, 1986, 1996). Habermas' conception of the Ideal Speech Situation (1984/ 1987) has often been taken as a model for educational practice, as in the work of Robert Young (1992). Habermas sees democracy as renewed and social progress achieved through unconstrained discourse when each party can be confident that what the other says is sincere, true, and appropriate, or at least is in a position to question this in a spirit of open dialogue. The postmodernist Lyotard, by contrast, sees communication not in terms of arriving at agreement but at new meanings including new disagreements: at dissensus rather than consensus. Reflection on actual social intercourse easily dispels the myth that only one of these processes is at play. Those gathered at a dinner party, family gathering or bar tend to engage in a number of communicative purposes, including but never solely embracing, coming to agreement, stimulating debate, enlightening and bewildering; even the business meeting among a group that works well together has to involve moments of playfulness and iconoclasm to cement social bonds before returning to the formal agenda.

It can also no longer be assumed that only human beings are possessed of language, or, in a broader sense, mind. This issue will be explored more fully in Chapter 4.1.

Fourthly, taking the three points above together, a social ethic begins to emerge, comprising the following elements. Respect is due to all persons (at least) on the basis of our shared humanity, or potential for humanity, and our mutual difference. History, identity and difference should be respected, but not intransigence. A respect for cultural heritage should not override an embracing of cultural change. Just as there is no uniformity in life experience, so it is mutable over time. Change is inevitable as is a degree of continuity; even the human species will ultimately change, divide and die. This implies both recognition of aspirations that have become traditional or conventional, and scepticism regarding them. For example, respect is due to those who value the trade union movement for its achievements on behalf of workers in its early days, but such respect may or may not determine loyalty to its practices in any current context; the same argument might apply to respect for the aristocracy or for financial institutions. On the other hand, there need be no ethical inconsistency in supporting moves to increase the number of women parliamentarians as a short term pragmatic move, while opposing gender-based affirmative action as a long term policy commitment. Whatever the outcomes of such debates in both cases it is inevitable, and not morally indefensible, that both continuity and contingent response should play a part in decision making. Such an acceptance may often prove challenging for those with strong ideological commitments from any point on the political spectrum, including both conservative traditionalists and ideologically committed social reformers. Actually, neither of these groups is in a position either to give voice to the experiences and aspirations of the mass of people nor to assume they know what they want. To this degree, a policy argument based on a fully semiotic position is inevitably liberal-pragmatic, though even adherence to this position runs the danger of becoming a totalizing move. However, there is clear support here for a policy emphasis on what Isiah Berlin referred to as negative liberties (i.e. 'freedom from'). These are the basic human rights that allow freedom of association, belief, conscience, movement and speech on the grounds that there are no ethically valid reasons for curtailing such freedoms other than under conditions of ramified harm where others might be endangered. On the other hand, there is a case for caution regarding policy moves to ensure positive liberties such as the institutionalization of affirmative action on the basis of gender or ethnicity, as such moves tend to define persons by means of group affiliations, whereas on the present account, it is ultimately impossible to prescribe what other people want, or (up to a point?) even 'need'.

The ethical, political and practical issues raised above will be examined more fully in Chatpers 3-5. Chapter 2.2 will lay more of the groundwork for these applied debates by examining the idea of rationality in the context of the present argument.

2.2 SEMIOSIS AND (THE MYTH OF?) REASON

'Philo-sophy' means 'love -(of)- wisdom'. To the Ancient Greeks, wisdom, moral goodness and rationality were not distinguished: each was *arete*, the excellence that characterised the best way of living, leading to *eudaimonia* (happiness, or fulfilment). Philosophers strove to attain this excellence. Philosophy was its pursuit.

In effect, most modern philosophers are not aretaic, but construe philosophy as 'love of' reason or rationality, as one form of excellence among many. The dominant mode of current philosophising, analytic philosophy, is the pursuit of the rational and logical through rigorous analyses of delimited concepts and issues, rather than the proposing of grand schemes. It is strongly anti-metaphysical. Noting Wittgenstein's famous remark that 'Whereof I cannot speak, thereof I must remain silent' (Wittgenstein, 2001:$7), some philosophers since at least Hume in the 1700s have become sceptical about whether logic can serve to resolve all issues in ethics, aesthetics or metaphysics. Thus modern philosophy is generally limited in scope compared to that of the Ancients.

The slide from universal *arete* to specific logic began recognisably with Plato's postulation of really existing conceptual forms, such as beauty and justice, the truths about which can only ultimately be accessed by those who have studied dialectic (philosophical debate) at the end of a curriculum that had begun with bodily discipline and music and graduated through mathematics for those deemed capable of following it so far. Rationalism, the belief that the highest state of humanity is that in which universal truths are properly understood that do not disclose themselves fully in human sensory experience, was fully launched by Plato and reinforced through Descartes' *Cogito ergo sum*, albeit Descartes grounds his rationalism on the subjective, empirical fact of the thinking being (i.e. even if I doubt I exist, there is still an 'I' that doubts my existence: Descartes, 2010.)

It is important to stress from the outset that this will not be an argument against reasoning. Rather, it will be an argument against assuming the universal validity of any particular process of reasoning. On one level, to attempt to explain anything is to attempt to construct a rational argument about it. What is at issue in the debate about philosophical rationalism is not whether people rationalise, or even whether we rationalise to create the criteria for (rational) judgment of others' rationalisations: indeed, we inevitably do this, otherwise we would have no means of judgment. (As Wittgenstein argued in the *Philosophical Investigations*, there can be no private language: all our thinking is rule bound and conventional in some way.) The question is whether there can be a final, culture-free, transcendental form of rational judgment. Reason construed thus has absolute external validity: a rational argument, on this account, is not merely coherent in the sense of being fit for purpose, but corresponds in some way to actually existing facts or propositions in the world beyond human experience. Both ethically and epistemologically, the question is whether there is an ultimate Right and Wrong, the existence of which validates human accounts. There are only three possible answers to this: 'yes', 'no' and 'don't know'. It seems suitably cautious to operate on the basis of the third of these unless or until one can be convinced of either the first or the second, by rational argument, empirical evidence or (better still, to most modern commentators), a combination of the two. Philosophy, on all accounts, should seek the answer rather than assume it.

Let us consider some common assumptions about reason in terms of this simple but universally significant problem. These assumptions are:

1. that reason is the capacity to think reasonably and deliberately, in a considered, logical way, exercising good judgment;
2. that reason is (in the natural world) unique to human beings;
3. that rational structures relate to the real structure of reality beyond human perception and thus have universal validity, so can discover the laws or operating rules of the cosmos;
4. that reason is consciously exercised; and
5. that reason is transcendent, whether or not God-given.

First, let us consider these five assumptions in terms of their internal coherence as a set. Two of the assumptions (2 and 5) are 'two-world' assumptions: that is, they suggest some conception of the supernatural, in the literal sense of that which exceeds the normal functioning of natural entities. 2 divides humans from animals; 5 liberates humans from material constraints. 1 implies coherent truth; 3 implies truth by correspondence. 1 is analytic (it simply redefines reason); 2-5 are synthetic and inferential; 2-5 are also speculative: reason here is taken to be something which is not directly empirically verifiable. While supporters may find evidence for them, they cannot be easily tested through experiments that attempt to falsify them, so are weak hypotheses according to, for example, Popper (1959).

Evaluated empirically, we might reformulate 1-5 as follows:

1E. Reason, as commonly understood, incorporates and implies one or more of the following: the capacity to think reasonably, deliberately, logically and exercising judgment.
2E. We use the term 'reason' to apply to what humans do and other entities appear not to do. To test whether other entities are actually capable of some of the things we consider reasonable would require both a tighter working definition of reason than is current and research techniques that have not yet been devised or employed.
3E. We can test whether (or rather, to what degree) our rational conclusions can serve as means to effect change, as we perceive it, in both the human and non-human worlds. This can include the development and use of metatheories, such as the formulation of universal physical laws. As we are limited to our own perceptions of what happens, however, we cannot determine the degree to which such processes work because they are either

self-referential or attuned to real extra-phenomenal processes (true by correspondence). We are limited to determining what 'works' or not according to criteria which may or may not themselves be valid universally. For example, we know that history has involved fundamental changes of mind about modes of human understanding, but we cannot tell whether our current understandings are objectively valid or will be subject to further radical overhaul.

4E. Consciousness is a contested concept which is commonly taken to incorporate the sense a person has of him or herself as a thinking being. However, there is no tight, agreed definition, and thus no way of ascertaining firmly whether or not other entities can validly be held to be conscious.

5E. Reason appears to have some transcendent property insofar as human beings (at least) can make plans for currently non-existent situations, involving memory and projection. Note that this does not necessarily imply mind-body dualism, as argued in Chapter 2.1. However, animals also appear to do this to some extent, though this is commonly referred to as instinct. It is not evident that animals evaluate their condition as humans do. Nevertheless, this human propensity does not necessarily give humans transcendent knowledge; the ability to combine examples of contextual knowledge to create new contextual knowledge does not necessarily imply a 'view from nowhere' (Nagel, 1986). It is clear that animals do make associations, for example, and act on them accordingly.

In short, we can analyse reason in terms of its apparent components and analogs (logic, judgement etc.), but cannot empirically validate any of the loftier claims that are made for it: that it is uniquely human, relates to the real structure of the extra-phenomenal world, is uniquely associated with consciousness, or is transcendent. We are on safer ground in regarding reason as a social construct, therefore, than as a prime mover. However, analytic philosophers, who tend to value the possibility of empirical justification over grand claims, are often dismissive of social constructionism. On the ground that the latter is a vague concept, this is justifiable, but if the aim of philosophy is to determine and examine that of which we can be most sure, then constructionism trumps rationalism.

Many of the claims made about reason are necessarily experience-dependent. Without experience, no claims about reason could ever have been made. Reason is ultimately parasitic on experience, therefore, but is not always testable through experience. Suppose you ask a carpenter to make a door. Both you and the carpenter know what a 'door' is without having to show this through concrete examples. The Platonic rationalist argument is that there is an actually existing door form, and that this accounts for our ability to talk to the carpenter. However, this is not a necessary prerequisite, for door-ness could simply be known by experience; the same holds true for beauty, justice or education: when people argue that certain things that happened in school were not 'real education', this does not need a Platonic explanation but can merely show that there are conflicts within the myriad uses of the term that cause us to question what we mean by it in a particular context when aspects of that context conflict with features we associate with the concept through other experiences. On this empiricist account, abstractions such as justice, beauty and education really are abstracted from experience rather than prior to it. They are generalizations. There is no compelling reason to believe, for example, that any other highly evolved life form would have any such concepts to share with us, or even that *homo sapiens* has evolved with a stable set of concepts.

Contrast this with the analytic position of the London School philosophers of education of around the 1960s and '70s. It is tempting but simplistic to base a definition of what education 'is' through selective and contextual analysis of ordinary language, rejecting (for example), uses of the term in phrases such as 'that was an education!', after something unpleasant has happened, as ironic or invalid:

> R. S. Peters has argued very cogently that, unless we extend the term education as Rousseau does, we would not say that X is educating Y if he is fostering undesirable and morally objectionable dispositions or using undesirable and morally objectionable methods; for example, if he is helping Y to form bad habits and false beliefs, or if he is using harmful drugs, brainwashing, or hypnotic suggestion (*Concept of Education* [1967], pp. 1-6). This seems to be correct. It is true we may say that what X is doing then is "bad education," but we would be more likely to say it is not education at all. Education is, normally at least, a laudatory term and its laudatoriness seems to be built into it. If one says that X is educating Y, one must be thinking that X is cultivating desirable and morally unobjectionable dispositions (excellences) by similar means. Education must foster dispositions and use methods that are desirable and morally unobjectionable, or at least regarded as such, otherwise it is not education. (Frankena, 1973: 1).

Such a jumping at definitions through over-selection can lead to the analytics' fatal error, from the point of view of the present argument: assuming the Is and then deriving the Ought from it. In this case it is questionable whether the Is is valid, for parties may not agree on the moral desirability of dispositions. How many non-Buddhists would argue that education should foster disillusionment, for example? It could, however, be argued that any learning involves seeing that what was held to be no longer is (dis-illusion, literally). And what of people who claim in all seriousness that they did not learn much from their education? On what grounds are their ordinary language uses of the term invalid while others are suitable as the basis for a definition? It seems more likely that this conceptual analysis is normative, even prescriptive, through and through: it is analysis skewed by aspiration. Analytic philosophers of education who are complacent in their definitions of education, seeing them as fit basis for application to numerous contexts, are being reductive, and can be dangerously so, through justifying practices and the expenditure of large sums of public money on those practices when the view that such practices may not unquestionably serve individuals' or communities' aims has been ruled out of court. On a fully semiotic view, that does take as full account of context as possible, such a fixed definition of education cannot be relied upon; indeed, can cause more problems than it resolves. The analytic approach to philosophy of education associated with Peters and his followers in the London School[56] takes clarification of the concept 'education' as the first move in improving schooling on a logically coherent basis, whereby decisions about, for example, curriculum and teaching methods are derived as logical expressions of the aims of education that are themselves logically derived from clarification of the concept. The present argument is that such conceptual analysis cannot validly do the work Peters *et al* claimed, on various grounds, including the impossibility of deriving all values from logical analysis and the fact that different curricular practices (e.g. mathematics and social studies) are, in effect, different language games or forms of life whose aims do not cohere[57].

Reason operates through signs (as Locke acknowledged: see Chapter 1.1), yet that sign use may or may not be reasonable. We therefore do not have grounds to make final assumptions about the extra-phenomenal world from the cultural practices that drive our own experience. In Wittgenstein's terms, 'Whereof we cannot speak, thereof we must remain silent' (*op cit*).

Appeals to absolute reason are therefore highly speculative. Less speculatively, we act according to what experience prompts in use, whether or not this prompting inspires (necessarily contextualised) reasoning or conscious reflection. Implicated in the consideration of reason here is that of cause. We have to be on guard against the fallacy of single causation: the fallacy that assumes that there is an invariate relationship between identifiable single events in the past and the future. What experience prompts and what agents thus do can never be fully understood on a simple one-to-one level.

Experience always being to some degree various, it is possible to state with some certainty that universal conclusions cannot validly be drawn from contingent premises. Reference to natural laws generally implies laws of predictability, but 'universal conclusions cannot validly be drawn from contingent premises' is effectively a law of unpredictability. Given that the set of factors leading to an experienced event, nor its context, can ever be fully repeated, it is never possible to state with certainty the outcome of a set of conscious processes. History may often nearly repeat itself but it cannot ever fully repeat itself. This 'law' is broken over and over again in areas such as educational policy and other forms of social planning where outcomes of a particular identified set of circumstances are supposed to be repeatable. In fact, neither the circumstances nor the outcomes are ever fully repeatable. In the luxury of the scientist's laboratory, factors can be reduced to numbers that seem small enough to identify clearly and handle in terms of experimental design. After significant reduction, the effect can be gained that a certain human intervention will always have the same outcomes. The social world never offers such laboratory conditions (even accepting science as infallible, which is unlikely). Variables cannot be isolated, measured and used to predict social or personal outcomes with anything like the degree of certainty often naively assumed by policy makers and those who advise them.

Experiences are not singular, discrete entities, so do not prompt singular, discrete responses, hence 'what to do' is not immediately self-evident. This results in the activity that we deem thought, judgment or deliberation. To say something is reasonable is always a post-hoc, propter-hoc argument. All we can say for sure is that experiences seem to follow from each other[58]: thus perceived causation and rationality. Rationality as a construct is ultimately experience-dependent. Hence it is the case for universal reason and not against it that demands proof. Plato's proof was weak. In the *Meno*, Socrates shows how an uneducated slave boy can perform mathematical operations assuming understanding of conceptual forms such as triangles. Socrates explains this in terms of the boy recalling this knowledge from the spiritual realm whence he comes, for he cannot have known it through experience. However, one does not need formal education to have experience. The intelligence of the slave boy can much more obviously be explained by his induction into the culture of geometry and calculation all around him than by reference to a supernatural realm of everlasting triangles.

Semiotic philosophy cannot assume parallel worlds. In semiotic philosophy, the sign, and its operation, constitute the focus of enquiry. The sign takes primacy over the referent insofar as the referent is understood as an extrapolation from the sign rather than *vice versa*. A sign need not be just a word, or anything consciously humanly fashioned. It is indistinguishable from a signal; it is a prompt, whether it's a line of Shakespeare, the white cliffs of Dover or, literally, a kick up the backside. (Note that signs are both one and multiple. Mathematics is a sign system, not the grounds on which to evaluate sign systems.)

G.E. Moore, one of the influences on the development of analytic philosophy, promoted common sense realism by drawing attention to empirical facts that we should take for granted as indicative of objective entities. He argued we should not cloud propositions such as that the earth exists and orbits the sun once a year by quibbling that it all depends on what we mean by 'the earth' and 'exists' and 'years': that this would be a misdirection of philosophy rather than an exercise of it: a charge of sophistry. The story goes that Moore put up one hand, said 'Here is one hand' then put up the other and said 'and here is another', as if this showed us something to be taken for granted. Semiotically, Moore was combining, or collocating signs. (*put hand up*) is a sign. The utterance 'here is one hand' is a sign...and so on. Each of these signs, taken separately, can mean something different according to context and receiver. (hailing taxi? Greeting? Strange nervous tic?) This approach effectively prevents us from taking full account of minority interpretations, just as (I would argue) in philosophy of education, counter views, such as that 'education' need not be a force for good, or that no 'education' exists beyond people's experiences of it, or that education often happens when you least expect it, can get squeezed out of the conceptual picture. These counter-perspectives do, after all, make things more difficult for professionals and policy makers. (John Lennon's song *Beautiful Boy* contains the lines, 'When you cross the street, take my hand. Life is what happens to you when you're making other plans' – as it shortly would to Lennon himself when he was shot.) In effect, the argument attributed to Moore here, like that of Peters and his followers, was closing down the definition of something through an appeal to the obvious, on the unprovable assumption that the sign refers to an empirically verifiable external reality, whether in the form of material object or conceptual proposition, even if only because such certainties seem necessary. This can become a circular and self-serving retreat into the myth of the obvious: the belief that X is an obvious indicator of Y, rather than only obviously being X. It allows for wishful thinking: the subtle elision of the 'is' into the 'ought'. Everything really does all hang on 'what you mean by' the putting up of hands or, indeed, by education. X indicates Y to one person at one time, Z to another at another. Of course, in any community, assuming Y may win over assuming Z, but that falls short of absolute legitimation. There is much difference between one rationale dominating in a certain context, and that rationale attempting to crush the other: look at the tensions between, among and within America, Israel and Islam. For example, Moore's exhibition does not prove there is plurality in the world (two hands), any more than it proves singularity (one body), or, indeed, that quantification is problematic. Similarly, consensual conceptual clarity in a given place or time about a term such as 'education' fails to grant that term objective legitimation.

Consider God: the prototypical God-word. Usually, the debate begins with 'does God exist'? At this level, and then through all its subsequent levels, this is a war starter. It posits a series of either/or decisions that are empirically unresolvable yet have dramatic consequences for human interactions, and for human interactions with the non-human world. It is put as though there is something – someone – out there (or there is not) which we must be right or wrong about believing in. This kind of simple binary thinking would not be adopted under a semiotic approach, which would begin with the acceptance that 'God' is, first and foremost, a word-sign. In semiotic philosophy, the sign is prior to its referent, thus it is what the sign evokes that is important, not what it objectively represents. Regarding 'God', people use it as a word for a range of possible entities, from cosmic Prime Mover or ultimate judge to personal guide and imagined friend, while aetheists may wish to substitute 'imaginary friend' for 'imagined friend'. (Note that the difference between these two positions seems much less great than on other accounts.) As the referent, on the semiotic account, can only be inferred from the sign, rather than taking the sign as expression of a taken-for-granted referent, there seems nothing here to fight over, for example. After all, even within one religious tradition, the word

'God' is likely to evoke some variation in responses and associations. The important thing is that looking at it this way should not start wars. We can never know all interpretations or fully understand their provenances. However, we can be assured that they will both endure to some degree and change to some degree, just as the sign 'God' itself will: we know the word is not consistent between languages or across time. These interpretations can neither be undone nor everlastingly perpetuated, neither by fighting nor by any other means.

A semiotic, non-rationalist philosophy therefore is relativist though not anti-realist. The weakness of relativist positions is that they fail to offer criteria for judging between competing value claims. However, this point has already been addressed in Wittgenstein's Language Game argument (and elsewhere). There are no universally recognisable criteria, but each language game, and each form of life to which it relates, manifests its own norms and values. Pragmatism is generally consistent with this: meaning is always meaning-in-use. On a fully semiotic account, everything is a matter of semiosis, of response in context, and no meaning adheres over the long term. (It is tempting to think that 2+2 always equalled 4, but it was not so, and still is not so for some cultures, such as the Amazonian Piraha, who have no arithmetic at all: Everett, 2008. To speak of there being four things in the world without any concept of four-ness is entirely meaningless.) Dichotomies do not work as absolutes, with their terms as always qualitatively discrete and fixed, but rather as pragmatic contrasts useful only in certain contexts: thus there are occasions in which it is helpful to talk about mind or body, or to differentiate between theory and practice, but these terms do not represent discrete substances, or even discrete practices in many contexts, so are often not helpful, and are rarely helpful when taken as absolute. For example, it is easy to forget, when contrasting body and mind, that these terms are merely being used to contrast aspects of human action (such as when tennis coaches stress that it is a 'mental game', or a garrulous person is criticized for not putting his brain into operation before he opens his mouth), or that the theory-practice division in education operates within the field rather than trumping it, so that both those committed to theory and those committed to practice are interested in furthering education. In educational discourse, while it may often make sense to contrast relatively theoretical discussion from concrete material actions (for example, theories about classroom management from the act of arranging tables and chairs), everything that goes on in education, intentionally or otherwise, has something of theory and something of practice about it, because every educational act or opinion is a response to education, and this is insufficiently recognised. A fully semiotic approach warns us against sharp divisions and prevents their use as argumentative shields, as when one party accuses the theorist of not understanding practice and the other accuses the teacher of not understanding theory. Semiotically, the challenge is always to respond to the other's response, which involves an attempt to understand it; there is no retreat from semiosis. There is no end point, and certainly no good reason to take any of the great philosophers as having the last word on any of these matters. Furthermore, semiosis always results in challenges to received views and contributes to personal change, and in this sense is always educational.

Much of the rest of this book concerns the implications of taking this semiotic, pragmatic position as fundamental. The rest of this chapter will set the groundwork for this by setting forth briefly some basic principles.

First, (contextual) reasoning is inevitable and inevitably involves deliberation and judgment. These categories do not become redundant as a result of rejecting universal rationalism. All judgment and deliberation involves 'if-then' considerations; this is even true of a cat hunting a mouse, so on this level, rationalising is an inevitable aspect of life beyond the human. It is a survival imperative, but necessarily contingent and selective. Nevertheless, within my phenomenal world (MMN), many things 'seem as if' more generally: it seems as if cats are natural hunters of mice, for example. However, as Hume argued, what seems like the expression of a natural law need not be so. In my experience, and in the experience of others I have encountered, cats hunt mice, but both cats and mice are likely to evolve or adapt such as this practice does not continue forever. The force of the present argument is not to deny the consequential power of (particularly) human action, but rather to acknowledge its contextual dependency and, as a result, some inevitable unpredictability of outcomes. In short, reason is a function of semiosis, not the reverse. As has been acknowledged within Humean scepticism, analytic philosophy, and some versions of pragmatism and semiotics, human reasoning is always constrained and contingent. Therefore, to believe it could provide a complete Theory of Everything, for example, would be hubristic.

Secondly, semiotics and pragmatism both problematize the body-mind distinction and thus, by extension, the distinctions between theory and practice, and between philosophical and empirical research. While, in all these cases, the distinctions are useful in context, none is absolute. However, it could be argued that this assertion depends on accepting the present argument as fundamentally empiricist. Perhaps so, but the appeal is not to the impoverished form of empiricism that reduces experience to measurable observations, in laboratories, and using telescopes, microscopes and other forms of scientific instrument.[59] Rather, experience is implication in the events and processes that, collectively, constitute the universe. Any research programme that arises from such considerations must inevitably, therefore, include approaches that are conventionally considered as both philosophical and empirical and methods that are both qualitative and quantitative. Ultimately, however, there must be recognition that research informs judgment so that, in this important sense, the qualitative always trumps the quantitative. In relation to this, taking meaning as meaning-in-use means taking actors' experiences, including (but not merely comprising) their perceptions seriously in all endeavours to understand. Thus scientific research cannot divorce itself from either its ethical responsibilities or its dependence on culture beyond itself.

In the remaining chapters, these issues will be worked through. Chapter 3 will focus on the development of the human being, considering the definition of the human (Chapter 3.1), literacy and the semiotic as umbrella concepts in discussions of learning (3.2) and the role of educational institutions and organisations (3.3).

CHAPTER THREE

THENS WITHIN NOW

3.1 HUMANITY AS ASPIRATION

In this chapter, I shall problematize the boundaries of the human, arguing that 'being human' is not a clearly defined or definable state of being. It is more strongly a normative than a descriptive concept. To be fully human is an aspiration by adults, yet both children and adults are fully human insofar as they work towards attaining full humanity, which cannot be attained. Humanity is therefore as much a regulative ideal as a species descriptor: like 'beauty', 'justice', 'truth' or 'perfection', it is regarded as worth striving for even though it can never be fully attained.

This argument will be made more fully in Chapter 4.1, as the basis of a universal ethical proposition, but the present chapter has a more limited focus: that of consideration of the child *vis-à-vis* the adult. To discuss this, I shall differentiate between the terms 'human animal' and 'human being', using 'human animal' in the sense of 'the biological species that strives for humanity' and 'human being' as the state that is aspired to. It is pertinent to do this here as childhood is a state of not-yet-full-humanity, albeit variously understood (Stables, 2008). Human beings are animals with an aspiration towards a state of full humanity; they are in a state of human becoming. This aspiration is certainly strong within Western liberal culture but is not necessarily universal, though a sense of species preference and preservation (i.e. generally valuing the human animal over the non-human animal) is necessarily a feature of species membership. In relation to this, the Aristotelian argument is that education is about revealing or fulfilling the hidden and potential human essence of the child while the adult state is that in which this potential is fulfilled. (For a fuller discussion of the Aristotelian position, see Stables, 2008). In non-essentialist terms, the aspiration involves encouraging activity that approximates to the ideal of the human insofar as this is actually a guiding ideal for any social or cultural group at any time.

Tangential to the main argument is the acknowledgement that the problem of the infant, or of the not-yet-fully-human of any age, overlaps with the problem of the animal. Neither is fully human, yet both have human characteristics. To complicate this further, and *contra* Aristotle, the adult human animal is striving for full humanity as well as the child, though whether the adult animal is striving, and towards what, is not empirically verifiable from the human perspective. In the case of the human species, a greater realisation of human potential is certainly regarded as possible in the infant. However, this involves some trade-off against the respect owed to other animals. Many human cultures now only look down on non-human animals where they used to look both down on them and up to them according to context. Modern Western cultures are strongly self-referential in this respect, their humanisms little attuned to a sense of ecological interdependence. For this to change, child-rearing would have to acknowledge the incompleteness and dependence of the human animal as well as its specialness. Even we, human animals, are never quite fully human.

In support of this proposition, note that there is no universal agreement about when human life, as animal or being, begins and ends. In the case of the end of human life, the controversy is limited. There is some scientific, legal, moral and philosophical dispute about what should constitute the moment of death, but this is not currently an issue of much live public contestation. The same cannot be said of the first attribution of human status, however (for human status is attributed, however much it seems to reveal itself). With respect to the beginning of a human life, there is much greater uncertainty. Of course, the independent breathing of the baby after birth seems superficially to mark the beginning of a life, though even this is not so clear, for a baby can be 'stillborn'. Even the moment of birth is not clear, therefore. To those who have attended births, the moment of bonding with the baby may seem more clear; that is a moment of attribution. That bonding is necessary, however, for, at first, the newborn is alien.[60] For the mother who suffers postnatal depression and rejects the child, this moment of alienation may not have been overcome. (Mothers in other species occasionally fail to accept their infants as well). In any case, both legally and morally, birth is not taken as the sole beginning of a human life, as the enduring debates around abortion show. For some, including orthodox Catholics, a human life begins at conception: a conjunction of sperm and egg deserves the protection accorded to all the human species. For others, some conception of viability of the foetus determines this point. It scarcely needs noting that many who take the first view are appalled by the second. As with many important issues, what seems obvious to one group is far from clearcut to others.

As it stands, in law, full human recognition comes in two stages. The first relates to protection, as indicated above; the second to the holding of full adult rights and responsibilities. The first marks the infant as dependent human; the second marks the adult as autonomous. Once granted, the second set of rights is not easily removed. The dying centenarian with advanced dementia may not exercise his or her rights to, for example, vote, but still holds those rights, whereas the seventeen year-old waiting to take up a scholarship at Harvard University does not. Hitherto, British prisoners were not allowed to vote until the European Court of Human Rights dictated otherwise. Note that there are significant differences in both these areas (protection and adult freedoms) between cultures. 'Western' culture stresses both. In his study of child-rearing in America, Mintz (2004) noted the differences between European settlers and Native Americans in this respect. The latter were much less restrictive, if not protective, yet their adult culture was less individualistic and narrowly anthropocentric: their children were less dependent but their adults less autonomous.

In conclusion, the boundaries round what constitutes a human life, even biologically, are blurred and indistinct. On one level, humanity is a closed system biologically, since inter-species breeding is not possible. However, even this is not clearcut, as recent research indicates former extensive interbreeding between *home sapiens* and Neanderthals.[61] The human species will inevitably either die or split in the future, as all species will. Nothing lasts forever, including humanity, as animal or as aspiration.

The human system that intuitively seemed closed is not so, and consideration of those who exist on the borders of human recognition exemplifies this. The problem of the non-rational infant is, in many respects, the problem of the criminal, of the mentally incapacitated, and of the animal. (Feminists may argue that is also the problem of the woman. See, for example, Guenther, 2009, responding to Derrida. Socialists may argue that it is the problem of the working class, and even of the bourgeoisie). Amongst this uncertainty, there is the select club of those fully recognised as human, but how far membership of this club extends is, again, hard to determine. Who enjoys full and untrammelled human rights, enjoying complete freedoms of worship, assembly, speech or travel? We cannot always meet whom we choose or go where we wish to go: we cannot meet the dead, or those who do not wish to meet us, or those we cannot afford to visit, and we cannot visit two places at a time, for example. It can be argued that 'full human rights' represents an aspiration towards which different subsets of humankind have made different levels of progress. If the adult did not (also) fall short of the ideal of humanity, there could be no ideal to aspire to. We all are human insofar as we are becoming human, or attempting to do so. No group of people has the legitimation, on this account, to assume their humanity as a touchstone for that of others, or to impose it on them.

So far, the focus has been on what divides those, who are apparently equally human (non-human animals excluded). It is now appropriate to ask what unites these various categories, and – as this is a book about human development and education – to focus in this on the category of the infant, of the emerging, pre-rational, not-yet-fully-human being.

The embryonic human begins life as a combination of cells. (There is no significant body of thought, at least in the Western tradition that sees the individual life pre-existing this assumption, though it might be argued that various conceptions of reincarnation challenge it). These cells began as components of different bodies, the mother's and the father's, subject to the various influences on those bodies. Once combined, the new cell combination's growth, within the mother, is affected by factors affecting the mother (or surrogate host; in these cases, the situation is even more complex). These factors include hormonal balances, illnesses and other toxins. Who can say what the result of a stressful period at work for the mother will be for the personality and life of the infant growing within her, for instance? We are the products of experience, but not simply of our own.

It is helpful to understand life as *semiosis* here, rather than in terms of identity. It is clear that the embryo responds; it is not clear who or what the embryo is in relation to its full humanity. On one hand, the human embryo is a form of animal embryo. On the other, there is something distinct about it: it will develop into a human, not a cow, reptile or insect. Again, semiotics, in the form of biosemiotics, can explain this.

The field of zoosemiotics, or biosemiotics (the latter term now more often employed) derives from the work of the biologist Jacob van Uexküll, and was developed into a discipline by, principally, Thomas Sebeok (1920-2001). It has now developed into a field of study in its own right, subdivided into zoo-, bio- and eco-semiotics (Maran, 2006). It regards all life as operating in a signifying environment, comprising external reality (the *Umwelt*: the blade of grass that might be a snack for a cow or a pathway for an ant) and a subjective mind-map or *Innenwelt*. The physical substrate thus 'speaks' or signifies to each species in a distinct way, this making it appear that each species has 'semantic closure' (Pattee, 1995): that is, that each species appears to be distinct from all others, breeding within itself and growing virtual copies of itself. Over time, this closure is shown to be incomplete, as species mutate, interbreed and evolve. In the terms employed in Chapter 2.1, species, as well as individuals, inhabit overlapping phenomenal worlds.

Suppose that a human life begins at conception. In what senses is such a life human, and how does it develop its humanity?

In childhood and pre-childhood, others help to make us human; in adulthood, we are supposed to help ourselves. The latter is what the philosophers imply by 'rational autonomy'. Under most cultural arrangements, the emerging embryo enjoys human status in terms of legal protection, often as part of the body of the mother (to be disposed of at her wish), though sometimes (as in the preferred Roman Catholic settlement) as a recognised being of itself. It is not supposed that the early embryo exerts any conscious control over these matters, any more than it does over its own growth. However, as with all living organisms, the embryo draws selectively on its biophysical context to operate within its own *Umwelt*; unfortunately, this selectivity does not render it invulnerable to, for example, potentially damaging hormonal changes or drug misuse by its host. However, it will grow towards viability for human birth, or will not, regardless of its will.

Nobody chooses to be born, although Hindu and Buddhist concepts such as *kharma* allow a role for actions in past lives to determine fortunes in the life to come. If being human is being rational and self-conscious, then we are not human when we are born as human. Lack of choice notwithstanding, however, we are born as cultural operators. Infants are goal-directed, and soon learn the cultural conventions around them, including the language in its local form, to get their way. To quote Wittgenstein, the neonate 'knows how to go on'. Culture thus construed is a stronger force than conscious reflexivity, shaping our beginnings and our ends. It embraces and thus transcends rational autonomy. It comprises all variations in the ways in which groups of the human species do things, not just those that are conscious. Cat and human represent between-species variation; culture represents within-species variation. Presumably variations also exist within other species; they have been shown to exist among birds.[62]

The human baby is therefore culturally attuned and goal directed but not self-consciously rational. This obliquely raises questions about the degree to which it is inappropriate to talk about other animals in terms of culture and goal-directedness. Whatever the view of other animals, however, it is clear that if human life is characterised by conscious, partly linguistic self-reflexivity, then babies are not human. However, if living is accepted as a process of semiotic engagement, of interaction between an *Umwelt* and an *Innenwelt*, language only emerges as a problem if it is regarded as absolutely qualitatively different from other sign systems. A fully semiotic perspective does not allow for such absolute qualitative difference. Thus, in the absence of other intervening variables of which we are unaware, the commonly held differences between human and animal consciousness are likely exaggerated.

Following Aristotle (see Stables, 2008), it can nevertheless be argued that what renders a human 'human', the infant included, is not the practice of linguistic self-reflexivity (Descartes' *cogito*) but human potential. We nurture babies because we believe they will attain this human status, because it is somehow within them. (This does not explain why other animals nurture their offspring, though it might help to explain why they do not nurture them for so long; they may simply have fewer assumptions about potential). Interestingly, however, we do not remove human status from those who have clearly lost their rational powers and will almost certainly not regain them. Indeed, respecting the elders is common, if not quite ubiquitous, among human societies. Similarly, we do not judge people in terms of how human they are with respect to how far they activate this potential; indeed, those with limited cognitive capacity but much personal warmth are often regarded as more 'human(e)' than those oppositely endowed. Humanity, understood as rational, partly linguistic self-reflexivity is always a partial state: incomplete, vulnerable, changeable and attributed. Being human is never more than becoming human (or becoming less human): there is no human essence, unless essence is taken as synonymous with potential. Thus Aristotle's argument holds only up to a point: human potentiality does guide human living, but the adult human has not fully realised her or his potential.

This is not to argue that the human species is identical to, say, the cat species, though the cub or kitten realises the potential (usually) of becoming an adult cat. As well as observable differences, humans assume there are differences in terms of mental processing and other experiential attributes that are not so directly verifiable. However, these obvious and assumed differences should not render us forgetful that there is much that cannot be known, including the extent to which a cat is self-aware, in the way in which a human understands self-awareness. We cannot know how much is communicated by the 'language' of cats or how far they plan ahead or are aware of the possibility of their own deaths. We can only compare them with us and find them wanting in certain respects.

Interestingly, however, most modern societies that have rejected animism have also rejected the many ways in which human beings have traditionally looked up to animals as well as down on them. Though cows are still sacred in India, there is decreasing evidence in the developed world of rituals involving taking on animal spirits. Such rituals effectively recognise in other species characteristics that are present but relatively undeveloped in humans. One might seek the agility of the cat or the perceptive acuity of the eagle, for example, so attempt, through dance, music, narcotics or other ritual means, to invoke those spirits and thus strengthen the human. As strategies for survival and flourishing, such practices are surely as logical as those of eating animals, consuming their products (milk and so on) or exploiting them for labour (as transport, or to pull the plough). If one can enter into the experience of the lion, one will (literally) become more like it. The dwindling of such practices in modern societies indicates a narrowing of anthropocentrism, even if the human viewpoint is acknowledged as inescapably anthropocentric. It could be argued that our humanity is reduced rather than enhanced by this narrowing. After all, there is evidence of increased dependence on animals, rather than the reverse; note the rapid increases in meat consumption in developing economies. This has been accompanied by a decreased capacity for humans to see themselves in relation to other animals in a fuller sense.

Technology also problematizes the boundaries of the human, as explored in the literature on transhumanism, a movement dedicated to expanding the potential of the human through technological enhancement (e.g. More, 1990). Of all the movements definable within the container concept Posthumanism, transhumanism is perhaps that which attracts both most active support and most vehement opposition. Nevertheless, though some visions of a posthuman cyborg future may seem horrific to many, there is no doubt that certain technological innovations have become accepted as part of the human condition. A person's spectacles can certainly be understood as part of that person, as might a hearing aid, an artificial limb, or even a motor vehicle or computer. Even clothes can be understood as technological enhancement.

In conclusion, regarding the human system as open rather than closed enhances and empowers humanity.

All this points in the direction of acknowledging the specialness, of the human, but not allowing a view of human life as either completely qualitatively distinct (God-given when other life is not, for example, or biologically self-sufficient) or as fully rationally and self-consciously controlled.

Modern societies attempt to induct the young into full humanity through educational systems.[63] Educational systems in technologically advanced Western countries, however, often manifest both of these tendencies.

Specifically, formal, compulsory schooling falls prey to a series of fallacies:

1. that the point of schooling is to bring up children (who are not yet fully human) to be adults (who are);
2. that schooling is an important element in this because it helps people to learn; and
3. that the tighter the rational control over schooling, the more predictable and potentially desirable its outcomes.

1.fails to acknowledge that human thriving does not cease at the onset of adulthood. (Indeed, it may well strengthen at this point as the means of material survival are no longer provided).

2.fails to acknowledge that learning is inevitable. If it is feasible to understand all living as semiotic engagement, then learning must be an aspect of living. (See Stables, 2005, Chapter 2). It might be argued that learning has a special status as a form of living because it is sort of behaviour, or action, that brings about changes in behaviour. However, as has been argued, there is always an element of unpredictability in human response, as habit and convention are always subject to revision and reinterpretation in always different contexts. Thus it is the process of living itself that produces behavioural change; it does not require an autonomous rational agency or a particular configuration of the brain. (Of course, without a brain there would be no living and no learning). Learning is therefore inevitable; formal education channels it by guiding the student's attention, rather than creates or enhances it in any absolute sense. This argument will be developed in Chapter 3.3.

3.fails to acknowledge that cultural forces extend beyond the remit of conscious rational control, involving traditions, habits, beliefs, prejudices, attachments and resentments, all of which motivate human action. Becoming (more) human may be an aspiration for all human animals, and adults wish to make their children as fully human as possible. However, acknowledging this falls short of claiming that these human aspirations are the same, and equally prioritised, for all groups and individuals. It is self-evident that human virtues are ranked differently, if not understood differently, among and between cultural groups: note, for example, the variable roles of honour/dishonour, tolerance and tradition.

The narrow rationalisations above also apply to views of the human *vis-à-vis* other species. This narrow rationalistic anthropocentrism not only fails to grant respect to non-human animals but also runs the risk of channelling repressed pre-rational instincts into either cruelty or unreflecting sentimentalism.

Finally, this narrow rationalism has potentially disastrous political consequences, as implied above. As we strive for the first time to construct a global civilisation, it is imperative to acknowledge that all versions of the human animal are striving for full humanity in different, if overlapping ways, and that none has fully achieved it. For one group to regard itself as fully human is inevitably for it to reject deviation from its norms as inferior.

It almost goes without saying that this happens, and that it threatens global security and the possibilities of peace and progress.

The following chapters turn to more specific aspects of the development of the human being, individually and collectively, on this fully semiotic account. Chapter 3.2 considers what personal and social development might amount to in terms of semiotic engagement. Chapter 3.3 asks what formal educational institutions actually do, on fully semiotic terms, developing criticisms 1-3 of compulsory, formal schooling above, and thus how their collective role might be construed on this revised account of human growth and development.

3.2 FROM LITERACY TO SEMIOSY: LEARNING AS SEMIOSIC DEVELOPMENT

The present argument posits living as semiotic engagement, on the basis of an opposition to absolute mind-body dualism being transferred to a similar problematisation of the sign-signal distinction. However, so doing runs up against several problems in language.[64] In one case, the educational development of a thoroughgoing semiotic position is constrained by a lack of terms for semiotic or semiosic capacity. The person who can read and write words is literate and is blessed with literacy; there are no equivalent semiotic terms. On one level, this is self-evident insofar as everyone 'reads and writes the world' so no special term might be deemed necessary. However, if the educational task is, as in the present argument, to be construed as that of developing each person's range of semiotic resources as far as possible, on the basis that a collapsing of the sign-signal distinction is a valid basis for regarding all living as semiotic engagement, then a suitable terminology is called for. This lack is rendered the more telling by the ubiquity of ways in which the narrower concept of literacy has been co-located in recent years and thus made to apply to facets of life that have little or nothing to do with the capacity to read and write: emotional literacy, environmental literacy, computer literacy and so on.[65]

This chapter will, therefore, consider the following. Firstly, it will briefly rehearse the well-worn argument that fully human (adult) status in the modern world requires literacy, and that modern forms of education have been specifically devised with the production of literate adults – at least functionally literate adults – as end result. What counts as literacy has, however, been problematized and broadened in Late Modernity, or Postmodernity,[66] such that childhood can no longer be seen so strongly as preparation for literate citizenship. Second, taking as its scope the fully semiotic, rather than the merely literate, it will consider what it would mean to be functionally, culturally and critically 'semiate'. The chapter will conclude with a broader consideration of what semiosic development, or progression in 'semiosy' might involve, as an alternative to the mystification of 'learning' as a core educational concept. Curricular implications will be considered. This provides the background to a critical reappraisal of the role of schools and other educational institutions in Chapter 3.3.

While literacy, in the traditional sense of reading and writing, has generally been seen as an aspect of learning rather than the whole of it, it has assumed a central role in thinking about education and personal development for many centuries.[67] Postman (1994) advances a literacy related theory of childhood, arguing that the development of mass literacy resulted in only the literate citizen being regarded as fully adult. This in turn required a formalized and structured education into literacy as enacted in modern schooling. Postman also argues that literacy is necessary for abstract thought, thus he sees a reduction of focus on traditional literacy development as cause for concern. He is correspondingly unenthusiastic about the increasing ubiquity of both televisions and computers. Regardless of one's position on these specific matters, it seems indisputable that in latter years, 'literacy' has become increasingly broad and ill-defined. This is evident in the number and range of collocations that embrace it, including 'computer literacy', 'ecological literacy' and even 'emotional literacy'. This rash of literacies may be due in part to a not fully articulated move towards a more fully semiotic position, as academics in a range of fields became increasingly aware of the inseparability of language from thought, cognition and other semiotic systems (cf. the work of Vygotsky, 1962, 1975, and his increasing band of educational disciples), and in part to a concomitant carelessness in employment of the term. Either way, there seem to be many instances now of 'literacy' being tacked on to some other term to imply little or nothing more than knowledge, skill or understanding. Once literacy had become 'visual', for example, it could become almost anything.

A related problem to that of defining the boundaries of literacy is that of defining the boundaries of text. This is, of course, an operational problem for teachers of literature and language arts, as the following (entitled *Text Riddles* attempts to show)'Riddles', not 'show':

> If a story is a text, is a cartoon a text?
> If a cartoon is a text, is a storyboard a text?
> If a storyboard is a text, is a series of pictures a text?
> If a series of pictures is a text, is one picture a text?
> If a picture is a text, is a mural a text?
> If a mural is a text, is a painted wall a text?
> If a painted wall is a text, is a coloured wall a text?
> If a coloured wall is a text, is any wall a text?
> If a wall is a text, is a hedge a text?
> If a hedge is a text, is a tree a text?
> If a tree is a text, what is an English teacher? (Stables, 1995: 18).

There is no unobjectionable point at which the boundary of 'text' and 'non-text' can be set: a realisation neatly embraced in Jacques Derrida's '*Il n'y a pas de hors-texte*' (deliberately ambiguous in the French but literally translatable as 'there is nothing of outside-text': Derrida, 1976: 158). Consequently, there is no universally agreed point at which the concept of literacy in relation to an activity becomes or ceases to be justified. Note that this is not an anti-realist argument, since Derrida is always insistent on their being an Other to the text, albeit that Other cannot be understood in terms of anything essential or fixed.

What perhaps brought this problem to the fore was the increasing interaction of verbal and non-verbal communicative forms, in film, advertising, cartoons, computer interfaces and elsewhere. This, combined with insights from philosophical and theoretical movements as apparently disparate as logical positivism (e.g. Carnap, 1959), ordinary language philosophy (e.g. Austin, 1962), cybernetics (after Wiener, 1948) and structuralism (after Saussure, 1916) has resulted in a rich vein of new forms of study but a serious, and perhaps, fatal attack on the clarity of the concept 'literacy'.

One way of attempting to bring back some sense of order into this increasingly fragmented field is to, firstly, take the term 'literacy' seriously in collocations such as 'computer literacy' and even 'emotional literacy' and then to break it down in ways that are both acceptable within the traditional literacy debate and applicable beyond it.

A conventional analytic breakdown of literacy is into the forms functional, cultural and critical. This has become accepted for standard textbooks such as Williams and Snipper (1990).

Employing this tripartite distinction, functional literacy defines the ability to read and write (initially) to a standard that enables effective day-to-day functioning as an adult citizen: in other words, the ability to decode and encode script to the point at which everyday functions can be effectively be carried out, including the understanding to enable appropriate response to what has been read (so that one actually stops on reading a Stop sign, to take a simple example).

What counts as functionally literate is highly contingent, inevitably varying from place to place and time to time. For example, a Nineteenth Century farm worker in England had very little need to read and write, and thus very little was required to be functionally literate. Many could not even write their names on parish registers at their weddings, but the presiding priests were not in doubt of their identity so remained content with a scribbled 'X' or some such. The Twenty-First Century farm worker, however, has to understand how to operate dangerous and powerful machinery and how to mix, distribute, and monitor the consequences of distributing, potentially extremely toxic chemicals, as well as being expected to complete a self-assessment tax form. Startling revelations such as that over 40% of the Scottish population may be functionally illiterate, echoing recent concerns in England (http://news.scotsman.com/literacyinscotland/Scotlands-appalling-literacy-rate.2273515.jp, retrieved 22 December 2009) are moderated by the knowledge of the extreme relative demands of contemporary society in terms of traditional print literacy. It can come as no surprise that literacy levels are much lower in less developed than in more developed countries, yet there remain high levels of functional illiteracy in the latter. This does not ameliorate the problem in either context, however, as the functionally illiterate are seriously disadvantaged within their social contexts.

Cultural literacy is a contested concept. It can be associated both with commentators whose commitments are greater attention to the cultural practices of minority, suppressed or indigenous cultures (e.g. Bowers, 1974), and with those concerned with integration, or even assimiliation of minorities into dominant culture (Hirsch, 1987). E. D. Hirsch's prescription of 'What Every American Needs to Know' (1987: subtitle) is arguably the most influential expression of the latter position. In both cases, however, the argument for cultural literacy is that persons are disadvantaged, and may also be disadvantaging others, if they do not understand the significance of key events and of individuals and places within a culture. For example, a student teacher in Wales talked to a class of 12 to 13 year olds about Bonfire Night: the traditional 'celebration' on November 5th of the Catholic plot to blow up Parliament led by Guy Fawkes in 1605 and commemorated by the ritual burning of a 'guy' on a large municipal bonfire and the setting off of fireworks. Bonfire Night, irrespective of how one regards its motivation, is a fixed item on nearly every British child's calendar. When asked what Bonfire Night commemorated, none of the class of (low-achieving) Year 8 pupils knew; one of them asked, 'Is it when Jesus was born?' Such examples remind the culturally literate of just how disadvantaged students lacking such forms of knowledge can be, irrespective of whether they are able to read and write. In addition, cultural literacy directly affects reading and writing, not only in terms of what is understood but also in matters such as choice of appropriate register: the same student teacher had great difficulty with one member of the above class in getting him to write a Christmas card for his mother, not because he could not write but because he did not know the appropriate form of address.[68]

Critical literacy is also contested. In the liberal-humanist tradition – in conventional Twentieth Century approaches to the teaching of history, or the literary canon, for example - to be critical was to be able to develop an individual response that stood up to external scrutiny: the polished argument was good, the original polished argument best of all. In the socially critical tradition, critique is more centred on cultural analysis rather than individual brilliance in interpreting cultural heritage (though whether this makes as much difference to what is ultimately lauded as is sometimes claimed is open to question). Here, the emphasis is on understanding the ideological forces that shaped the text, or other cultural artefact, in order to be able to subvert those dominant power relations and thereby become empowered. The most influential application of this broad approach to the practical educational field has perhaps been that of Paolo Freire, whose approach to development education was grounded in a commitment to indigenous and suppressed people devising their own solutions rather than slavishly following experts from the developed world (Freire, 1972).

A certain amount of work has been done in applying this Functional-Cultural-Critical framework to new or extended literacies such as those implied in the collocations referred to earlier (e.g. Stables, 1998). Thus, to take the example of computer literacy (CL), it might be assumed that functional CL involves the ability to conduct key functions such as using email, word processing, spreadsheets and internet search engines; cultural CL involves knowing what to make of what is available on the Net and thus how to make informed choices about, for example, what kinds of research for a school assignment are likely to be valid or valuable; critical CL involves understanding the internet as a means of potential manipulation and learning how to use it as a tool for empowerment rather than the reverse. This brief example serves to show both how these forms of literacy overlap and how differentiating between them offers the possibility of a more focused educational appraisal than can be gained by simple adherence to the blanket term 'literacy'.

There is already an implicit assumption in many of these collocated literacies that the concern extends well beyond the narrow limits of spoken or written language. Often when we use 'literate' we would mean 'semiate' if the term were in common use. Taking the liberty of adopting this neologism, therefore, it is appropriate to consider what might be understood by functional, cultural and critical semiosy, and then how this might be instantiated and developed in any particular field. Note also that, if (but only if) living can validly be regarded as semiotic engagement, then semiosic development can serve as an alternative concept to learning as a whole, and not merely to literacy development, variously understood.

Because semiosy is a broader concept than literacy, the lines between the functional, cultural and critical are harder to define. For example, use of colour in the Chinese and Anglophile worlds tends to involve some different traditions. On arriving in China, a Westerner may be struck by the vibrancy and particular use of colour on posters and notices, but may not be aware that, for example, white is the colour of death and funeral celebrations in the Chinese cultural context, whereas it tends to function either as neutral background or as symbolic of freshness and innocence in the Western; red tends to signifies good fortune in China, but danger and sensuality in the West. There must be many other examples. However, it is possible to maintain the distinction between the functional and the cultural here. Functionally, the newly arrived Westerner needs to understand what is going on at the simple level of survival: to distinguish between an advertising poster and a shop sign, for example, or to be able to locate a restaurant or lavatory. This does not necessitate knowing that white symbolises death and red good fortune, for the new arrival is likely merely to look for what s/he can recognise from the Western context and act accordingly. However, a knowledge of Chinese colour conventions is just one small way in which the visitor's experience can be enriched, and such enrichment increases the possibility of cultural integration and success in the new context.

Critical semiosy is a problematic concept not least because criticality is generally associated with language use and semiosic response may or may not involve language. Arguably, considering the cultural-critical distinction from a fully semiotic perspective serves to problematize it altogether. However, there remains a difference, albeit subtle, between recognising the cultural traditions on, say, a Taiwanese election poster and having the sort of understanding of how the medium is manipulated to attract votes that results in real personal or collective empowerment. The latter involves knowing how to go on as a propagandist as well as an elector, in Wittgensteinian terms.[69]

It is, therefore, possible to differentiate between different forms of semiosy, as of literacy. Nevertheless, the former is of a different order from the latter. If living is semiotic engagement, then everyone is semiate, while not everyone is literate. It could be argued that within the whole of life engagement (semiotic engagement) certain forms of semiotic activity need teaching while others do not: traditionally conceived literacy and numeracy, for example, are specialised activities that children, in general, learn best in schools. This, of course, is a standard educational position, though the problems attendant to treating literacy and numeracy as discrete sets of teachable skills are well recognised within the literature.

As noted above, everyone is and becomes semiate while not everyone becomes literate. There are grounds for stating that person A is more literate than person B but not that s/he is more semiate. (To regard A as more 'learned' would be to employ a restricted definition of learning as equating to traditional scholarly activity). Each person is differently semiate, however, and patterns of response to life events generally are what determine differential levels of success and wellbeing. Some people are better than others at increasing material resource; some are more content with their lot. Whether these traits, along with the social and cultural circumstances of one's birth, are determined or not is a philosophical question the outcome of which is not only indeterminable but also of little consequence to the present debate. It may, after all, be the case that all learning is predetermined, but that does not remove the feelings of satisfaction and personal growth that can attend it. All that can be achieved is a clearer understanding of what it is about some people's semiotic engagement with the world that leads them to greater human flourishing than is granted to others, even where external circumstances and constraints seem comparable. Related to this are notions of deficit and disadvantage: while there may be little perceived need to regard one person as more 'semiate' than another, there may well be value in identifying certain 'semiosic deficits' that impede normal development. For example, the concept 'dyslexia' often lacks a clear working definition, taken sometimes as narrowly relating to reading and writing difficulties and at others as 'specific learning disorder'.[70] The former is regarded by experts as overly narrow, while the latter can be seen as almost uselessly vague. In such cases, a view of learning as semiosic development may prove helpful in clarifying and (perhaps even more importantly) communicating the issues at stake here.

Drawing on a range of traditions, the following characteristics of the highly semiate person might be identified:

- Relatively more successful people have a greater range of knowledge, understanding and skills than less successful people; they either select carefully from this range or deploy a greater range; this in turn often but not necessarily implies they have been more educationally successful;
- More successful people respond less often through avoidance. If they are fearful, they overcome their fears or find alternative strategies to avoid them. They are not risk averse and do not make excuses;
- More successful people both utilise memory strategies well (use the past to inform the present) and appreciate the present more fully; it might be said that they live more mindfully.[71]

This raises the objection that semiosis has now become so vague an analytical concept that it has become effectively empty, leaving no more than a set of psychological truisms. The above list reads like the introduction to a course in positive psychology, and raises the question of what a focus on semiosis really adds to an understanding of human development.

The answer is counterintuitively simple. While semiosis is never fixed or entirely stable, it also has no fixed hidden depth or structure: the responses that people have to events, involving their biophysical organisms, in the present, are their responses and provide all the data that are required to work on. Unlike 'learning', the concept carries with it no unhelpful mystification, as expressed in constructs such as 'learning how to learn' or 'enhancing learning'. There is no necessary recourse to hidden depths and structures, whether to the subconscious mind, the division of labour or the logic of reasoning. Nothing hangs on distinctions between cognitivism and behaviourism or between personal and social concepts of mind. Just as Saussurean language theory evolved to concentrate on the endless variety of *parole* and to reject the necessity to recognise underlying structures of *langage* and *langue*,[72] so semiosic development as a response to learning theory can simply accept the variety of human interpretations and responses as they appear. Every person's response to every event both necessarily draws in shared cultural resources and is individual, as the context of that response is always to some extent unique. Insofar as it is historically determined, that historical determination itself eludes complete understanding. Education that is attentive to individuals is not, then, education that accepts certain responses as normal and certain as pathological by reference to some external totalising scheme, nor education that attempts to define students' progress according to rigid measures of 'ability', 'potential' (drawn from standardised tests), gender, social class or any other objective measure, but rather that both accepts and questions all responses. This is not to sanction all responses as carrying equal value in society – nobody takes someone seriously who insists that 2+2=5, as this is not how the language game of mathematics 'goes on' – but to accept all responses as they are and to challenge and develop them by confronting them with other (often, but not always, 'standard') responses. Thus the conservative student benefits from exposure to radical perspectives and the immoral student to ethical reasoning. This is not to determine what each student's response will be to that questioning, as that can never be determined.

On one level, this begs a simplification of teaching and its attendant bureaucratic processes; on another a greater sensitisation.

The richness of human experience and meaning cannot be reduced to simple Right and Wrong. On the other hand, no knowledge is judgment-free and all judgments are necessarily social judgments. Education is, in this sense, always judgmental, as, implicitly, is all social policy. (For example, a decision to increase tax on alcohol and reduce it on organic food would imply a clear judgment about what constitutes healthy consumption). However, what is required is a move from exclusive to inclusive judgmentalism. Exclusive judgmentalism allows for only certain persons' judgments to be articulated, and does not allow those judgments to be challenged or encourage them to be revised; teachers' personal professional judgments are not to be trusted, and students' judgments even less. Inclusive judgmentalism would not remove judgmentalism but rather universalise it. Everyone involved would be expected to make real judgments, with real consequences, and learn from the consequences of those judgments with a view to refining them in future (bearing in mind that judgments cannot simply be repeated in any case as contexts for judgment never repeat themselves exactly). On this basis, the educational process becomes one of continuous challenge to preconceptions, in which what A means by X is always confronted by what B means by X, with reference, overt or tacit, to what C means by X where C refers to the person or group with the greatest power over the discourse: the government, experts in the field or examiners, for example. However, this does not remove either A or B from the responsibility of taking considered action and facing the consequences of it. This is an educational system with no place for censorship or other forms of totalitarian control over thought and response, even where this is paraded under the banner of political correctness. At the same time, it is a system that values process and product equally, as interdependent but discrete processes, in which discussion and communication lead to committed responses that have real consequences for both teacher and taught. In short, it is, in contrast to extant heavy accountability procedures, a system of high trust.

Again, this has implications for social policy more broadly. Take, for example, the issue of climate change. There is a scientific consensus, though not uncontested, that human-induced emissions of carbon dioxide have contributed to global warning in recent decades. Governments have important responsibilities in relation to this and a number of possible avenues for action. They can affect both supply and demand sides of the economy through, for example, tax and incentives. They can offer grants and subsidies for 'green' energy and for energy conservation: for solar panels on domestic dwellings, for example, or for roof insulation. They can alter building regulations and planning laws. In addition, they can conduct policy as public education in various respects, and in this they have a clear choice. One option is to use the mass media, including the WorldWideWeb, to promote the approved messages, in order to encourage the desired behaviours. Another is to promote the free flow of information and debate so that members of the public are encouraged to confront the issues and come to their own conclusions. That the former has been the preferred path of the UK government in recent years is evidenced by the role scepticism is granted in the debate. To be a climate change sceptic is to be construed as a climate change denier, with the implication here that 'climate change' is partly human-induced. This can be seen as an example of exclusive judgmentalism in relation to policy as public education. It can be justified, to some degree, on the grounds that the issues are difficult and the statistics impossible for a non-expert to make sense of. Notwithstanding these concerns, an inclusive judgmentalism in this case would involve putting everyone in the position of having to address the issues as far as possible, presenting them with not merely the officially approved 'facts' but with the scientific data and the scientists' interpretations of them, both where these cohere and where they differ. If inclusive judgmentalism were the policy driver, scepticism would be seen as antithetical to denial. The latter might be seen as a much more risky strategy, and maybe the situation concerned needs exceptional treatment because of its extreme seriousness. Nevertheless, there is an educational principle here. Scepticism and openness can both be seen as strong educational virtues, and a democratic polity relies on a thinking, as well as a minimally informed populace. In the longer term, and taken across the entire range of policies, encouragement of inclusive rather than exclusive judgmentalism must surely, on this account, be the more empowering path.[73] Similar, perhaps less controversial, arguments have been made in relation to issues of obesity and body image, with commentators such as Rich arguing that public messages on this matter often serve to disempower rather than the reverse (e.g. Rich, 2011a,b.).

Semiosic development, thus understood, becomes the key issue of educational concern, of more importance than 'learning'. Human beings are both semiate from birth (or earlier) and become increasingly, or increasingly acceptably semiate as they learn to 'read and write' situations in increasing sophisticated, appropriate or effective ways. As all living is semiotic engagement, this implies that any development in semiosy must be seen as a matter of social judgment rather than pure growth, though it could be argued that the move from dependence to autonomy (however construed) transcends cultural difference. Either way, somehow our capacities to respond to situations develop such that we can, or at least appear to, increase our and others' flourishing.

It seems appropriate to consider, therefore, what the implications of considering semiosic development might be for, in turn, overall educational policy, the management and leadership of schools and other educational organisations, curriculum, teachers and teaching, and, finally, students and learning. These aspirations for education provide a context for the critical appraisal of formal education in Chapter 3.3.

In all these cases, the central tenets of a fully semiotic approach to living and learning are first that meaning is interpretation (where interpretation need not be conscious) and secondly that outcomes are never fully predictable. As far as overall policy is concerned, this surely implies a limit to the extent to which outcomes can, and should, be predicted. Until about the 1980s, this might not have been a controversial position to take, at least in a liberal state with a concomitant commitment to educational for rational autonomy, such as the U.K. However, educational policy in many countries since then, like much social policy, has been developed according to a strict accountability model, in which actors are, at least in theory, held responsible for meeting agreed or imposed targets. Taking semiosis as foundational, however, militates against such an approach. Understandable though the impulse to make large service providers accountable for the money spent on them is, it is doomed to failure: targets cannot and will not always be met. Furthermore, there is no guarantee that meeting the imposed targets will deliver the service that all the users will prefer.

Against this, investment in services must be evaluated somehow. The most obvious step-change here would seem to be from principally quantitative to principally qualitative forms of evaluation. That is, measurement of outcomes could take a secondary role to measures of customer satisfaction. The implications for schooling policy in the UK, to take one example, would be obvious and stark. Successful schools would be those their users considered successful, not those with good league table positions; failing schools would be those deemed failing by their users, not necessarily those with the worst examination results. Perhaps users in this context should be considered in this order of importance: first, students and former students, then parents, then employers, then other members of the community, however defined; in other words, in order of their degrees of personal investment as users. That this is not the current approach may be explained easily by confronting an uncomfortable dilemma: the more qualitative the measures, the less they can be directly orientated towards achieving greater equality of outcome or other overriding policy objectives, all or most of which are set with good intentions. However, if outcomes cannot be so predicted or engineered, to pursue them may not be feasible. The choice is, on these terms, stark.[74]

The same dynamics are at play in the management and leadership of organisations, such as schools. Here, too, taking a fully semiotic view surely leads to a welcoming recognition of differential interpretation and action rather than a purely performative view that understands effectiveness in terms of simple delivery of objectives through line management systems. The school in which discussion is open and differing views are welcomed is, on this account, preferable to that which groans under the weight of a false, imagined or imposed consensus. In effect, a fully semiotic account renders all systems as open, even where they are generally considered closed. There are no firm limits to what constitutes a school, a manager, a teacher or a pupil, for example; on close inspection, all these boundaries are less clear than they first appear. (Where exactly does Harvard University begin and end? When is the author of this chapter a teacher and when is he not? Is a student a student during the school holidays?) Schools are communities of living persons, not just ships that can be steered – and even ships are in constant interaction with the elements that move them and attack their boards. Good management and leadership should surely acknowledge and welcome such uncertainty, being ever watchful and responsive to inevitable but unpredictable change. This is after all, perhaps, a more obvious construal of the idea of public service than that encapsulated in the obsession to meet fixed targets.

In the same spirit, the work of teachers cannot effectively, so should not (on this account) be highly prescribed. Of course, as in the other cases, there is a balance to be struck here. Parents, students and others reasonably expect to know roughly what children will be taught, that the examinations they will take will be of comparable value to those taken by others, and that they will have been thoroughly prepared for them. However, within these broad parameters, teachers have to use their professional judgments in dealing with young people of varied interests, abilities and backgrounds. A system that insists on too much standardisation can only restrict the potential for this judgment to be exercised. Again, however, there is a tough choice to be made here, for increasing emphasis on teachers' professional judgments means reducing the emphasis on achieving overriding social aims such as 'raising (pre-specified) standards' or 'improving (quantitatively measurable) life chances'. Only a robust educational theory enables one to make such difficult choices. If semiosis is regarded as foundational, then over-emphasis on the latter simply does not work.

Similar tough choices emerge in consideration of issues of student choice. Well behaved, compliant students are *prima facie* more likely to succeed, but students who are motivated to achieve are most likely to achieve. It is interesting to recall at this point the work of Andrew Pollard and his colleagues looking at pupil learning identities. For example, Pollard and Filer (1999) identify four clear types: conformist, re-definition, non-conformist and anti-conformist. Perhaps counter-intuitively, both conformist and anti-conformist positions can be antithetical to ultimate success since they both involve risk aversion in the classroom context. Ultimately more successful students are those who resist stereotypical positions, who seek recognisable individual identities and who, better still, actively seek to develop their own identities rather than stay with them. In some earlier work, Pollard had identified 'Jokers' as the most successful classroom group, implying by this those pupils who took an active role (in collaboration with, not in opposition to, the teacher) in the progress of the lesson. It might go without saying that students who take risks may pose more problems for teachers than those who are passively compliant. However, if the inevitability of individual response is acknowledged, then all teaching should seek to encourage such response, and teaching should be problematized by encouraging difference as students problematize their own lives by waking up to the endless possibilities of action that confront them rather than either simply following instructions or, even worse, rebelling against everything that schooling offers them.

For all these actors – policy makers, leaders, managers, teachers and students – an emphasis on becoming increasingly semiate involves a movement towards a more high-trust, personally responsive regime than that offered in highly centralised and controlled systems. It involves a reaffirmation of personal responsibility, including a more open acceptance that students, too, make their own choices and that these choices have real consequences for themselves.

It is in the spirit of the present argument that it should stop short of detailed prescriptions for action: if the argument is accepted, then actors will interpret it in their own ways. However, it might be noted that there are other commentators who, notwithstanding their lack of exlicit engagement with the idea of semiosis, have begun to move in similar directions. Pollard's case has been noted above. Rom Harré's work on identity development and personal positioning (Harré, 1983, 1998) stresses the need for individuals to balance social and personal identity, and his construal of identity development in terms of a cycle of Conventionalisation, Appropriation, Transformation and Publication has been cited as a model for teaching and assessment that values personal creativity while acknowledging the importance of public feedback (Harré, 1983; Ross, Radnor, Mitchell and Brierton, 1993; Stables, Morgan and Jones, 1999). Gert Biesta (2006) draws on Hanna Arendt's concept of natality in his 'Beyond Learning' thesis (title) to separate the categories 'education' and 'learning' and to argue that teachers' roles should not be primarily to transmit information or values but to engage with students so that newness is constantly emerging into the world. In all these cases, and many more, there is a recognition that something is missing in an education system, or indeed in any system of social welfare, that attempts simply to deliver pre-set objectives through effectively top-down structures (for if the structures are not effectively top-down, the objectives cannot be assumed to hold), however desirable the specified outcomes may be. Unfortunately such outcomes are unachievable. People are born and die as semiotic engagers, both interpreting and, little by little, changing the semiotic structures they inherit. Their ways of engaging with the systems of meanings that constitute their environments will change, and some of that change is construed as development. This is particularly so when the outcomes of the changes are approved, either by the individual concerned or by interested others. This is a far cry, however, from the claim that educational experts can ever really know what it is good for students to learn. Consider, for example, what the outcomes might have been of sticking to a strictly prescribed 'Curriculum for the Twentieth Century' devised in 1910, based on the considered predictions of well meaning experts.

Formal education takes up a good deal of a young person's time and therefore should offer myriad opportunities for significant events from which they learn and are deemed to have grown. Such growth should place help them become more successful and fulfilled citizens when they leave school. A belief in this fundamental power is in no way diminished by a refusal or inability to state exactly what it is that people need to know and to do to become highly semiate; rather, the switch of emphasis from literacy to semiosy serves as a reminder that there is much more to living and learning than the acquisition of a set of clearly defined skills. While certain skills clearly are important in the adult communities of given societies, there is no case for basing education simply around their acquisition *via* purely top-down systems. Rather, a semiotically rich education will, as Biesta, Harré and others effectively suggest, entail the appropriation of existing cultural resources into the evolving worldviews of the people it is supposed to serve. The end result of any education system is the sense students come to make of the world and their place in it. This is a matter of constant negotiation and interpretation.

Given this, there is a need to reappraise schools, and the almost universal assumption that what they do is *ipso facto* good. This critical examination of the role and function of formal, compulsory schooling is the focus of the Chapter 3.3.

3.3 WHAT DO SCHOOLS DO?

The position so far developed is empiricist, semiotic and pragmatic. It maintains that all sentient beings operate in a physical transcendent present (PTP). That is, they have a sense of Now in which they operate as observers of a moving world. They know this world and how it operates from past experience (empirically), understanding elements within that world in terms of how they are prone to operate, and therefore in terms of their effects and uses (pragmatically). The cat recognises the mouse insofar as it recognises the behaviour of mice. It knows what sort of thing the mouse will do and can preempt this to some extent. Every Now has, therefore, a Then dimension that comprises past and future aspects. Every sentient being has an *Umwelt*, its environment comprises signs to which it reacts (semiotically). At times one's *Umwelt* changes, never more dramatically than at the time of birth: the foetus's *Umwelt* was within the mother; the infant's outside.

Returning to the human species, no two people have precisely the same *Umwelt*, though the basic signifying structure is inherited culturally. Within this shared set of inherited meanings,[75] however, individuals respond differently. There are people with enhanced or diminished individual senses, for example, or formative experiences that render commonly held meanings alien to them: the idea of the parent as loving and protective, for example. Then there are inherited meanings specific to cultural groups: an example might be the different cultural responses to dogs, cows or pigs.

This chapter is about the effect 'education' has on all this, but first the term must be given a working definition, lest it be taken as either unfeasibly broad or over-subject to particular interpretations.

There are a number of terms that overlap with 'education' but are not synonymous with it. These include 'learning', 'teaching', and 'school' (or 'college'/'university').

From a fully semiotic perspective, it is impossible to identify 'learning' as a qualitatively distinct form of life (Stables, 2005: Chapter 6). If all living is semiotic engagement, and learning is an element of living, then learning is also semiotic engagement. I have suggested in earlier work that 'learning' is most accurately defined as 'a term applied retrospectively to changes in the life story' (Stables 2005: 67). The saying 'We live and learn' is a wise one: by living we learn, and we cannot avoid learning. Old people in physical and mental decline have to learn patience and toleration of dependence even as they approach the very end of their lives. Learning is, therefore, inevitably part of what comprises education, since it accompanies every changing stage of life. It is a necessary but not sufficient condition of education, therefore. 'Education' is normally taken as comprising other elements, including that of teaching. Also, not all learning is generally taken to be educational, as it may not comply with what are considered educational aims.[76]

Teaching too, however, happens all the time. When my partner tells me the dishes have not been washed, she has taught me something and I have learnt something. (Whether I have 'learnt my lesson' depends on the relationship of 'teaching' to that of 'curriculum': there are strong social norms governing what should and should not be learnt). Teaching does not happen only in classrooms. Teaching always leads to learning, however trivial, however, though learning does not require direct or recognisable teaching. Teaching is therefore also a necessary but not sufficient condition of education. Again, not all teaching may be regarded as educational, if one takes the view that an education in drug-dealing is not really educational, for example.

For present purposes, 'school' or 'schooling' will be the term employed for formal educational establishments and certificated processes, given that alternative terms such as 'college' imply elements of ambivalence around conceptions of formal instruction, curriculum and compulsion. Schooling does not happen all the time. It happens in highly constrained environments and largely at tightly specified times. As it does not have a monopoly on either learning or teaching, schooling also is not a sufficient condition of education, but it is a necessary condition, if and only if one accepts what goes on in any particular school as educational. It is quite possible to conceive of a school in which people were not doing anything regarded as of educational value, though it would not be possible to conceive of a school in which nobody taught anybody and nobody learnt anything. This suggests that 'schooling' is (as are 'learning' and 'teaching') in some respects a broader term than 'education' while in other respects a narrower one. Just as not all teaching and learning might be seen as educational, so not all that happens in school is educational. Now, it might be argued that 'schooling' implies only the educational aspects of 'what goes on in school': that 'schooling' is directed along educational lines. Against this, one might note that the institution of schooling forms a necessary element in the social fabric of so-called 'advanced' countries. If it were to be shown today that no school offers anything of educational value, the schools would still likely open tomorrow as schooling, in the broader sense above, has a child-minding function. Schools (arguably colleges and even universities) keep (mostly) young people out of the way, leaving (most) adults free to continue with economic life.

To sum up, 'education' is generally taken to comprise as necessary elements the following, though none alone amounts to a sufficient condition of it: human change and development in a socially approved direction; learning; teaching, and usually participation in schooling. 'Schooling', however, is not entirely synonymous with education. Education in total is a necessary but not sufficient condition of schooling. (Few would deny that schooling should be educational). Schooling, however, has two distinct features. First, its control function involves elements that are not otherwise seen as educational or desirable, such as the tight control of students' time and movement. Secondly, learning through schooling is highly controlled (or rather, strong attempts are made to control it), in that its association with teaching is more tightly specified and contextually specific than in life in general, *via* norms of instruction, both didactic (in terms of how things are taught) and curricular (in terms of what is taught).

It need hardly be noted that there is no shortage of people willing to advise on what schools should do. Given this plethora of expertise and quasi-expertise, it is notable how relatively little work is done on what schools actually do. Funded educational research is often either evaluative or developmental: looking at issues of school effectiveness and improvement. Such approaches do not warrant or welcome critical interrogation of either the aims or the actual merits and demerits of schools, other than against sets of predetermined criteria. Alongside this narrowly instrumentalist agenda, there often go unchallenged certain assumptions. These include that schools exist to teach people how to learn, as well as to give people learning, and that the learning in schools comes from teaching. 'Learning' may often be seen as the scarce goods that only schools can provide, a view shared by those in the teaching profession who wish to counter any suggestion that they might be regarded as 'child-minders'.

The preliminary remarks above show none of these assumptions to be more than partly justified. Schooling does not teach people to learn, though it may teach them certain kinds of learning process, such as the conduct of science. Young, for example, has argued that schooling offers universal access to a range of discourses that would otherwise be denied to children from less privileged backgrounds (Young, 2009). While it is not justifiable to assert 'You go to school to learn how to learn', therefore, it is at least partly justifiable to assert, in most cases, 'You go to school to learn how to learn science'. Similarly at the level of content, while living would be impossible without learning some scientific facts, school may be the only environment in which many encounter the specialist scientific knowledge. How much of this knowledge is retained or subsequently deployed remains open to question, but at least school introduces young people to it. On the other hand, teachers clearly are employed in part as childminders. However, teachers are not merely childminders; cheaper childminders could be sought were that the case.

Consider a child beginning her career at a new school. Let us call her Tess.

Tess's first encounters with the school happen before lessons begin. Indeed, they may have happened on a preliminary visit. From her physically transcendent present position, her 'My Now', her senses are regaled with a fast moving succession of images, part familiar, part strange. She recognises other pupils as familiar children, whether personally known to her or not, and that they are moving from place to place. However, she does not know yet where these places are. She knows they are moving to and from lessons, but she is not sure exactly what those lessons will be like. Perhaps most importantly to her, she knows something about how to fit in with this environment, but she does not know how she will be received; she does not know which, if any, of these children will be her friends, or which, if any, of the teachers will value her contributions. She has a sense of who she is in relation to this new *Umwelt*, but also a sense of deep uncertainty about who she will become in relation to it.

Now consider there are two Tesses. Tess 1 is the daughter of a teacher at the school, was a highflyer at her previous school, and already has friends at the new school. Tess 2 did poorly at her last school, comes from a family with little interest in or sympathy for formal education, and has no friends yet at the new school. Perhaps she was sent here as a result of the disruption attributed to her previous friendships. Both Tesses live in the PTP; each has a ' My Now'. Tess 2's is likely to be more fearful, less confident than Tess 1's. There is little doubt that Tess 1 is likely to fit in better, get better marks and be regarded as the more 'able' student. (Partly examined concepts such as 'ability' and 'effort' form important elements in the discourse of schooling[77]). Tess 2 will almost inevitably struggle. However, each is engaging with her *Umwelt*; they are equal in that respect, at least. Indeed, it could be argued that surviving the school is a far greater challenge for Tess 2, whose immediate *Umwelt* seems generally less inviting than Tess 1's. Tess 2, in short, may well learn more and try harder (that is, expend more energy) while also receiving lower marks for her work and less encouraging feedback about her 'ability'. Tess 2 may learn more overall but learn less about the curricular, examined subjects. Tess 1 may simply carry on as normal and be praised for her effort and intelligence.

In short, what schools actually do is present people with a mass of sensory data that they will make sense of according to their conditioning (partly from within the school, partly from without) and their context. (Note that self-image, for example, involves both conditioning and context. Many children may enter certain classrooms convinced that they 'cannot do this'; for many others, the case is reversed). In general, this sensory onslaught has certain common characteristics, and to survive amongst it requires certain skills and resiliences. Inevitably children learn from going to school. Ultimately, however, what they learn is unpredictable.

There is much evidence to show that school tends to reproduce academic success and social advantage, so that Tess 2 will almost (but not quite) inevitably do worse there than Tess 1.[78] However, attempting to understand it from a fully semiotic perspective, wherein learning is inevitable, encourages emphasis on the extra-curricular and social learning that attending school must promote. Both Tesses will have had to negotiate the complex social matrix of school life, particularly with respect to peer group acceptance.[79] School also inevitably teaches one more about the web of power relations that drives society beyond the family gates. At the same time, it might be borne in mind that much learning of this sort could take place in an alternative setting to a school.

Taking all these elements into account, it can be inferred that schooling is a powerful, though not all-powerful, form of socialisation. This socialisation function is undertaken on several levels. First, as the Tesses' fears show, there are the challenges of socialising, of struggling for acceptance, affection and respect among peers. Secondly, there is the induction into socially valued forms of thinking and (to a lesser extent) other forms of 'doing'. This is the socialisation into thinking like a mathematician, a historian or an artist. How far this succeeds with many children, given the time they spend in school (in two school careers, primary and secondary) is open to debate, as is the range of forms of induction that are offered, for craft and art skills are little developed in most schools. There is a long idealist philosophical tradition, strongly identified with Plato and Hegel among others, that sees induction into conceptualisation as of central importance in the fulfilling of human potential, though it is important to note that, for Hegel, merely abstract conceptualising was not enough: the subject must be actively engaged in the struggle towards universal knowledge;[80] there is also a more recent sociological argument along the lines that only formal, compulsory schooling can offer induction into facilities of reasoning the possession of which is a necessary prerequisite for access to positions of social advantage (Young, 2009). This aspect of the socialisation function of the school is, therefore, widely regarded as of central importance in determining the overall value of schooling. Finally, schooling socialises insofar as it filters and selects. Many would argue that the advantage Tess 1 begins her school career with is effectively the advantage she is likely to end it with. There are exceptions, but in general school rewards cultural and social capital (Bourdieu, 1986) with more cultural and social capital, at least for those whose stock of capital is fairly high at the outset; whether it offers a good return on the limited capital brought by Tess 2 remains a matter of controversy.

These general remarks about schooling, it might be argued, downplay individual students' agency. That is, some Tess 1s will make little of school, while some Tess 2s will thrive, perhaps finding education a wonderful escape route from relative deprivation. As to the extent to which such motivations are intrinsic or socially determined, the debate may never be closed. It is certainly the case that generalisations about schooling cannot predict individual outcomes other than in terms of probabilities. It is also the case that the provision of education is not the sole determinant of the educated person: educational success (if that is the same as being an educated person – see, for example, Hodgson, 2010) requires certain dispositions in the student and may be little dependent on, for example, the quality of teaching or curriculum.

Society requires knowledgeable, sociable and capable individuals, but also innovative and courageous ones. Schooling in general focuses on the first set of qualities (though the range of capacities it directly seeks to develop is limited), yet many innovative and courageous individuals have had very conventional schooling. Indeed, the case might be made that those members of society most widely recognised as creative, or as showing qualities of leadership, come predominantly from the most traditional and conventional schools. Insofar as this is valid, it might be explained in terms of three contributory factors. Perhaps such schools offer more challenges to students, and thus make them develop their capacities to problem-solve and take initiatives. Perhaps schooling is not the main contributory factor here, as these pupils come from backgrounds that predispose them to excel in other ways. Perhaps perceived traits such as innovation, courage, creativity and leadership are merely inevitable responses to high levels of knowledge and other forms of socialisation, though it is not universally assumed that the most 'schooled' individuals are also the most entrepreneurial in any sense.

Whatever one's position on the questions above, schooling seems a broadly conservative institution. That is, schooling socialises in various ways. Some students may exploit this socialisation in exciting and fruitful ways, but such exploitation is not the formal business of schools, which tends to be that of cultural transmission rather than cultural reform. Note, for example, Biesta's argument that education construed simply as learning inevitably concerns itself more with socialisation than with the creation of the new: Arendt's 'natality' (Biesta, 2006; Arendt, 1958).

Living in the PTP relies a great deal on the taken-for-granted, and it is questionable whether schooling challenges the taken-for-granted as much as it might. Just as Tess 1 and 2 come to school with certain, not fully articulated, assumptions, so we all live through each moment largely on the basis of assumption: of knowing what things are and what they are likely to do next. For example, before writing this, I took the dog for a walk as the sun was rising. I assumed that the path in front of me led where it led before, and I assumed the sun was beginning a new day in the sky, that will end at sunset. The dog assumed certain things too, though I cannot be sure exactly what. Neither of us knows for certain that any of these things are the case, but we proceed on the basis of conditioned certainties. (See Wittgenstein, 1975). For schooling to be deeply transformative, it must challenge some taken-for-granted certainties (inevitably not all of them), and not merely offer access to new facts or discourses. Tesses 1 and 2 will each be introduced to the methods of historical analysis and experimental physics, yet it is not necessarily the case that schooling will challenge those strong assumptions that drive their orientations towards these activities, and thus determine their levels of enjoyment and success with respect to becoming historians or physicists.

While school is undoubtedly challenging, and brings much of value in terms of both developing and challenging a student's self-identity, it is also remarkable how many dispositions it does not challenge. Take, for example, a basic emotion such as disgust. Human beings tend to feel strong emotions of rejection towards certain objects that Kristeva has termed 'abjects' (Kristeva, 1982). Abjects are psychological objects that are both of us and not of us; we find them disgusting, according to Kristeva, in that they help us to define the limits of our humanity by indicating what must be excluded from it. Strong examples include corpses, vomit, urine and faeces. Weaker examples might include saliva (spitting), half digested food (eating with your mouth open) and earth on the body (dirty fingernails). To a racist, other ethnic groups are abjects; to a sexist, the opposite gender.

There is a common tendency to regard the strong emotional objections we feel to such abjects as rational. Surely it is right to be disgusted by faeces because they are 'dirty', might carry disease, smell foul? This, assumption, however, masks historical and cultural variation. Not all human groups react with equal vehemence against the sight of human faeces, just as some societies find the exposing of female flesh in public offensive whereas others do not. Similarly, urine was seen as a valuable resource in many human societies in the past (Magnusson, 2010). Abjection and disgust comprise a flexible category that overlaps with, for example, offence. Barrow has argued that a liberal education must not be held back on the grounds that it might occasionally cause offence to certain groups: education necessarily sometimes risks offence, a risk we should all be prepared to take (Barrow, 2005). If there is educational value in inviting, or at least risking, offence, there might also be educational value in confronting disgust.

Intuitively, many may feel that a sense of disgust marks a transition from emotional to rational, from barbarism to civilisation. However, disgust is emotional. Historical and social investigation might suggest that this intuitive response is quite misleading. Rather, the progression has been from rational to emotional. It may be that modern people react with disgust to human urine (particularly that of others) because in the past it was assumed it carried disease, whereas current received wisdom is that it does so only rarely. There is a case, therefore, in reassessing urine and thus training young people out of their disgust, or, at least, trying to make them question it.

There are two other, connected, potential important aspects of the 'urine question'. First, a huge amount of environmental resource is currently used to dispose of it, through the flushing of toilets and sewerage services. What is being flushed away and treated here is a potentially rich resource, and in the past was recognised as such. Ecologically, our unproblematized collective disgust is exrtremely wasteful and costly. Good use could be made of urine, both domestically (for example, a garden fertiliser, when diluted) and socially, including commercially (for example, as dye or fixing agent). These uses of urine were common but have now been marginalised by an overriding sense of disgust. Secondly, our collective uninvestigated disgust may damage rather than enhance personal health and hygiene. Plague spread more when people assumed that bad smell carried disease (thus prompting a quite natural emotional aversion to certain smells) than it did when the realisation came that the disease was carried by rats. Similar examples abound. In recent years there have been public health scares over various forms of influenza. Many people have worn face masks, a response of limited use (Cohen, 2009), but science has increasingly acknowledged that inadequate washing of hands and bringing of the hands to the mouth and nose are much stronger carriers of such diseases than infected breath (CDC, undated). However, people in general are much less disgusted by the contacts their hands make with surfaces that others have touched than they are by foul-smelling breath. This surely is where education, in whatever form, might play a stronger role. However construed, education is always about challenging and developing the self, including self-identity, self-image and the individual's assumptions and prejudices, yet when it comes to an everyday reaction such as that of disgust, schooling seems to offer little in terms of challenging ingrained assumptions, even where these assumptions have been scientifically shown to be mistaken.

There are feasible limits as to what schools can and cannot achieve. More accurately, the provision of schooling has a significant, but inevitably limited effect on the overlapping phenomenal worlds of the many students that pass through it. In terms of My Now, what I encounter at school will both reinforce and challenge my assumptions, the necessary certainties which allow me to plan for my survival. The sense each person makes of the school experience is dependent on that person's habitual ways of responding and on her context: for example, Tess 1 may generally be comfortable about tackling most school lessons but not on a day when she does not feel well or is worried about a problem outside schooling. Whatever the explicit aims of schooling, what it actually achieves is not fully predictable, least of all for any individual student.

Nevertheless, there seem to be areas in which schools could go beyond their dominant role as conservative culture bearers and aim to play a stronger role in cultural renewal, through challenging the taken-for-granted. Barnes and Sheeran (1991) have shown how academic success is dependent on taken-for-granted 'ground rules' which come naturally to experts, such as teachers, and are therefore rarely articulated, yet the command of which determines success in schooling. The same principle applies more broadly. If students are fixed in their assumptions and prejudices, including those that seem integral to their self and cultural identities, then their scope for meaningful learning is much constrained. Teaching, thus understood, is always an invitation to challenge what was assumed: it is a matter of more or less controlled identity disruption, but of a sort that aims to prompt reappraisal more than retrenchment. A Buddhist might describe the learning process thus aimed for as one of awareness leading to disillusionment, in the literal sense of coming to see that which was taken as true as no longer so, on the path to enlightenment: a process of finding the self that involves losing the self, a theme echoed in other religious traditions. In ordinary language philosophy, the work of Cavell and his interpreters, drawing on Emersonian perfectionism and Thoreau, also promotes attention to the ordinary as the key to significant personal growth (Cavell e.g., 1992, Saito and Standish, 2010). Unfortunately, a teacher cannot ultimately control whether a pupil reappraises or retrenches, but what schools and teachers can conceivably do is engender situations of potential reappraisal by engaging students' interests, so that their attention is focused on exploring the taken-for-granted, however briefly.

The extent to which schools can be cultural recreators rather than merely culture-bearers is, then, variable. Some students will use the most traditional and transmissive education in creative ways. Others, however, may well respond positively to challenges to their assumptions that are not routinely offered by most schools (such as deliberate engagement with the disgusting), though it may be beyond the power of schooling to prevent some people from retrenching into cultural inflexibility. However, given that this retrenchment happens anyway, schooling has little to fear from attempting to be somewhat more daring in relating formal instruction to students' otherwise unquestioned assumptions and self-image. The worst that can result is offence, but judicious choice of subject matter and treatment of it can reduce that potential offence to a (perhaps necessary) minimum. The alternative is that schools do nothing to challenge Tess 2.

While the argument developed in this book is not, in many respects, Hegelian, Hegel makes a number of remarks about philosophy in *The Phenomenology of Mind* that can equally be applied to education, and which have been echoed by many commentators since, including A. N. Whitehead in his dismissal of 'inert knowledge' in *The Aims of Education* (Whitehead, 1916). Hegel argues that the true philosopher always engages the subject in the subject matter, for to deal in abstractions without relating them to self-exploration is superficial and unproductive. Progressive understanding must be dialectical and thus involve increasing awareness of how the known exists only in relation to the unknown. Thus, in the famous 'Master-Slave dialectic' Hegel considers whether the Master, whose needs are met through the labour of the Slave, is in one sense less liberated than the Slave, who has to labour for the (dependent) Master (Hegel, 1977: $189-196). As Wood has remarked in relation to Hegel's educational thought, 'the otherness of the object is overcome through a struggle with it' (Rorty, 1998:5).

For people to make something of formal education, and to value it fully, a similar level of personal involvement is desirable. We live in the physical transcendent present, assuming we understand what we encounter and reacting as we see fit. New experience gradually (sometimes quickly) modifies our reactions. If, however, Tess's reaction to a science lesson involves watching something from a distance that she assumes has little to do with her real interests, then its effect on her life will be very limited indeed. For teaching to succeed, it must tap into the real concerns of students and challenge that which they take for granted. This is risky, and may occasionally seem confrontational, though it need not be aggressively so. Unfortunately, schools are necessary to society for reasons beyond the educational, so poor teaching in this respect can often win out. It may be considered preferable to avoid complaint and litigation rather risk uncertainty and offence. When schools do what they do most safely, they may be doing very little of lasting import.

In conclusion, schools are not necessarily well placed to provide education of the highest standard, as they are necessarily risk-averse. However, the more they can promote challenge (which society does not demand of them as an immediate need) alongside protection (which is a perpetual necessary concern for schools), the more they can offer in terms of empowering, rather than simply reproducing, citizens.

BE(COM)ING RESPONSIBLE: HUMANS, OTHERS AND ETHICS

4.1 TOWARDS HUMAN RESPONSE-ABILITY

Being human is always becoming human. Full, or complete, humanness is therefore an aspiration rather than a state. It is what Kant referred to as a regulative ideal (Kant, 2000). The argument of this chapter develops that of Chapter 3.1, extending its scope to a broad discussion of ethics.

This is not the usual way of regarding the human condition. Commentators are generally concerned that some people regard others as less than human. Indeed, it is never difficult to cite evidence for such a position: Hitler, Pol Pot, or the 'ethnic cleansing' in Rwanda and the Balkans in the 1990s, for example. Finkielkraut (2000) goes as far as to suggest that humans have never regarded others as fully human, and that the thin universal tolerance of the global Millennial tourist amounts to mere indifference rather than respect. Such arguments, while superficially compelling, rest on two assumptions: that there is a common human essence, and that there is a universal rational set of criteria for making such judgments.

While such arguments serve a moral purpose in encouraging greater mutual respect, or at least tolerance, they can be construed as negative and divisive, based on the premise that 'we' (however defined) regard ourselves as human, but others as lesser beings. The present argument challenges this default position on two grounds. First, in ordinary language, the concept of the human is presented both as actual condition and as aspiration. Secondly, to regard the human condition as qualitatively distinct from the animal-species condition demands a form of mind-body dualism that is unjustifiable in the context of current scientific and philosophical understanding.

With regard to ordinary language, it is clear that the idea of the human is both descriptive and normative. Descriptively, it defines a species: the human animal. Normatively, it proclaims a set of aspirations, variously realised in terms of the humane, humanitarianism, collocations such as 'human decency' or 'human feeling', and human rights. Failure to meet these aspirations amounts to 'behaving no better than an animal'. Given that the normative senses cannot be completely divorced from the descriptive, it is therefore valid to argue that no one is fully human.

The standard view sees the human as an animal, but of a special sort: specifically, the rational animal. As rationality cannot easily be explained in biological terms, and has not been generally so explained throughout history, the assumption of this account must be that rationality is imbued in humanity from some extra-biological source (traditionally the divine), or has evolved in terms of a form of consciousness that is so far immune from biological explanation. The former is a strong two-worlds argument, in which the divine and earthly realms are regarded as discrete; the latter is a weaker form of such an argument, that implies a form of 'second nature' (McDowell, 1996) that has evolved in human beings such that they are qualitatively distinct from other animal species in some ways, operating in a 'space of reasons', to use Sellars' term (see Sharp and Brandom, 2007). Either view demands a form of mind-body separation that both science and philosophy either struggle, or do not attempt, to justify in a manner that enjoys widespread acceptance, either in expert or lay communities.

The present argument, as that of Chapter 3.1, proceeds on the basis that full humanity is a regulative ideal: that is, we are all guided in our actions by a conception of a good or perfect human being. In this sense, we are all not yet human, and never to be fully human. Inevitably, such perceptions will sometimes be shared, and sometimes be culturally, if not individually, distinct. There is no universal test of reason to apply to human aspiration. For example, a girl may aspire to a somewhat different ideal of womanhood, or female humanness, in some parts of Europe as opposed to some parts of Asia. Similarly, ideals of the citizen may vary between American liberals and Chinese Confucianists. There would be no argument in philosophy if there were no such scope for diversity in this respect.

Aspiration to full humanity is far more humbling on this than on the standard humanist account, whereby we are imbued with a human essence that we might betray but can generally only express rather than improve. On the standard account, we may improve the lot of others who have fallen below what we expect of humans like us, but this potentially patronising stance does not involve acceptance that we, too, fall below that level; the standard account does not breed humility or sympathy. The proposed approach is more challenging, as fully human status is always both desired and simultaneously out of reach. It cannot ever be attained fully, though everyone who aspires is trying to attain it. Also, this perspective explains why each cultural group disapproves, to some extent, of others, without implying that this amounts to damning them. From the personal perspective, if I am aspiring to a state of humanity that I can never fully reach, then, while your behaviour might seem strange, and even at times distasteful, to me, I can sympathise with your struggle and sense of incompleteness as, in that respect, we are alike. For example, religious differences might lead me to regard you as narrow-minded. However, each of us is aspiring to goodness, as our religious beliefs demand, thus our mutual religiosity should serve more to unite than to divide us. On a more particular level, consider the problem of bullying among children. Both the bully and the victim are likely to feel excluded from some ideal human state: the bully's actions and the victim's sufferings both attest to this. Each wants to be accepted, on the basis of the false belief that there is some attainable sense of complete belonging and acceptance that each aspires to but neither has attained. If, however, there were more of a universal realisation that all feel excluded, incomplete, and unable fully to meet their own expectations, there might be correspondingly less bullying.

Consider human rights. These are often construed almost as desired possessions: as goods that people should possess, and often as goods possessed by some but denied to others. They are not part of the natural condition of being human, understood either biologically or historically. On this account, some people have, for example, freedom of assembly, while others do not. On the alternative argument, no one has complete freedom of assembly, though many, perhaps most, people aspire to it. Freedom of assembly is, on this revised account, a universal, or widespread, human aspiration, variously met but never fully realised. No one can have full freedom of assembly: we cannot be wherever we would like to be, be in more than one place at a time, meet the dead, bring others together as we wish, travel wherever we like, or afford the time or the costs involved in realising all our aspirations. However, by feeling the frustration of simultaneously aspiring to such freedom but only partially being able to gain it, it is possible to sympathise with others whose opportunities in this area are less than our own. The standard account, in regarding such freedoms as on-off switches – either we have this freedom or we do not – encourages lack of sympathy on the individual level and crudeness of policy on the collective.

A non-essentialist account places great emphasis on responsibility. This is not a quality that is possessed by some but not by others, but rather becomes on this account variable, contextually realised and always to be struggled for. Responsibility here entails more than compliant postholding; it should entail response. Response-ability, as this understanding of responsibility might be construed, is realised in process; it involves being in dialogue with a challenging call: in this case, the call to be human as we think a human should be.[81]

This and the following chapter discuss ethics and morality. In developmental semiotic terms (the basis of the alternative account), Chapter 4 concerns semiotic engagement that is approved of in the context of an espoused value system. On this account, to be ethical or moral is to do (what is taken to be) the right thing, judged by social norms rather than appeal to universal reason. In a liberal democratic polity, ethical and moral behaviour includes commitment to, for example, equality under the law and basic human rights such as freedom of conscience, of expression and of assembly. Those imbued with such values, including the present author, wish both to enjoy such freedoms and to have others enjoy them. However, two mitigating factors should be borne in mind. First, not all cultures necessarily have the same aspirations, or have them in the same balance; secondly, nobody can realise such aspirations in full. This set of assumptions carries certain implications for social and educational theory and policy that will be considered in this chapter and the next. The present chapter will focus on the development of a more response-able society in terms of human interaction. Chapter 4.2 will take as its starting point the post-humanist turn that is implied by the acknowledgement that we are never fully human, and will consider the implications of this for our relationships with other species, that are not fully human either, though they do not aim to be.

Response-ability implies interaction. This in turn implies the precluding of fixed borders, as interaction inevitably brings together beings that are different but not entirely distinct. As argued elsewhere (Stables, 2005), a fully semiotic account – that is, one that sees all living as semiotic engagement – also sees all systems as open even where they at first appear closed.

This argument rests on a problematisation of the sign-signal distinction as a logical extension of the problematisation of the mind-body distinction (as by Dewey, for example: Dewey, 1925; Stables, 2008). Semiotic theory after Peirce tends to proceed on the basis that not all action is semiotic, but that semiosis involves interpretation (e.g. Deely, 1990); however, this interpretation may not be conscious, as in animal behaviour studied from the perspective of biosemiotics (Sebeok, 2001; Maran, 2006). Further, some commentators have suggested that Peirce himself was moving in his later work to a position of recognising the fundamental workings of nature as, if not interpretive, at least habitual rather than law-driven.[82]

A fully semiotic perspective can go further than this, however. On this account, 'sign' is traditionally associated with 'mind' and 'signal' with 'body': in other words, only (minded) human beings are traditionally conceived of as sign users, while non-rational entities simply respond to signals. (It is acknowledged that the term 'signal' is not used entirely consistently among relevant literatures). However, if mind cannot be neatly separated from body, nor can sign (or its distinctions as icon, index and symbol, after Peirce) from signal. The resulting sign(al) is a prompt that cannot be tidily categorised or quantified: in short, there is no clear point at which 'sign' ends and 'signal' begins. Thus there is no clear demarcation point between the human and the non-human. Rather, the continuum of sentient beings is one of overlapping phenomenal worlds (Chapter 2.1). Thus, for example, a man can have a relationship with a dog.

Just as between species, so within species. In relation to the latter, consider the boundaries of an organisation or institution. A school, for example, rather as Anderson conceived a nation, has no fixed boundaries, but is rather variously and collectively imagined by those engaging with it (Anderson, 1983; Stables, 2003). More controversially perhaps, on this account species boundaries cannot be seen as fixed, any more than there being a fixed boundary between what constitutes a dialect and a language. (In recent decades, Serbo-Croat has moved from being widely seen as one language to being recognised as two, while the Flemish language has more widely been accepted as a dialect of Dutch. The political implications of both these changes are self-evident). The theory of overlapping phenomenal worlds developed in Chapter 2.1 renders even species distinction a matter of interpretation, subject to change over time.

The key to the development of the response-able human being is the acceptance that there are no firm boundaries. As being human is rather aspiration than essence, there is no firm boundary between who is human and who is not. There is a species boundary, of course, but it is not absolute: we share many things with other species. Similarly, there is not a point at which the non-human, pre-human or becoming-human child becomes the fully human adult: the quest towards full humanity is endless. We live in overlapping phenomenal worlds, the human ones among which share a sense of what is worth aspiring to as human.

What seem to be immutable categories of human existence are, on the alternative account, roles: that is, attributions of status within a particular social and cultural imaginary that may or may not be strongly mirrored in other social imaginaries. For example, consider the general state of being alive, and the more particular one of being a parent. If it were self-evident where human life begins and ends, there would be no dispute over either abortion or euthanasia, albeit the debates about the former are more explicitly addressed in terms of life rather than, say, capacity to reason. Beginning of human life could before conception (if we are reincarnated), at conception, at the point of viability of the foetus, or at birth. Arguably, full human life does not begin until rational autonomy is reached. Life's end could be signalled by the failure of the heart, the brain or, on a more brutal account, by the loss of reason. Similar controversies lurk within definitions of more precise roles. For example, while it might be obvious that a parent has a child, consider the following: the adoptive or foster parent; the parent of a deceased child; God the Father; Mother Nature. Furthermore, all these definitions depend on some agreement about the nature of a 'child'.

At this point in the argument, it may be worth considering how this alternative account relates to the dominant counter-trend in educational theory since the Enlightenment. Here, 'counter-trend' refers to that tradition in educational thinking that is sceptical of linear progress built on beliefs in autonomous rationality and social progress achieved through a positivistic commitment to experiment and innovation. This emphasis on educational and social reform in terms of linear progress is characterised by a relatively narrow gap between conceptions of physical and social science (i.e. a belief that even if society is not law-driven, it can be treated largely as if it were), and concomitantly by a means-end rationality characterised by the strict application of methods drawn from the physical sciences, assessed by performance indication measures such as benchmarks, targets, objectives and league tables. The alternative set of accounts referred to above as the 'dominant counter-trend', often broadly associated with Romanticism as a cultural movement, tends to see educational value (for example) in terms of the psychological quality of the life of the child or the community rather than on more easily measurable outcomes, such as indicators of material wealth. Recent moves towards measurable indicators of human wellbeing or happiness perhaps indicate a desire to integrate the latter set of values into the former; nevertheless, there remains a recognisable split in emphases between the two broad camps.

One of the strongest representatives of this broad Enlightenment-sceptical trend is Rousseau. The alternative account developed here overlaps with that of Rousseau in certain important respects but differs in others.

In *Émile*, Rousseau objects to too-early socialisation on the grounds that it leads to the development of *amour propre*: self-identity based on comparison, judgment and envy. Instead, early education should be aiming for *amour de soi-meme*: the natural confidence that comes from healthy self-respect and leads to sympathy for others, as opposed to invidious comparison (Rousseau, 1991). Thus far, the present argument is Rousseauian. There is an unfortunate mass of evidence that many young people, in the West at least, have fragile senses of self-worth based on premises including how popular they are, how thin they are, how good-looking they are, how good at sport they are, and so on. Implicit in such views is that they are less than fully human, while others are not so lacking. Such feelings have very unfortunate consequences including eating disorders and other manifestations of deep anxiety; their long-term effects are harder to chart but may be equally as damaging.

The present argument is not fully Rousseauian, however. Rousseau clings to the concept of a state of nature that is essentially fulfilling, and from which the mass of humanity has erred. As such, he can be seen as a social contract theorist in the broad tradition of Hobbes and Locke, though he differs radically in his conclusions. Hobbes, Locke and Rousseau all contrast a state of nature with a socialised condition: to Hobbes, nature is violent so humanity submits to authoritarian rule for its own protection (Hobbes, 2009); to Locke, nature is essentially good, and so is society, in which free individuals choose to achieve more by collaboration than they could alone (Locke, 1692); to Rousseau, however, the state of nature is fundamentally good while all existing societies are corrupt, therefore human development should eschew society for as long as possible.

By contrast, it can be asserted that it is a mutual acceptance of human lack that brings real sympathy and consequent growth. The world is not divided into the Haves, who are in touch with nature, and the Have Nots who are over-socialised. Rather, the world comprises a mass of people who, somewhat similarly and somewhat differently, are aspiring to what they regard as the ideal state of being human. The chief difference between the present argument and that of Rousseau, therefore, is with respect to the idea of human completion. As Storme and Vlieghe have argued, what characterises the human condition is universal potentiality rather than actuality; thus, they argue, the retrieval of any meaningful notion of childhood from the reductionism of the instrumentalist 'learning society' must be one that embraces child and adult alike: that is, a recognition of the lack, rather than the fulfilment that gives meaning to human life (Storme and Vlieghe, 2011). To Rousseau, such a lack is always negative. Rousseau's educational and social prescription, most fully articulated in *Émile*, is that of developing self-confidence (*amour de soi-meme*) in isolation from society, as all existing societies are corrupt and will therefore promote and envious, competitive and unhappy form of self-identity: *amour propre*.

Dominant accounts of human development all have an end point: Aristotle's citizen who has achieved *eudaimonia*; Plato's rational guardian; the autonomous, Enlightenment rational adult conceived variously by Descartes, Spinoza, Locke and Kant; the man (*sic*) – even the child - who is more than a citizen as conceived by Rousseau and then subsequently by Romanticism, Nietzsche and Existentialism. On all these accounts, fulfilment comes largely with achievement; on the present account, as on Storme and Vlieghe's, human fulfilment is evidenced by its opposite: a mutually salient mixture of the feelings 'I can' and 'I cannot'. Aspiration and disillusionment, evinced by the capacities to plan, regret and reconstrue, characterise us; we are most fully human when realising we cannot be fully human. We are both members of society and transcend it, yet we are simultaneously never fully either of these, for all these final positions are, after Derrida, deferred.

The ethical challenge, therefore, is to respond sympathetically to the lack in others from the sense of our own lacking. From a belief in overlapping phenomenal worlds comes a faith that engagement with others is as valid as it is uncertain. Indeed, it may even be valid beyond the boundaries of the biologically human: the next chapter addresses this. The remainder of Chapter 4.1 will consider the social and educational arrangements that are best likely to promote such engagement.

As *eudaimonia* (happiness/fulfilment) is rather a process of aspiration than a state to be achieved, it cannot be engineered. The emphasis in a society that aspires to full humanity must be on the most opportunity possible. Such a society will encourage moves towards full human rights for as wide a range of people as possible, including non-adults. Laws will therefore be geared towards increasing the freedoms of expression, conscience, travel and so on. Note that this calls for a more progressive state than one that assumes these rights are already possessed for, on the alternative account, they can never be fully realised.

Such a policy cannot be evaluated against traditional criteria of political or economic Left *vs.* Right, though it would be clearly anti-totalitarian. Social institutions would exist to enable, prevent and punish just they do now, but in the spirit of aspiration towards rather than realisation of its goals. Such a society might be described as socialist insofar as it would regard aspiration as classless and be committed to the greatest possible opportunity for those with very little; however, it would be aware of the dangers of centralised rational planning with its universal dispositions, and would not proceed on the basis that one class, gender or ethnic group enjoys full human rights that others do not have. Such a society might be described as liberal in its commitments to human rights for all and its acceptance of differential human aspirations and market mechanisms for transacting them, but it would not glibly assume that the granting of certain legal rights and freedoms marks the end of the road in terms of reform and progress. Such a society might be described as conservative insofar as it would acknowledge that individuals, alone and in their own chosen collectivities (families, professional groups and so on) should be free to aspire to their own conceptions of fulfilment, as free as possible of state interference; however, it would not be a society that sought to preserve the *status quo* or valued order over aspiration. It might, therefore, have a government of the Centre Left or Centre Right on current understandings, but it is hard to see how it could have an extremist government, that forced adherence to one strong ideology on all its people.

Whether full human rights are construed as achievable or to be aspired towards, laws and other social arrangements seek to empower and enable but must inevitably also constrain. On the present account, both enablement and constraint are grounded in recognition of overlapping phenomenal worlds. One individual's aspirations and perceptions will partly coincide with and partly differ from another's. The enabling context is thus defined by individual aspirations: many people may want easier access to their doctors, for example. The constraining context is defined by mutual limitations: the amount of resource other people are prepared to give to doctor-access may be small relative to other priorities. Thus, for example, the level of tax is effectively determined by taxpayers. Of course, this is not fundamentally different from current democratic arrangements insofar as voters can decide between low and high tax parties and differing sets of policy commitment. However, there tends to be a rigidity in current arrangements explicable in part as adherence to ideologies and in part, relatedly, to a belief that various human goods can be achieved rather than variously struggled towards; this encourages inflexibility.

Education of the young is one of the fields that might be most radically altered by such a shift of emphasis, for childhood would no longer be seen simply as a preparation for full human, adult life. Both adults and children would now be regarded as simultaneously fully human and pre-human. (See also Stables, 2008). Adults would be seen as learning through play as much as children would be seen as having serious aspirations and plans. Consider the child pretending to be, say, a teacher, and an adult being one. There are certainly quantifiable differences between them in terms of knowledge, and therefore competence, and in terms of social recognition and payment. There is also a difference of expectation. Qualitatively, however, these differences are not so great as often imagined. Both the child and the adult are trying to be teachers – are acting the role of teacher – to the best of their ability. Those engaged in training to teach might be painfully aware of how tenuous the distinction between 'playing at it' and 'being able to do it' actually is. It is a matter of playing a role within a social arrangement whether it is the child in a game of schools, the student-teacher in the classroom, the actor in a school drama, or the experienced teacher monitoring the playground. Each is aspiring to a version of that role that is in part shared and in part individual.[83]

The principles of enablement and constraint must operate with respect to childhood and schooling as with respect to other facets of social life. However, giving both giving full value to childhood aspiration and realising that no human aspiration is ever fully met invites some problematisation of what have been considered educational certainties. On the standard liberal account, grounded in Locke's belief that children are both infinitely trainable and capable of reaching rational autonomy (Locke, 1692), rational autonomous adults decide what is best for pre-rational children. On the present account, the enabling force in educational policy must be the aspirations of children (which, judging from their play and interests, are not radically different from those of adults), while the constraints are grounded in both the need to protect children from the naivety and even potential cruelty of each other, and by a series of adult factors, ranging from the desirability of keeping children out of the way while economic life progresses to the (doubtless related) urge to protect children from dangers they are not yet equipped to face. What education does not need to be grounded in is an overriding obsession with what children should learn. If children play at being nurses or engine-drivers, for example, they are self-evidently keen to learn what it takes to be a successful nurse or engine-driver; if they have to be forced into learning skills relevant to this, the approach to teaching has not been a good one. Children always want to play a fulfilling part in the society they see around them: these are the resources they have to play and imagine with. Education can be more easily diminished than enhanced by overprescribing what children should learn; in any case, there is always a degree of unpredictability in what people actually learn, as contexts of interpretation differ. The best education helps young people to do the best they could possibly do at the activities they aspire to do, given that particular aspirations change over time. Thus good education is minimal on one level: it does not impose unnecessary external aims and constraints. On the other hand, good education provides development of that which enables both the fullest development of current aspirations and the greatest flexibility for future aspirations. Thus, both literacy and numeracy are indeed very important; however, as Dewey stressed, the richest learning is likely to occur when these abilities are exercised in meaningful, aspirational contexts, and that is where much education continues to fall short. (Dewey, e.g. 1916)

The question arises as to how best the form of ethics proposed here is best understood in terms of the established debate.

It is possible to construe the above argument as that of a modified Kantianism insofar as humans are not regarded as ends in themselves but rather as end-orientated. While the Kantian categories are categories of understanding, underpinning Kant's ethical thinking in the *Metaphysic of Morals, Critique of Practical Reason* and elsewhere, the moral Categorical Imperative[84] is expressed rather differently. In effect:

CHAPTER 4

- Treat each moral principle as a universal law. (If something is right, it is right in every context: the standard argument against the Nazi guard who claims he was only acting under orders, for example);
- Treat humans as ends in themselves; and
- Act as if you live in a kingdom of ends. (Judge in relation to ends, not means.)

Categorical Imperatives are moral laws, to be contrasted with Hypothetical Imperatives, which are merely moral maxims (to address the problem, 'If I want X, then I must do Y'). Hypothetical Imperatives might suffice for consequentialist ethicists – pragmatists, utilitarians or postmodernists, for example – but they will not do for a deontological ethicist such as Kant. The present argument proposes a deontology of lack, respecting each person not as an end in herself but as seeking such an end and always falling short. Insofar as an end is always a goal, this may seem a nice distinction. However, it is possible to distinguish between respect for the person *per se* and respect for the person's capacity to work towards an ideal state. The latter leaves space for the expression of human diversity while necessarily entailing certain constraints, as aspiration towards full human rights implies having such aspiration for others; therefore, the exploitation of others is necessarily unacceptable. While this delimits aspiration minimally along traditional liberal lines (that is, it would not allow as aspiration to full human rights practices such as slavery or the sexual abuse of infants), it would allow for very considerable variety in conceptions of the good life. It would be able to accommodate adherence to differing comprehensive value schemes, religious or ideological, insofar as they failed to suppress the aspirations of all parties towards their own conceptions of full humanity. This is akin to Rawls's conception of political, as opposed to comprehensive liberalism (Rawls, 1993). However, it is important to note that the concern here is never with the absolute expression of a full human right, but with working towards that expression. Thus, to take a concrete example, persons and groups who did not share dominant Western assumptions about men's and women's dress codes should be judged not on, for instance, whether women should wear veils to leave the house, or whether men should wear ties to work, but on whether open debate and the possibility of change are allowed. All societies have dress codes, and it is inevitable that some will seem inappropriate to others; no individual has absolute freedom in this matter. However, it is, on the present account, an ethical duty to embrace the possibility of social change in these matters through respect for all parties' views on how dress codes might best reflect the aspiration towards the richest human flourishing, as conceived by present actors in delimited contexts. Therefore, while all societies also inevitably police dress codes to a degree, there must be constraints on the extent of that policing. After all, it is not unfeasible that the French schoolgirl banned from wearing her headscarf to school is attempting more strongly to enact a conception of human dignity than some of her jeans-wearing colleagues. While her behaviour is doubtless transgressing a certain social norm in the context in which she finds herself, therefore, a justification for denying some students access to education on the grounds of dress should be stronger than an appeal to either tradition *per se* or an abstracted notion of cultural cohesion. Institutions often have dress codes, and perhaps always will. These, however, should be open to change when proposed changes allow for greater expression of aspiration towards full human rights while not impeding that aspiration among others. The question in relation to the headscarf wearer is thus whether or not her so doing in any way limits the valid aspirations of others, just as the question in relation to the adoption of certain European dress codes in certain Asian contexts might have the same effect.

On the other hand, insofar as what is being proposed concerns the fulfilment of contingent human preferences rather than fixed outcomes, it might be considered a form of utilitarianism. It is, however, not self-evidently consequentialist, insofar as measurable outcomes are not reliable guides to how far a course of action serves as aspiration towards an unattainable ideal. Again, the key issue is that persons are free to experiment in pursuit of such ideals provided such pursuit does not impede the valid pursuits of others.

In a limited sense, the proposed scheme might also be seen as virtue-ethical insofar as it respects aspiration in conjunction with other-orientation, but there is no agreement about the specific virtues that should be developed or encouraged. Rather, the encouragement is of the debate around virtues: for example, concerning the value of the concept of honour, the valid application of courage, or the dividing line between compassion and sentimentality.

In conclusion, ethical schemes tend to be either outcome orientated or absolutist. What is proposed here is rather a deferred ethics, always respecting the yet-to-come. On this account, persons are construed as potential insofar as they are potential prior to actions and share the potentiality to aspire to a human ideal, but they are not, as on some readings of Aristotle, pre-existing potentialities.[85] Under such an ethics of possibility, actions are justified according to their capacity to promote human aspiration. Thus actions are justified by their effects but their effects can never be reduced to final outcomes. Such as account might be construed as deferred pragmatism. In terms of outcomes, it can be helpful to think in terms of what, after Deleuze and Guattari (1987), has been construed as 'rhizomatic consequentialism' (Stables, 2004) rather than in simple means-ends terms, as the richness of contextual and cultural variables that determines how human aspiration is played out in a particular context is such that no observer could ever predict exactly how development of that aspiration might express itself. In terms of process, think of respecting the human (and the non-human) as yet-to-be: the ethics of possibility, but not of foreclosed potentiality.[86]

However, the proposed scheme is complicated by fact that human phenomenal worlds overlap with those of non-human sentient beings. Thus the next chapter will consider the implications of this ethical position for human relations with the non-human.

4.2 POST-HUMANIST ETHICS: RESPONSE-ABILITY BEYOND THE HUMAN

The sense in which the construct 'posthumanism' is employed in the present argument is not the dominant sense. For that reason alone, the term will appear here as hyphenated. The chapter will begin with a brief overview of three construals of the posthuman, ending with an account of the sense to be employed in this case.

The first involves a simple rejection of humanism as a guiding principle, with no particular focus on biological or cognitive change among the human species. This construal associates posthumanism with anti-humanism: in brief, rejection of the idea that there is some fixed human essence that necessarily guides ethics and morality.[87] This definition therefore embraces structuralists, poststructuralists and others who see language and other signifying systems as constitutive of the human condition, rather than *vice versa*. On this account, both Peirce and Derrida are posthumanist, for example, though arguably Dewey was not.[88] Most commentators associated with this position do not use the term 'posthumanism'.[89]

The second construal dominates the literature, associating the posthuman with technological destabilisation and development of the human body and psyche. Here the idea of the posthuman resonates strongly with those of the cyborg and the transhuman. Bostrom (2005) plots the range of perspectives at play here on a spectrum from transhumanism to bioconservatism:

> Positions on the ethics of human enhancement technologies can be (crudely) characterized as ranging from transhumanism to bioconservatism. Transhumanists believe that human enhancement technologies should be made widely available, that individuals should have broad discretion over which of these technologies to apply to themselves, and that parents should normally have the right to choose enhancements for their children-to-be. Bioconservatives ... are generally opposed to the use of technology to modify human nature. A central idea in bioconservativism is that human enhancement technologies will undermine our human dignity. To forestall a slide down the slippery slope towards an ultimately debased 'posthuman' state, bioconservatives often argue for broad bans on otherwise promising human enhancements. (Bostrom, 2005: 202).

Writers in this field often appropriate 'posthumanism' entirely as relating to their own concerns, thus effectively excluding the two alternative accounts presented here.[90] Most posthumanists with a transhumanist orientation are concerned with possibilities of human development beyond human biological limitations[91], extending a trend that began with tools, developed spectacles and hearing aids and, more recently, devised prosthetic limbs and other devices that effectively enhance the body. Thus such thought is largely progressivist and optimistic in tone; its emphasis tends to be technological rather than ethical, descriptive rather than normative. In general, the focus in this tradition is the problematisation of the human through technology rather than relations between human and non-human entities, which comprise the focus of the third approach.

Ecological post-humanists might argue there is a residual humanism in each of the above approaches, though proponents of each might make the same charge: that it is, in effect, impossible to deny some distinctness to the human when it is used as an analytic category, and when all judgments are made from a human perspective. Nevertheless, ecological post-humanism differs from the other forms in not being solely and directly concerned with human interest. That is to say, non-human life is credited value ostensibly on its own terms, even though it remains arguable whether anything more than human interest is being served in the long term. From the perspective of the Western liberal tradition, ecological post-humanists, particularly of the more pragmatic sort, might be said to be acting on the basis of enlightened self-interest where that self-interest is best served by a valuation of the non-human entities with which humans interact. This can be seen as an extension of the Lockean position on the social contract: that free individuals co-operate with others (in this case, including non-human others) for mutual advantage. Taking Hobbes, Locke and Rousseau as three of the leading 'social contract' theorists, Locke's position is most apposite here. All three posit an original state of nature which is transformed by human reason into society. Hobbes regards humans as essentially competitive and destructive of others ('nasty' and 'brutish': Hobbes, 1651: Ch. 13, para. 9) in the state of nature, so needing to submit to the rule of a sovereign for self-protection; Rousseau sees the state of nature as benign but human society as largely malign ('Man is born free and everywhere he is in chains': Rousseau, 1762: $1). Locke sees both nature and society as essentially benign, with free individuals choosing to co-operate for mutual benefit on condition of the mutual recognition of the rights to life, liberty and happiness, *via* freedom of thought, the accrual of private property and the division of powers (e.g. Locke, 1690, 1692).

However, others associated with environmentalism, whether or not explicitly engaged with the idea of the post-human, draw on other traditions, including Marxism (e.g. Huckle, 2010), Buddhism (e.g. Cooper and James, 2005) and 'deep ecology' (Naess, 1973) which regards itself as a radical break from mainstream political philosophy. Thus ecological post-humanism might be characterised as a set of concerns spanning radical animal rights (e.g. Horsthemke, 2010, who argues for animals as moral agents), and opposition to economic growth (e.g. Stibbe, 2005) at one pole, and mainstream economists who support carbon trading and other forms of evaluation of 'natural capital' at the other (e.g. Jansson, Hammer, Folke and Constanza, 1994). What all these positions hold in common is a sense that progress and success can never validly be measured in purely human terms: both economically and ethically, human flourishing is dependent on the flourishing of non-human entities with which humans interact. Some commentators (e.g. Bonnett, 2004) argue that an awareness of such dependence demands a sort of phenomenal shift, in terms of a revised attitude to nature, in the broadest sense.[92]

Cutting across these distinctions is the ethics of alterity (the Other), as articulated by Levinas (e.g. 1967) and Derrida (e.g.1995) in particular. These influences are apparent in both Biesta's rejection of humanism and Petrilli's 'semioethics'. In each case, what is resisted is retreat into a sealed conception of identity:

> That which unites each one of us to every other is the otherness of each one of us, that which cannot be reduced to any form of identity. (Petrilli, 2010: 225).

Nor is this an idea entirely born of postmodernism. The importance of encounter with other worldviews has been stressed epistemologically by Vygotsky (1978) and by social constructionists such as Berger and Luckmann (1966), and ethically by Durkheim (1973, first published 1925). Where Levinas and his followers differ from this tradition, however, is in their insistence on the persistent alterity of the Other. In other words, to fully know or understand the Other would be to appropriate it into a newly fixed self-identity, whereas the Other will, in fact, always escape attempts to pin it down in this way. Regardless of the radicality of such a view, however, there is still arguably a humanist legacy insofar as neither Levinas, Derrida nor Petrilli denies the specialness of the human response. Petrilli is explicit about this, arguing that humans are semiotic while animals are merely semiosic, as human semiotics is metasemiotics: humans have signs that reflect on signs (Petrilli, 2010: 194). Indeed, Petrilli at one point argues overtly for an enhanced humanism:

Can the properly human supersede the space-time of objects, the space-time of identity? (Petrilli, 2010: 213)

Thus while the present argument has much in common with Petrilli's, the stress on problematising the sign-signal distinction demands a greater distancing from the humanist tradition than is evident in Petrilli or, indeed, in any of the above commentators with the possible exceptions of the deep ecologists and Horsthemke. However, even Horsthemke and other radical animal rights proponents carry some humanist baggage in their focus on the animal, rather than merely the human. In such work there is an assumption that humans and (other) animals are qualitatively distinct from the rest of nature.

The present argument can be construed as one of post-humanist pragmatism[93]; as such, it is a philosophy of effect that denies special status or sole consideration to effects on, and directly emanating from, humans. Nevertheless, it remains somewhat anthropocentric as it adopts a human viewpoint and is inevitably primarily concerned with the human interest. Nevertheless, it differs from Peircean pragmaticism, as interpreted by, for example, Petrilli (2010) and Deely (1990), in problematising the human as a closed system on any level, instead understanding the universe in terms of overlapping phenomenal entities (Chapter 2.1), and experience as implication in events or processes (Chapter 1.4). On this account, it is impossible ever to be sure where (for example) my phenomenal world coincides with, or differs from yours, whether there are any absolute divisions at all between human and non-human animal, or where these lie, or whether there is any absolute division between sentient and non-sentient entities, or between life and non-life. It is on this basis, acknowledging the inevitable anthropocentrism alluded to above, that an ethics of human action in relation to both the human and the non-human must be based.

Such an ethics can be seen as broadly Levinasian. That is, it demands response to another (responsibility as response-ability) where that Other touches aspects of the Self but always remains ultimately unknowable and, furthermore, where the contact always occurs in the context of a greater, always unknowable Otherness which may be referred to as God or Nature: a totality that frames the terms of engagement, whether or not these are construed as essentially moral, but full knowledge of which will always remain elusive.

At issue here are beliefs, attitudes and actions relating to the non-human (animals, plants and the physical fabric of space-time), and to those on the borders of the human, such as the unborn, the very young, those excluded by criminality, and the mentally ill. In contrast to Chapter 4.1, the remainder of this chapter will focus on ethics in relation to non-human entities.

What is suggested is an ethics of relative thriving. The relativity here is demanded by the constrained nature of experience (the My Now: Chapter 2.1). The untenable extremes are those of collective solipsism and disinterested equality, for each denies the context-dependency of the ethical agent.

'Collective solipsism' refers to the human tendency to take the immediate community or society not only as the norm (which is perhaps inevitable) but as the sole consideration. In practice, humanism often operates reductively, pitting 'us' against 'them', regarding the former only as fully human and seeing the in-group's interests as the only valid criterion in any ethical debate.[94] By extension, all humanism or extreme anthropocentrism can be regarded as a form of collective solipsism, since it tends to disregard the effects of human actions on the non-human environment except where there is an immediately recognisable feedback effect whereby those actions are clearly seen to damage the human: extreme air pollution, for example. Collective solipsism is unjustified on the present argument because it assumes firm boundaries between in and out groups.

'Disinterested equality' refers to radical egalitarianism that seeks to regard all within its remit as absolutely equal: for all animals to have equal rights analogous to human rights, for example. Disinterested equality is untenable because it does not take account of differential interests. While acknowledging, for example, that animals might feel pain or enjoy the sensory richness of life in the open air, as opposed to captivity (i.e. by accepting overlap between human and non-human phenomenal worlds), it fails to take full account of the inability of one perspective ever to embrace all, and the consequent impossibility of, for example, knowing what it is like to be any animal, while acknowledging that rewarding relationships of different sorts (emotional as well as instrumental) are possible between persons and non-persons.

Ethics of relative thriving take for granted both the inevitability of the limitations of the human interest (including variation within it) and the inevitability of some overlap between human and other-animal responses. Let us consider how appropriate treatment of three animal groups might be inferred from these premises: farm animals, domestic pets, and wild animals. Here 'animals' is used as an umbrella term for *fauna* and can be taken to include insects, birds, reptiles and amphibians as well as mammals. Similarly, 'wild animals' will include *fauna* not evidently under human control, including both those species seen generally as benign (for example, most birds) and those seen as generally malign (including many insects: the malarial mosquito or tsetse fly, for example).

Farm animals owe their continued existence to humans. If the world were to turn vegetarian, most farm animals would not be set free; they would die out, for they owe their births and protection as well as their deaths to human beings. We cannot be sure of what the best interests of, say, cattle are. However, we can identify certain bovine responses that are analogous to our own, such as reactions of apprehension, fear or uncertainty (it is difficult to differentiate), or the desire to seek shelter, where it is available, in rain or snow. On this basis of limited knowledge and somewhat more supposition, it is possible to arrange for cattle's relative thriving without invoking absolute rights, on the basis of humans' enlightened self-interest. For example, fields can be well fenced, thus stress-inducing intrusions can be kept to a minimum (though it is evident that cattle often show an interest in human visitors, for example), and shelter can be provided in the form of trees or copses (a common habit in the Eighteenth Century but not so far in the Twenty-First). Similarly, the effects on cattle's general health and immunity of varying levels of demand on them in terms of, for example, milk supply, can be monitored and adjusted accordingly. The argument here is not necessarily for organic or free-range farming *per se*, but rather for farming that is sensitive to the interests of animals and does not see them merely as short-term production units. To some extent, a Kantian argument is invoked here in the form of a categorical imperative: each species should be respected as an end in itself, even if only because its capacity to serve us, directly and indirectly, is likely to be linked to its overall wellbeing. However, the Kantian approach is insufficiently relativistic, lacking recognition that even human interest is not always self-evident, and that respect for the cattle as Other must always assume elements of the yet-to-be-known and never-to-be-known. Thus farm animals should be treated with the utmost possible sensitivity and with constraints on human confidence that animals can be increasingly commodified without effect on their flourishing.

Domestic pets may be victims of a different sort of narrow humanism or extreme anthropocentrism, through being posited as human companions and thus assumed to have interests virtually identical with those of their owners. Social acceptance of this is so strong that the obvious inconsistencies between treatment of pets and of animals in other contexts are generally overlooked. However, on the assumption of overlapping phenomenal worlds, a particular pet's interests are no more or less likely obviously to coincide with a pet owner's than a farm animal's with a farmer's or a holiday maker on safari with a lion's. It follows therefore that a pet owner's loving treatment of an animal may be unnecessarily cruel. The determining factor is the degree to which the owner's care for the pet is grounded in sensitivity to the pet, as opposed to the immediate emotional concerns of the owner. Insofar as pets are often regarded as protection against loneliness, the danger of owners' emotional needs not being in the animal's best interest are increased. Again, the ethical way forward here on the present account would be to seek to respond to the animal's Otherness rather than try to mould it to suit one's preconceptions, wishes or needs.

In an attenuated sense, many wild animals are, in effect, domesticated, insofar as their existence and flourishing are encouraged by humans, who find them life-enhancing. Thus the wild animals in a national park are, broadly, analogous to pets: they are encouraged to thrive because people like them, and are given licence to roam within broad parameters. Of course, their freedom is constrained (as all creatures' is, including the human) and debates will inevitably continue as to how far the preservation and regeneration of their habitats should be policy objectives. The ethical challenge does not reside mainly with regard to such creatures, but rather to those who are seen by humans as malign. Many, though not all, such species are insects, from annoying flies to death-bringing malarial mosquitoes. Here the human interest to control and destroy is very strong, and often inevitably overrides the creature's right to life. Even in these situations, however, human power to control can become hubristic and ultimately self-defeating. Although knowledge of natural systems, in terms of issues such as food chains and the dynamics of disease, may be impressive compared to even a few decades past, it would be extreme to claim that all is known about the potential indirect value of any species to the human, or to any other of which people generally approve. In the perpetual absence of complete knowledge, which on a theory of overlapping phenomenal worlds, can never be attained, there is an argument for allowing, even encouraging, the flourishing of such species, albeit in necessarily very carefully constrained contexts.

This brief discussion of issues of animal welfare can serve to problematize dominant conceptions in areas such as animal cruelty. Also important is the extent to which it can inform human attitudes towards the Other in all its forms, within and beyond the human species.

PROMOTING HUMAN PROGRESS

5.1 RELATIVE SAFETY? DIFFERING CONCEPTIONS OF THE GOOD

In the Platonic, rationalist tradition, understanding of the Good is sought through reasoning. For Plato, Aristotle, Descartes and Kant, disciplined contemplation (Aristotle), dialectic (Plato) or self-examination (Descartes, Kant) promote virtue as well as cognitive clarity, as understanding develops of what is what is objectively Right as a corollary of what is objectively True: Aristotle's Golden Mean[95], and Kant's Categorical Imperative[96], for example. For present purposes, this position can be characterized as ethically realist[97].

By contrast, ethically relativist positions are often associated with empiricism. Aristotle argued that experience and habit (*ethos*) were important in developing virtues[98], though he did not question the objective nature of the virtues themselves; he also moved on from Plato in stressing that different activities have different ends. Locke stressed the importance of ingraining good habits in the *tabula rasa* of the child's mind (Locke, 1692). Hume went further in urging recognition that what is known is never objective cause and effect bur merely experience of what follows what, and that there are no grounds therefore for inferring the Ought from the Is (Hume, 2009). Pragmatists and Utilitarians both evaluate actions according to their consequences.

Certain Continental philosophers, grounded in the Hegelian tradition of regarding truth as both objective and transitory, defined by negation, are also effectively ethically relativist. Derrida's *différance* and Levinas' Other[99] who must be respected for her Otherness, though never fully known, both imply ethical relativism. Arguably the most forceful and explicit rejection of the ethically Realist position comes from Nietzsche and the Existentialist tradition, wherein ethical relativism is a matter of active creation, not merely an accident of differential experience. Nietzsche's Superman (*Übermensch*: literally 'overman' rather than Superman) creates his own rules to live by and Christianity is explicitly rejected as a slave morality.[100] (Even Sartre's position is more accommodating than this, as Sartre acknowledges an apparently objective distinction between living in good and bad faith[101]). For Nietzsche, morality is an expression of creativity.

In the rationalist tradition, it is possible to become fully, objectively human in the sense that true ethical knowledge can be attained. Empiricists and Existentialists must make the most of their own experiences of life, never sure of the degree to which such experiences mirror those of others or are ultimately rational.

On the present account, full humanity is always an aspiration, never a settled state. Thus the argument is ethically relativist. The challenge for ethical relativists is always that of justification, of agreeing the criteria for evaluating different ethical claims. (See, for example, Siegel, 1987). Without such criteria, it may appear that 'You should' becomes no more than 'I want you to': subjective preference overcomes objective truth. On the other hand, if no such objective truth verifiably exists, 'You should' may always be seen as no more than 'I want you to', as in the actions of generations of totalitarian leaders claiming to act in the name of God, nation or socialism.

While ethical realists may accuse relativists of allowing the subjective to trump the objective, the latter can point to the intersubjective as a missing element in the debate. Judgements need not be construed as either objective or subjective, but can be understood as social and, in a limited sense, therefore, as collective. (The sense is limited in that individuals' interpretations of judgments can never be guaranteed to cohere even though their agreements to those judgments do). 'You should' is a natural corollary, therefore, not of 'I want' but of 'We want'. (Many dictators in the Big Brother mode have appealed publicly to this sense of collective interest either deludedly or for private gain). Given that ethics serves to hold societies together, guiding both law and interpersonal relations, consensual judgment is of utmost social importance, whether or not is it objectively rational. Similarly, in a globalised world, consensual agreements between groups with sometimes very different values are also of utmost importance. Liberals might wish to define such agreements in terms of Rawls's Political Liberalism, though even the term 'Liberal' should presumably be open to debate (Rawls, 1993). In the *Philosophical Investigations*, Wittgenstein argued against the impossibility of a private language (Wittgenstein, 1967). Preferences can only be expressed in publicly agreed terms, whether or not others see them as moral; even Nietzsche's Superman was reliant on society to this degree.

Contingent ethical consensuality can be a viable aspiration for both ethical realist and relativist; it may not be enough for the realist, but at least it ensures open debate and offers the possibility of peaceful coexistence and justified action. 'Contingent ethical consensuality' implies agreement on judgments but assumes subsequent variability in the interpretation of judgments. Thus it allows for both the implementation and enforcement of laws, rules and conventions, but it also calls for their constant revision, and for continuous dialogue with those both within and beyond a defined social group. Untrammelled by the final demands of reason, it calls forth maximum reasoning.

The argument for contingent ethical consensuality builds on three key aspects of the broader argument so far: specifically, (first) the idea of the human as constantly developmental and aspirational, (secondly) the primary importance of the sign, and therefore of ordinary language, and (thirdly) the idea of overlapping phenomenal worlds.

The constantly developing and aspirational human may or may not believe that there are, for example, universal laws; the salient point is that the quest to discover, or subvert, them is never complete. Thus ethical judgments can never be final, and there can never be final agreements about them. This is because each agreed judgement effectively introduces a new sign into the discourse and, inevitably, this sign will be interpreted in the context of its reception, thus somewhat variously. This inevitable inconsistency will call forth further judgment.

Most decisions are not directly concerned with universal laws, if such there are. Consider the agreement to introduce a 70 mile-an-hour speed limit on motorways. The noun phrase '70 mile-an-hour speed limit' thus becomes a sign, a lexical item in everyday discourse. There is, thus far, agreement on the speed limit. However, what exactly this limit means (implies and infers) for individual drivers will vary. Three common interpretations may be: first, that one should never exceed 70 miles an hour as indicated on one's speedometer (even if overtaking a truck doing 69.5 miles an hour in the outside lane, thus causing a stream of cars moving much faster to slow down violently behind you); secondly, that one should not maintain an average speed significantly above 70 (say about 10% above); thirdly, that the 70 limit is intended to be a warning that a driver runs a significant risk of punishment if consistently travelling well over this speed (say, 95m.p.h.). There are others, of course. Each of these interpretations may well be held by sincere, responsible and generally law-abiding citizens. The variety of interpretations may or may not cause a problem that calls forth a collective re-evaluation: in this case, either tightening or abandoning the limit or producing clearer public guidelines about its implementation. The issue is certainly ethical, as it is concerned with providing guidelines about human behaviour with respect to the safety and wellbeing of others. Consensuality is essential in such a case. However, such consensuality will always be limited.

Both broadly semiotic and narrowly 'ordinary language' approaches prioritise the sign over its referent, regarding the sign as empirically verifiable and the referent as implied or inferred but not empirically verifiable. Thus the important consideration in relation to centrally important concepts such as 'God', 'science' or 'liberty' is not that they simply point to empirically verifiable realities but that they have certain evocations. For example, there seems no justification for violence over the issue of whether the Christian God, for example, is an imaginary friend, as argued by Dawkins, or an imagined friend, as argued by devout Christians. The implications of this for ethical co-existence are self-evident. Public debate and the cultural cohesion which it serves are of paramount importance. However, there are two significant dangers. The first is that cultural beliefs, traditions and conventions become ossified, so that open debate is no longer possible; the second is that those in powerful positions lose touch with the public to the point at which they assume support for what others see as anti-social behaviour, as in the case of ageing despots who regard themselves as the liberators they might once have been.

It is often overlooked that the concept of the Good itself is interpreted in radically different ways. This is the case even if we limit 'Good' to a non-count noun, ignoring uses such as 'good' as the singular of 'goods', 'good' as an adjective, where it is often little more than an all-purpose sign of affirmation, or 'good!' as an exclamation, where it indicates general agreement and approval. Straughan's book, *Can We Teach Children to Be Good?* (Straughan, 1988), for example, assumes that the business of learning to be good is simply a matter of moral education. However, it can be argued that 'good' in schooling is rarely used morally, though whether the uses are ethical in a broader sense remains a matter for debate.

Considering the particular activity of education as schooling, three dominant conceptions of the Good might be identified:

1. The Good as moral. That which is good is good in its own right, and/or because it is good for others, either directly or indirectly *via* being good for oneself. Thus politeness is good;
2. The Good as achievement. That which is good is successful. The aim is to be 'good at science'. 'Good' here implies 'good at';
3. The Good as instrumentally useful. Just as a good hammer drives home a nail efficiently, a good command of a foreign language may help a student get a job, and this usefulness is in no way modulated by whether the job in question is that of missionary or safe-breaker.[102] Here, the Good is narrowly 'good for'.

Of course, many situations span two or more of these categories. Thus it might be 'good' to get enough sleep and eat well to get the most out of school; this should help bring service to others, success and personal advancement. Nevertheless, the official discourse of schooling, in England and Wales at least, has in recent times been almost exclusively concerned with category 2. Schools have been judged almost entirely on measurable test success, at the lower levels particularly in literacy and numeracy, and at the higher levels in terms of grades in public examinations (GCSE and A Level[103]). School 'league tables' that appear regularly in the popular media are constructed entirely on this basis, ignoring categories 1. and 3. completely, and this has been the case even when 'value-added' league tables have been experimented with, that evaluated performance in relation to prior achievement.

As Nietzsche pointed out in *Beyond Good and Evil* and elsewhere, the moral, specifically Christian, sense of the Good is historically contingent. British social commentators who bemoan the lack of social responsibility among some young people might consider how far any sense of moral Good is valued or promoted within formal education. A pessimist might argue that what is promoted is neither moral Good nor Nietzschean self-striving but rather narrow instrumental compliance, since being 'good at', say, science involves only success in following a fixed syllabus and does not involved creativity or critical thinking to any significant extent at school level. Either way, a great deal is overlooked in the easy assumption that the Good in education is either unanimously agreed or ethically verifiable.

A recognition that My My Now overlaps with Your My Now, accompanied by an acceptance of the impossibility of a private language, ensures that ethical relativism cannot fall into solipsism. Even when we talk to ourselves, we draw on a common language, and our actions cannot impact on ourselves alone. The deluded loner is dangerous not because he or she is entirely outside society, for if that were the case, no damage could be done to society. The danger lies in the nature of that person's partial adherence to social norms. Ethical consensuality is always contingent, but in the case of the sociopath even the contingent acceptance is lacking.

Consider the brief but unsettling riots in English cities in the summer of 2011. Inevitably, these sparked a set of responses, with the political Left broadly focusing on structural issues and the Right on moral decline as major contributory causes. In terms of the present argument, the situation might be explained as follows. Most people agree to, or at least acquiesce in, a series of legal, ethical and moral principles that are held to underpin orderliness in a liberal society. These include a belief in material progress for all, respect for private property, a belief in some conception of fairness or social justice, and a general adherence to the law. The young looters of August 2011 may have shared these beliefs to a large extent. Many may have felt that they were in some way entitled to material goods that many others round them clearly possess; they may have felt that property should be private (that theirs cannot be someone else's); they may have felt that it is unjust that (for example) rich financiers can enjoy massive incomes while others have very little; and they may have had strong senses of the importance of law in some way or another, even if only understood in terms of honourable loyalty to family, friends or gang. Where they differed from the majority was in small rather than large ways: they failed to respect the shops they looted as owners of private property; they failed to acknowledge that the law does not empower them to redistribute wealth as they see fit; they failed to acknowledge that those beyond their immediate circles have rights and interests that should have as much respect as their own.

This is not to excuse any rioter or looter, but merely to point out that the differences in worldview between them and the law-abiding majority may well be relatively minor. After all, there is common disagreement about how conceptions such as fairness and justice ('social' or otherwise) should be played out in social policy. Ethical interpretation is always various. What unites the law-abiding majority, however, is the active agreement to abide by a norm however variously it can be interpreted. Thus, in the spirit of contingent ethical consensuality, most people will accept that the present economic system, however flawed and contested, should be allowed to run free of disruption by individuals looting shops. Thus economic inequalities may remain a problem to be addressed (for example) but a consensual opposition to direct theft and violence holds. The young looters, like other criminals, fail to acknowledge the importance of such consensual agreement, however flawed and contested.

As there has always been a degree of lawlessness in all societies, it is probably not possible simply to find a total solution to problems such as these. However, in the spirit of contingent ethical consensuality, a solution, however partial, must always be sought. That solution cannot validly rest on the premise that everyone can be taught to see the problems in the same way, however.

Overlapping and sometimes incompatible views about ethical goods are not only inevitable but necessary to maintain a healthy polis. Following the global economic problems of the late 2000s, for example, there has been heated debate in Britain and elsewhere about the ethics of investment banking, and the huge financial bonuses some in that field continued to accrue even after the near collapse of the system. It seems inconceivable that free market capitalists and socialists could ever agree on all the issues surrounding this, as their political and economic philosophies are grounded in the inevitability of such disagreement. However, most people agree to continue peacefully, even amicably, among such disagreements. It is perhaps remarkable that there are so few rioters and looters.

The question is begged, therefore, as to what holds most people to an ethical consensus, however contingent and contestable. It appears that most people, in hitherto relatively stable societies at any rate, adhere to a set of moral principles which are never clear in terms of how they should be interpreted, but which nevertheless are sufficient to allow for the continuation of a high degree of social order.

Such social order is, therefore, neither the product of complete rational consensus (which is impossible in terms both of completeness and universal rationality) nor complete dissensus (which is logically impossible, as disagreement rests on comparison, which cannot be made without elements of compatibility).

Philosophical models that stress the trumping of either consensus or dissensus by its opposite are therefore flawed. These include Habermas's conceptions of communicative action and of the ideal speech situation (Habermas, 1984/1987), and Lyotard's argument that dissensus always trumps consensus (Lyotard, 1986, 1988).

Habermas argues that agreements are best reached when parties are convinced of the sincerity, truth and appropriateness, as well as the comprehensibility of the other's argument. This rightly draws attention to the qualitative difference between agreement and simply linguistic exchange, but it nevertheless rests on certain assumptions, including that sincerity, for example, is responded to as an absolute; judgments of the other's sincerity, insofar as they are made at all, are surely not yes/no judgements but are relative and contextual. For example, one might trust a political candidate relative to others and to undertake a specific task, whereas one might not trust that person at all in other contexts. Habermas's argument also is light on the extent to which agreement on terms may not be reflected in consistency of interpretations.

Lyotard, on the other hand, downplays the importance of consensus in making dissensus possible. One can only dissent from something that is agreed. To argue, for instance, that science progresses by paralogy is to ignore the necessary role that analogy plays to make this possible.

Consensus and dissensus are the two sides of the communicative coin that serves as social currency. Communicative value accrues from simultaneous public commitment and private dissensus: in Harré's terms, from an appropriate balancing of social and personal identity (Harré, 1984).

In pragmatic and educational philosophy, this has been an increasingly recognised position largely through the work of Stanley Cavell. Naoko Saito is one commentator who has stressed the democratic and educational potentials of Cavell's ordinary language philosophy, including Cavell's revival of the Emersonian idea of Perfectionism. Saito's interpretation of Cavell lays the blame for social disconnection and political disenfranchisement (arguably the problem of the young English rioters) on 'the irony of democracy's fate - that rift between, on the one hand, the fact that people's consent to society is a condition of democracy and, on the other, the fact that the life they lead is one in which they do not know what to say or even what they *want to* say' (italics in original).[104] What this calls forth is not just a recognition of each person's voice, in the thin sense of a mere call for political recognition, but rather a struggle to find one's own voice in the context of a desire 'to say and think what makes us intelligible to the world'.[105] The key concept here is that of struggle: the struggles both to know oneself and to be recognized in society are never ending, yet their pursuit is what makes life meaningful, and this pursuit can be carried out through examination of the ordinary language that each of us employs in our struggle to make sense of the world. On this account, it is surely doubly ironic that the disaffection of the young should be the cause of civil unrest, since that disaffection is the potential ground of their civic engagement, conducted in the terms of a language that they already possess. While eleven or more years of formal, externally imposed education was insufficient to prevent some people from looting, the confronting of their existential angst, in terms already known to them, would have been enough to begin to establish them as active citizens and peaceful political agents, on Cavell's and Saito's account.

In conclusion, the differences between the sociopath and the law-abider are likely to be small and will never be complete. All persons differ to some extent; phenomenal worlds overlap. As distinct embodiments of culturally shared resources, each person is, or is capable of being, a private ironist, in the sense of someone who reflects on his or her sense of being in the world while maintaining a degree of skepticism and a resistance to closure.[106] However, for social order, private irony must exist in tandem with public commitment. Contingent ethical consensuality thus involves buying into social agreements, including moral norms, in good faith, while constantly striving to renegotiate them with respect to oneself in the context of others. The spirit of active citizenship is thus one of 'Let's go with this for the time being and see what we can make of it.' As soon, and as far as possible, everyone should consider themselves part of the 'we' that constitutes the widest definition of society; otherwise individuals will either not reflect critically or buy into norms other than perhaps those of a very close circle, such as family, friendship group or gang.[107] There is no one simple prescription for achieving this, beyond stressing the importance of people growing up knowing that their words and actions count in terms of having real consequences for both themselves and society more broadly. What cannot be assumed is a stable identity of interests; rather, individuals' interests will overlap, and will therefore partly coincide. If social powers can both acknowledge and permit the variety of conceptions of the good that the above analysis implies, and can develop institutions as enabling structures to pursue these various conceptions, then the maximal conditions will be in place for persons to develop as the arational utility maximers they aspire to be, able to use their powers of rationalization (among their other powers) in the confidence that they will not be constrained by others' reductive assumptions about the Right and the Good, yet suitably protected from the dangerous excesses of others. A movement in this direction would be a movement towards really participative democracy.

5.2 ON HUMAN PROGRESS: KNOWLEDGE, NUMBERS AND TIME

The final chapter will reflect on the concept of human progress, both individual and collective, taking into account the central claims of the argument so far, which can be enumerated briefly as follows. First, life is better understood as process than as substance. That is, the universe comprises forces, processes and events that create, *inter alia*, material effects that seem to endure to a greater or lesser extents. This contrasts with a substance metaphysics, whereby the universe fundamentally comprises matter that moves and acts in mutual relation. Secondly, in the context of process having priority over substance, living (as part of the work of the universe) can be understood as semiotic engagement, broadly understood on the basis of inability to differentiate distinctly sign from signal, or mind from body. Thirdly, individual sentient beings inhabit phenomenal worlds, in which it is always Now. These phenomenal worlds interact and overlap but never quite coincide. Taken together, these assumptions serve to problematize three key aspects of the post-Enlightenment concept of progress: number, time and knowledge.

It is often assumed that the universe is inherently numerical, and that mathematics therefore has a particular privileged status. This effective worship of mathematics can be traced back as least as far as Pythagoras (c.570-c.495BCE) and is evident in the thinking of Plato. The epistemological basis of this is a correspondence theory of truth, whereby the fact that mathematical explanations (largely) explain natural phenemena is taken to show that those phenomena are expressions of fundamental mathematically regular processes at the noumenal level.[108] As Kant would argue very much later, knowledge is, by definition, always of phenomena and never directly of noumena, about which, therefore, assumptions only can be made. The present argument concerns the sign, or signal-sign ('sign[al]': Stables, 2005[109]) as a unit of meaning, and thus as unquantifiable. This inability effectively to quantify the sign runs through the semiotic tradition. Even Peirce, the mathematician[110], could not effectively quantify the sign, and furthermore questioned the extent to which the universe can validly be seen as law-driven (and thus mathematically regular) as opposed to habit-driven (and thus mathematically approximate: see Chapter 1.1[111]). The Derridean view of meaning as deferred certainly defies neat numerical analysis of the human condition, albeit Derrida might be seen by some as part of a semiological tradition that has little to say about the non-human world.

The present concern is with the human sciences, rather than with physics or cosmology. Nevertheless, the status of mathematics is of ontological, epistemological and, specifically, methodological significance. The basic non-countability of the sign renders the social sciences as of questionable value when they operate on a physical science model (which may itself be flawed) that assumes all life ultimately to be not merely broadly explicable, but actually driven, by mathematically regular natural laws. Pragmatically, statistics can always help to explain, but they only function effectively within the contexts of explanations that are not themselves ultimately statistically verifiable; they do not necessarily point to invariate laws.[112] Whether this is interpreted as an entrenched philosophical opposition between correspondence and coherence theories of truth or as a new insight for which semiotic pragmatism is responsible is a matter of debate; on either account, the claims of the social sciences to explain anything beyond the contextual and the cultural are challenged, as (on the pan-semiotic account) is the claim of the physical sciences to be on the path to realising a final theory of everything, as science cannot escape culture either.[113] This is not a fundamentally negative response to science. It by no means invalidates the scientific endeavours which continue to enhance human experience. However, as a pragmatic account, it construes effectiveness in terms of effects, which are always on culturally conditioned experiencing agents. Some may see this as limiting the scope of science, but on a fully semiotic account, opportunities are opened up as well as closed down.

An important issue here is that of natural resources: their availability, creation and availability.[114] There is a default tendency to regard natural resources as both given and in danger of being exhausted. That is (as commentators since Malthus have repeatedly warned), the Earth's ability to feed and nurture increasing numbers of human beings is threatened by human population increase and increased energy consumption generally. The present argument does not challenge that perception of danger. If the available food resources can be conceptualised as 100 putative food mega-units annually, and each billion of the human population requires 10 of these mega-units, then a world population of over 10 billion will be unsustainable; the same calculations can be made with respect to oil or any other natural resource.

However, the following deserve consideration. First, the world has not always been able to produce 100 mega-units annually (given that the production can be measured this accurately at all). Secondly, a food unit of resource is not given but is rather produced from a natural unit of resource; a natural resource has to be processed to become a human resource, at the very least by gathering, and often by much more sophisticated means. Thirdly, food supply may not meet food demand in all areas, even if it does overall. Fourthly, intervening factors, from disease to war, can affect food production and distribution. In relation to the first point, food production has so far increased in line with population increase, although no generation would have been able to produce what the subsequent generation did produce. In response to the second point, a natural resource is in fact a unit of meaning; it does not simply reside in nature to be consumed by a person. Even the simplest of natural resources – food – is a matter of knowing what to do with natural entities. Units of meaning are not given by noumenal nature. In response to the third point, a resource is not a closed system. For a food item to be food for a person, it has to be transported, for example, requiring further resource use. In response to the fourth point, further factors, whether natural (for example, weather or earthquake) or specifically human (for example, war or political dispute) can further intervene in production and supply.

The inferences from this offer both hope and alarm. In the context of the society in which he wrote, Malthus (1766-1834) may well have been right: the ability to produce food at that point would not sustain a larger population. Those who argue the same now are also correct. 100 mega-units will not feed more than 10 billion people on the calculation above. However, generations subsequent to Malthus have consistently proved themselves able to achieve what not only seemed, but was, impossible at the time: increased production beyond the feasible limit. This can happen because resources, while indeed finite, are never fixed, for the reasons given in the last paragraph. The common fault in reasoning around these issues is to assume that finitude and fixity are synonymous, and this can be construed as symptomatic of a worldview that is over-dependent on mathematical modelling, for the mathematics can tell us (approximately) what is available but not what will be available when technologies and other contextual factors change. The alarming conclusion is, therefore, that the world will indeed run out of food, and other natural resources, if we go on as we are; this is true now as it has always been true, though the time scales might change. The hopeful reading of the situation is that human beings will continue to innovate in unexpected ways, as, again, has been the case to date. However, implied within this simple observation is a radical suggestion relating to educational and social policy. If we teach the younger generation everything we know, the human species will die; it can only survive if subsequent generations continue to achieve what is currently impossible. It follows that educational and other social policies which seek compliance in any form may have the opposite effect from that intended, for rather than sustaining cultures, they may deprive them of the innovative thinking which, alone, can sustain them, albeit they will undergo change in the process. Learning is not enough. Each new generation must seek to do things anew.[115] Assuming that statistics have a normative, transcendental value can be harmful, as their value is contextual and descriptive.

Similarly, time as noumenon is unknowable. Experientially, it is always Now, and Nowness is experienced in terms of sequences (the Then dimensions of past and present: Chapter 2.1). Experientially, Now is all there is, yet Now is also deferred, as there is no absolutely still point of reference; think of the experience associated with saying 'I have made a decision!' Change seems ubiquitous and inevitable, and time and space are the means by which we construe it. Time is thus inextricably linked to narrative. Time is a tool of narrative, and *vice versa*: the link cannot be broken. Beginnings and ends always relate to specifiable narratives. We cannot conceive of a beginning and end of everything. Therefore, when cosmology offers us accounts of the beginning and end of the universe, this, in its linguistic, if not its mathematical form, is a new creation myth, for science expressed in language cannot escape language any more than science expressed mathematically can ever prove beyond doubt that the noumenal universe is fundamentally mathematical. Beginnings and ends are always contextualised within narratives. Although time, as human beings understand it, may be standardised in terms of clocks and measurement, and may therefore seem to transcend all forms of social construction, this is illusory, since narratives are always contingent.

As conceptions of social progress are time dependent, these are also contingent. As individual development and growth are experienced by the individual person and by those with whom that person interacts, so narratives of progress are dependent on the mutual experience of change as progress, and this is by no means inevitable. Social progress is therefore not inexorable, and this can be illustrated with reference to the value of formal education.

Bourdieu has explained various forms of social advantage in terms of financial, cultural and social capital (Bourdieu, 1986). A perspective on this from the liberal tradition (though not one offered by Bourdieu himself) is that personal and social progress might be evaluated according to the degree of return on the capital invested. Taking formal education as an example, successive generations throughout the past century have gained more materially than their parents. As a result, they are likely to agree that their education helped them, and they are thus further likely to be positive about the benefits of, for example, compulsory state-funded schooling. Under current global economic circumstances, particularly in Europe and North America, there is less immediate prospect of a return on one's educational investment. Thus, far from valuing formal education more as a means of escaping straitened circumstances, it may, on this account, be valued less. This construal therefore throws into question the value of perpetually seeing increased educational provision as the means of ensuring further social progress, though it by no means amounts to an argument for destroying educational opportunities for those who are motivated to take them up, and begs a more flexible and open-minded approach to policy provision that is increasingly responsive to shifting aspirations.[116]

Finally, in relation to knowledge itself, it is important to stress that the highly relativist positions adopted during the development of the present argument do not undermine its importance. The standard philosophical conception of knowledge as justified, true belief can be maintained if (and only if) justification, truth and belief are all socially validated, where 'socially' implies a sincere, if inevitably never complete, consensus. It is undoubtedly the case that there are dangers attached to this position: whole societies can get things very wrong, and powerful groups can exploit others' weaknesses or ignorance. However, there are also dangers in assuming that knowledge transcends cultural context and can therefore be taken as absolute and applicable regardless of context. If Nazi Germany can be seen as a symptom of the former danger, environmental degradation, nuclear accidents, and wars conducted on the basis that all the world needs or wants Western liberal democracy might be seen as symptoms of the latter. No knowledge can transcend context. To take one relatively unlikely, but by no means unthinkable, example, suppose that global temperatures begin, quite sharply, to fall as a new Ice Age encroaches. If it is still accepted that carbon dioxide emissions have a global warming effect, then oil and coal emissions could be encouraged to mitigate the effects of rapid cooling. It might be argued that this indicates a possible change in strategy rather than in knowledge itself. However, on a pragmatic account, what something is understood to be is constituted by its effects. The situation above would inevitably change understandings of resources as a corollary of changing their uses.

In conclusion, it is not valid to draw universal conclusions from conditional premises, whether in science or for society, albeit planning must proceed on the best explanatory model available. An alternative model of social progress is therefore sought to that based on simply numerically measurable improvements over time against criteria that are assumed to be universally valid. Rather, it is safer to regard such measurable trends as in service of the aspirations they serve, which are in turn in service of the people who set them in the contexts they found themselves.[117] In terms of evaluating and setting policy, there is a case for putting far more emphasis on subjective and intersubjective quality of experience, and only experiencing agents themselves can provide such data. As scientific relativity places experiences of time and space in the context of the observer, so education and social policy more broadly might take more account of those it purports to serve.

NOTES

[1] For very recent treatments of the issue, for example, see Finkielstein (2000) who argues that groups of humans throughout history have failed to acknowledge other groups as fully human, and Agamben (2004), who contemplates what would be left for the human if, as other commentators (e.g. Fukuyama, 1993) have suggested, the Twentieth Century somehow signalled the 'end of history.' (That is, on Fukuyama's account, the death of competing idedologies).

[2] See, for example, Stables, A. (2008a).

[3] It is not a universal trait of human culture to regard the young person as the same as the old. The linguist and anthropologist Daniel Everett, for example, was told by Amazonian villagers that when he visited them in the past, they were not there but others (whom Westerners would regard as the same persons but older) had been there. The Piraha people whom Everett studied also had no number system: another attribute often considered humanly universal (Everett, 2008).

[4] Consider, for example, the advertising concept of the Kidult, the origin of which is uncertain, as an example of a social shift from seeing the child and youth as aspiring to the skills and mores of the adult to a more confused situation in which, for example, adults often aim to emulate people much younger than themselves.

[5] This argument has been made briefly in Stables, A. (2008b).

[6] This builds on the argument in Stables, A. (2005).

[7] See, for example, Guenther, 2009, on Derrida.

[8] Stables, 2005, 2006a., 2006b., 2010.

[9] cf. Wittgenstein's argument that no one can speak a private language (Wittgenstein, 1967). See Chapter 1.3.

[10] Responding particularly to Semetsky's work, Marcel Danesi has coined the term 'edusemiotic' to define the growing body of work devoted to exploring semiotics in relation to education (in Semetsky, 2010).

[11] See Chapter 1.1.

[12] With respect to this, the argument is also, to a degree, Hegelian, for it is in Hegel that we find the roots of Twentieth Century theory of language as socially constructed systems of signs, within which individual items' meanings are not determined by correspondence to external reality but rather relationally to other items (Hegel, 1807).

[13] A key text here is Roland Barthes' *Mythologies* (2009, first published 1957), in which a series of written and visual texts, including a wrestling match, a striptease and a car advertisement, are subjected to a form of literary critical analysis.

[14] 'Social semiotics' can refer to two related but distinct entities. 'Social semiotics' without capitals is a broad, heterogeneous orientation within semiotics, straddling many other areas of inquiry concerned, in some way, with the social dimensions of meaning in any media of communication, its production, interpretation and circulation, and its implications in social processes, as cause or effect. 'Social Semiotics' with capitals is a distinguishable school in linguistics and semiotics which specifically addresses these issues. It is important because it synthesizes these issues, not because it covers those issues in a distinct or authoritative form. Social semiotics makes semiotics more broadly useful, and Social Semiotics assists in this process.' (Hodge, undated, retrieved 16 September, 2011).

[15] Timo Maran (2006) has written a very useful account of the overlaps and differences between the related fields of zoosemiotics, biosemiotics and ecosemiotics. Each of these develops a form of biological semiotics. Von Uexküll is a seminal figure, while the most renowned developer of the field has been Thomas Sebeok. (e.g. Sebeok, 1992).

[16] From the earliest days, Saussure has received a chilly reception from Anglo-Saxon academics. C.K.Ogden and I.A.Richards wrote: 'Unfortunately this [Saussurean] theory of signs, by neglecting entirely the things for which signs stand, was from the beginning cut off from any contact with scientific methods of verification.' (Ogden and Richards, 1923: 8).

[17] Plato's Myth of the Cave can be found in *The Republic* Book 7, Section 7. Retrieved from http://people.bridgewater.edu/~jjosefso/The%20Myth%20of%20the%20Cave.htm 16 September 2011.

[18] - or that which lies behind it; at the noumenal level, there may be no identity. There remains an element of mystery:

If, by the term noumenon, we understand a thing so far as it is not an object of our sensuous intuition, thus making abstraction of our mode of intuiting it, this is a noumenon in the negative sense of the word. But if we understand by it an object of a non-sensuous intuition, element of mystery:

element of mystery:

If, by the term noumenon, we understand a thing so far as it is not an object of our sensuous intuition, thus making abstraction of our mode of intuiting it, this is a noumenon in the negative sense of the word. But if we understand by it an object of a non-sensuous intuition, we in this case assume a peculiar mode of intuition, an intellectual intuition, to wit, which does not, however, belong to us, of the very possibility of which we have no notion—and this is a noumenon in the positive sense. (Kant 1781/2003: Ch.3).

[19] e.g. Sternfjeld, 2007.

[20] E.g. Burke (1966), discussed with reference to education by Rutten, Mottart and Soetaert (2007).

[21] For example, words can be construed as either icons or symbols.

[22] The argument that true science must proceed on the basis of potentially refutable hypotheses is perhaps most strongly associated with Karl Popper (Popper, 1959).

[23] For some detail on this, see Stables, 2008.

[24] To radical Peirceans such as Deely and Stjernfeld, only followers of Peirce can be considered as philosophical semioticians; the tradition from Saussure should be referred to as semiological after Saussure's term *Semiologie*. This ignores first that Peirce wrote about *Semeiotic*, not simply *Semiotics*, secondly that the term *Semiotics* is widely used as an umbrella term, including in film and media studies, linguistics and a range of other disciplines, and thirdly that limiting *Semiotics* to Peirce renders critique of Peirce within *Semiotics* logically impossible.

[25] For example, a colleague of the author claims he has told students that Analytic philosophers do not consider Continental philosophy philosophy, and that Continental philosophers do not consider philosophy enough.

[26] By 'tradition' here, I refer to the past century and a half, and to philosophy of language specifically. Peirce was as much influenced by Kant and Hegel as are those in the Continental tradition, though in very different ways. Ultimately, Peirce's rejection of Kantian dualism (the phenomenon-noumenon divide) and comcomitant commitment to a grant metaphysical scheme renders him much more a Hegelian than a Kantian, and thus closer to the Continental tradition than the traditional semiotics-semiology divide, as articulated by commentators such as Deely (1990) might suggest.

[27] First published (in French), 1913.

[28] We might remind ourselves that many influential philosophical works may appear structurally incoherent, including Wittgenstein's *Philosophical Investigations*. (Wittgenstein, 1967).

[29] Of course, the appearance of arbitrariness does not necessarily imply absolute arbitrariness (whatever that may be). It might be argued that Saussure is simply more cautious than Peirce on this.

[30] See below (main text) and Chapter 1.3 (Lyotard).

[31] Note that even atomic accounts have long since abandoned their initial premise: that (as originally conceived by Greek scholars including Democritus: BCE 460-370) the atom was the smallest, indivisible building block of matter.

[32] e.g. *The Realistic Spirit: Wittgenstein, Philosophy, and the Mind* (Bradford Books, 1991).

[33] e.g. "The Method of the Tractatus", in *From Frege to Wittgenstein: Perspectives on Early Analytic Philosophy*, edited by Erich H. Reck, Oxford University Press, 2002.

[34] For a discussion of this (quite varied) school of philosophy, see Alfred Ayer's *Logical Positivism* (New York: Free Press, 1959).

[35] Example not used by Wittgenstein.

[36] The Programme for International Student Assessment (PISA) tests, organized through the Organisation of Economic Organisation and Development (OECD) have repeatedly shown

such results through the 2000s. See, for example, http://news.bbc.co.uk/1/hi/7115692.stm retrieved 18 October 2011.

[37] i.e. thinking from data to hypotheses and theories, rather than explaining data in terms of hypotheses and theories (induction) and resorting to the best available explanation rather than enabling proof (abduction).

[38] It must be acknowledged that Peirce evades this dichotomy, but arguably at some cost. Peirce's evolving consciousness, like Hegel's, seems unable to acknowledge fully either cultural diversity or the historical tendency of scientific thought to spend considerable time following blind alleys, in hindsight.

[39] This is on a reading of Plato that assumes we can tell what he thought from his writing. Some Plato scholars deny this, arguing that Plato always resists answers (in the spirit of Socrates): e.g. Smith, 2011 (unpublished conference paper). Following commentators such as Smith, it would be preferable to state that the argument for ideal forms is a common interpretation of Plato.

[40] Retrieved from http://www.heraclitusfragments.com/index.html 30 November 2011.

[41] Wittgentstein; see Chapter 1.3.

[42] Whitehead, 1929b, various references.

[43] See Chapter 1.2.

[44] An event is here defined as a process identified.

[45] Hartshorne, 1991.

[46] See Chapter 1.2.

[47] Chapter 1.3.

[48] Chapter 1.3.

[49] In Stables, 2005, the signal-sign is referred to as the 'sign(al)' for written convenience (Stables, 2005: 8ff.). The sign(al) as unit of meaning (as Interpretant in Peirce's terms) is not a fixed entity but a unit of difference (Derrida) and so therefore cannot be precisely spatiotemporally located.

[50] One response to Zeno's paradox: 'getting there' is prior to 'getting half the way there', half the way again, and so on. One is either going all the way there or half the way there on each journey. Experience is not divisible into measurable units.

[51] The clear distinction between stimulus and response is problematized in Dewey's *The Reflex Arc Concept in Psychology* (1896), though it might be said to be implicit in the thinking of Hume (e.g. 2004).

[52] Note Wittgenstein's rejection of the possibility of a private language in *Philosophical Investigations*.

[53] See reference to Houser, 2000, in Chapter 1.1.

[54] The concept of stem cells is also salient here. The stem cell develops according to its context, reminding us that that the fundamental building blocks of life (or forces underpinning life forms, on a process account) are common and that differentiation is contingent. It remains to be seen whether, for example, animal stem cells could help regenerate a human brain. Such experiments may be limited on ethical grounds, but their very possibility renders them deeply suggestive.

[55] Bower, retrieved from www.sciencenews.org 7 December 2009.

[56] Mostly associated with the University of London Institute of Education in the 1960s and '70s, though still characteristic of the approach employed by some connected with that institution.

[57] See, for example, the author's response to John White on this in Stables, 2006.

[58] After Hume – see Chapter 2.1.

[59] See Rorty's *Philosophy and the Mirror of Nature* (Rorty, 1981).

[60] Derrida alludes to this state of alienation in *Structure, Sign and Play in the Discourse of the Human Sciences* in Derrida, 1978: 294:

Here there is a sort of question, call it historical, of which we are only glimpsing today the *conception, the formation, the gestation, the labor.* I employ these words, I admit, with a glance towards the business of childbearing – but also with a glance towards those who, in a company from which I do not exclude myself, turn their eyes away in the face of the as yet unnameable which is proclaiming itself and which can do so, as is necessary whenever a birth is in the offing, only under the species of the non-species, in the formless, mute, infant and terrifying form of monstrosity.

[61] 'According to a new DNA study, most humans have a little Neanderthal in them—at least 1 to 4 percent of a person's genetic makeup.' (Than, 2010).

[62] There is evidence of birdsong varying between urban and rural environments:

During the summer of 2008, birds were recorded in Washington, D.C. area backyards. Surprisingly, in areas with intense development (e.g. more pavement, buildings and roads), birds sang songs with a lower maximum frequency (the highest pitch of their song gets lower) and a narrower frequency range. *Effects of Urban development on Birdsong*, online magazine of the Migratory Bird Centre, Smithsonian National Zoological Park. Retrieved from http://nationalzoo.si.edu/scbi/migratorybirds/research/marra/development-changes-bird-songs.cfm 5 November 2011

[63] Dewey (1916) argued that it is only modern, complex societies that require this form of induction.

[64] By 'language' here, I refer to English. Other languages sometimes throw up other confusions. However, I am not aware of the concept of 'semiosy' as a broader conception of literacy existing in any language.

[65] See Stables, 2003a., Chapter 6, for a fuller discussion.

[66] Which of these terms is employed, in relation to social theory, tends to depend on the degree of optimism surrounding commentators' views on the progressive nature of modernity. Thus for Giddens (1991), Late Modernity encapsulates a sense of increased opportunity in a globalised world. For Lyotard (1986), Postmodernity is a condition of arational scepticism, of 'incredulity towards metanarratives' (xiv). Positions between the two include Beck's New Modernity, or Risk Society, characterised by the increased individualisation of risk, and Baumann's Liquid Modernity, with its emphasis on fluid structures (Beck, 1992; Bauman, 2000).

[67] Note, for example, that the original English grammar schools, such as Shakespeare attended in Stratford-upon-Avon in the 1570s, taught a curriculum entirely, or virtually entirely, comprising that which might now be called the language arts, particularly the broad field of rhetoric. For an argument to reintroduce rhetoric as a foundational concept for contemporary education, at least in the arts, humanities and social sciences, see the work of Soetaert, Rutten and others at the University of Ghent (e.g. Rutten, Mottart and Soetaert, 2010).

[68] These instances are drawn from the experience of a student teacher known to the author in the early 1990s.

[69] See Chapter 1.3.

[70] 'Findings show that the meaning of the label dyslexia is not settled in public consciousness.' Tassie, 2010: 109.

[71] For a discussion of the Buddhist conception of mindfulness, see, for example, Gunaratana, 2011.

[72] See Chapter 1.2.

[73] For a somewhat more extended discussion of this, see Gough and Stables, 2012.

[74] See also Stables, 2003b.

[75] (Unless we accept Peirce's speculative scheme, under which Interpretants have real existence independent of interpreters. There are no grounds for an empiricist to accept this. See Chapter 1.1 and ff.).

[76] See, for example, Frankena's discussion of R.S.Peters in Chapter 2.2.

[77] Murakami et al conducted a small-scale inquiry into how the various parties in a school construed the concept of effort, for example, showing how operationalising such a concept in a specific professional field is not simply a matter of adopting, or even interpreting, expert outsider perspectives, but is always part of a broader set of negotiations between self and environment (Murakami, Stables and McIntosh, 2010).

[78] Among the myriad of research papers and books on this, Ball (2003) provides one of many stimulating perspectives.

[79] Again, there is a well-established literature in this area. One well cited paper is that of Wentzel and Caldwell (1997) who found a strong correlation between peer group acceptance and

academic achievement, though critical sociological literature since Willis (1976) has stressed that the values that bind some groups of students together may be antithetical to those of the school.

[80] To quote Tubbs (undated):

Fundamentally Hegel views education and learning as 'experiential' ... But to have a philosophy of education or, better, a science or philosophy that is education, experience has somehow to experience itself, to recognise the educational development which is taking place ... An object is thought (known), then mediated in its being known as a thought thought again or known as not-known and finally known and not-known as both of these. This final stage is therefore not final at all, and its instability is its being educational or our continued learning from and about experience.

[81] Cf. Levinas, 1967. See also Chapter 1.2.

[82] See quotation from Houser, 2000, in Chapter 1.1.

[83] Cf. Harré's work on positioning discussed in Chapter 3.2.

[84] An idea introduced in the *Groundwork of the Metaphysics of Morals* (Kant, ed. Guyer, 1998).

[85] See Stables, 2008, particularly Part 1.

[86] That is, the kind of narrow judgment that, for example, presupposes a child's academic potential on the basis of test results. British schools, in particular, have been encouraged to do this in recent years, having their effectiveness measured in terms of their progress against benchmarks drawn from test results on sometimes very young children. On the basis of this logic, a school whose pupils do appallingly on entry but averagingly on exit is better than one whose students score highly on both entrance and exit.

[87] Note that on this account, humanism is not at odds with many religious traditions. For example, Roman Catholicism's objection to abortion, involving teaching that the human embryo is of moral consideration, is an example of a strong humanist ethic based on the idea of humanity (but not other species) existing in the image of God. Humanism unites fervent believers and radical aetheists, even though in some contexts (such as humanist organisations), it associates solely with the latter.

[88] Note the author's critique of Dewey relating to this in Stables, 2008.

[89] An exception is Biesta (e.g. Biesta 2006) who sees the human as social work in progress (building on Dewey). Thus he is a posthumanist according to the first definition here but not on the other two accounts, whereby he might be construed as a humanist, as he maintains the specialness of the human, though not as fixed essence.

[90] For example, Roden (undated): 'I take the term 'posthuman' to refer to hypothetical descendents of current humans that are no longer human in consequence of some history of technical augmentation' Retrieved from http://open.academia.edu/DavidRoden/Papers/399801/ Posthumanism_and_Instrumental_Eliminativism 15 November 2011.

[91] E.g. Hayles, 1999.

[92] The degree to which such a shift is possible has been a matter of debate between Bonnett and others influenced by Heidegger in this and the present author. See, for example, Stables, 2010.

[93] For an early articulation of this perspective, see Stables and Scott, 2001.

[94] E.g. Finkielkraut, 2000.

[95] *Nicomachean Ethics* (Aristotle, 350 BCE).

[96] *Groundwork of the Metaphysics of Morals* (Kant, 1998).

[97] It is important to note that it is possible to be, for example, an ethical relativist but an ontological realist. Indeed, the present argument is minimally realist (that is, acknowledges a substrate normally conceived of as physical forces or energy) but is strongly relativist in all other respects. At the metaphysical level, relativism is not opposed to realism.

[98] *Nicomachean Ethics. Ethos* has a broader meaning than the everyday sense of 'habit' in modern usage however. According to Miller (1974), for example, it is best understood as good character evidenced by habitual behaviour.

[99] See discussion in Chapter 4.2.

[100] *Thus Spoke Zarathustra.* Nietzsche, 2005.

[101] *Being and Nothingness.* Sartre, 1993.

[102] The author has been involved in research into how schoolchildren make subject and career choices, and has often heard comments such as 'There's no point in doing religious studies unless you want to be a vicar'. The influence of such narrow instrumentalism in children's thinking is often overlooked in the literature. (See, for example, Stables, 1996; Wikeley and Stables, 1999).

[103] GCSE = General Certificate of Secondary Education, generally taken in about eight subjects at age 16. A Level = Advanced level, generally taken by about half of all 18 year-olds.

[104] Saito, N. (2011) Quiet Desperation, secret melancholy: polemos and passion in citizenship education, *Ethics and Education* 6/1, 3-14, p.3. See also Chapter 3.3.

[105] *ibid.* p.5.

[106] This phrase is most closely associated with the work of Richard Rorty, particularly Rorty, 1989.

[107] It can be regarded as a failure of formal education, particularly at the level of compulsory schooling, that it often seems to fail to develop this sense. On the other hand, youth has always been associated with potential lawlessness. As Shakespeare wrote in *The Winter's Tale*, first acted in 1612, 'There is nothing between the ages of fifteen and twenty-five except....' Nevertheless, we should expect our educational organizations to do what they can.

[108] That is, at the level beyond human empirical understanding. To Plato, sense data often give distorted views of noumena: see the 'myth of the cave' in *Republic* Book 7 (Plato, 360BCE). Kant argued that although time and space are fundamental schema underpinning our understandings, and that we also tend to understand everything in terms of certain categories (such as quality and relation), we can only know for sure that these schema and categories exist as part of our mental apparatus (Kant, 1781/2003).

[109] Various references.

[110] See Chapter 1.1 .

[111] Of course, Peirce wrote about 'a' sign, but was not consistent in defining it, such that a word, an image or a thought can all be signs.

[112] So called 'evidence based' approaches to policy and research, for example, pay little heed to the theoretical frameworks within which the data operate. Without the challenge of theory, there is a danger of data simply being used to confirm or deny, rather than rigorously test.

[113] Among the body of work showing how scientists are inevitably constrained by the cultural resources at their disposal is that of Gooding on Faraday: Gooding, 2006.

[114] For a much fuller discussion of this, see Stables, 2010.

[115] For one of the most compelling developments of this idea in the context of schooling, see Biesta, 2006.

[116] The broader argument about the extent of the justification for compulsory education is explored in Stables, 2009, where the case for compulsion is considered in relation to four criteria: moral (is it morally either justified or required?); empowerment (does it empower the student?); equity (does it contribute to a more just society? and economic (does it promote economic growth and well-being?).

[117] On this basis, for example, disgust of the Nazis may be tempered by the sobering realization that much of what they stood for, particularly in the realm of eugenics and racial superiority, was widely shared among academic commentators of the time.

REFERENCES

PREFACE

Agamben, G. (2004). *The Open: Man and Animal.* Palo Alto, CA: Stanford University Press.

Everett, D. (2008). *Don't Sleep, There are Snakes: Life and Language in the Amazonian Jungle.* New York: Pantheon.

Finkielkraut, A. (2000). *In the Name of Humanity* (J. Friedlander, Trans.). New York: Columbia University Press.

Fukuyama, F. (1993). *The End of History and the Last Man.* London: Harper Perennial.

Guenther, L. (2009). Who follows whom? Derrida, animals and women. *Derrida Today, 2*(2), 151–165.

Hegel, G. W. F. (1807). *Phenomenology of Mind* (J. B. Baillie, Trans.). Retrieved November 22, 2011, from http://www.marxists.org/reference/archive/hegel/phindex.htm

Hume, D. (1975). *Enquiries Concerning Human Understanding and Concerning the Principles of Morals* (L. A. Selby-Bigge & P. H. Nidditch, Eds.). Oxford: Oxford University Press.

Kukathas, C. (1989). *Hayek and Modern Liberalism.* Oxford: Oxford University Press.

McDowell, J. (1996). *Mind and World.* Cambridge, MA: Harvard University Press.

Semetsky, I. (Ed.). (2010). *Semiosis, Experience, Education.* Rotterdam: Sense.

Stables, A. (2005). *Living and Learning as Semiotic Engagement: A New Theory of Education.* Lewiston, NY/ Lampeter: MellenPress.

Stables, A. (2006a). Sign(al)s: Living and learning as semiotic engagement (text of inaugural lecture delivered 30/11/2005). *Journal of Curriculum Studies, 38*(4), 373–387.

Stables, A. (2006b). From semiosis to social policy: The less trodden path. *Sign System Studies, 34*(1), 121–134.

Stables, A. (2008a). *Childhood and the Philosophy of Education: An Anti-Aristotelian Perspective.* London: Continuum.

Stables, A. (2008b). Semiosis, Dewey and difference: Implications for pragmatic philosophy of education. *Contemporary Pragmatism, 5*(1), 147–162.

Stables, A. (2010). Semiosis and the collapse of mind-body dualism: Implications for education. In I. Semetsky (Ed.), *Semiosis, Experience, Education* (pp. 21–36). Rotterdam: Sense.

Wittgenstein, L. (1967). *Philosophical Investigations.* Oxford: Blackwell.

CHAPTER 1

Theoretical Foundations: Semiotics, Process and the Language Game

1.1 Peirce and the Development of American Semiotics

Atkin, A. (2010). Peirce's theory of signs. *Stanford Encyclopedia of Philosophy.* Retrieved November 22, 2011, from http://www.seop.leeds.ac.uk/entries/peirce-semiotics/

Barthes, R. (2009). *Mythologies* (A. Lavers, Trans.). New York: Vintage.

Bogue, R. (1983). *Deleuze on Cinema.* London: Routledge.

Burch, R. (2010). Charles Sanders Peirce. *Stanford Encyclopedia of Philosophy.* Retrieved November 22, 2011, from http://www.seop.leeds.ac.uk/entries/peirce-semiotics/

Burke, K. (1966). *Language as Symbolic Action.* Los Angeles: University of California Press.

Cortazzi, M. (1993). *Narrative Analysis.* London: Falmer.

Deely, J. (1990). *Basics of Semiotics.* Bloomington: Indiana University Press.

Dewey, J. (1896). The reflex arc concept in psychology. *Psychological Review, 3*, 357–370. Retrieved November 14, 2006, from http://spartan.ac.brocku.ca/~lward/Dewey/Dewey_1896.html

REFERENCES

Dewey, J. (1897). My pedagogic creed. First published in *The School Journal, LIV*(3), 77–80. Retrieved November 16, 2006, from http://www.infed.org/archives/e-texts/e-dew-pc.htm
Dewey, J. (1915/1944). *The School and Society*. Chicago: University of Chicago Press.
Dewey, J. (1916). *Democracy and Education*. Toronto: Macmillan.
Dewey, J. (1925). *Experience and Nature*. La Salle, Ill.: Open Court.
Dworkin, M. (1959). *Dewey on Education: Selections*. New York: Teachers College Press.
Eco, U. (1986). *Semiotics and the Philosophy of Language*. Bloomington: Indiana University Press.
Fairclough, N. (1995). *Critical Discourse Analysis*. Boston: Addison Wesley.
Greimas, A. J. (1989). *The Social Sciences. A Semiotic View* (F. Collins & P. Perron, Trans.). Minneapolis: University of Minnesota Press.
Halliday, M. A. K. (1978). *Language as Social Semiotic: The Social Interpretation of Language and Meaning*. Maryland: University Park Press.
Hodge, B. (undated). Social semiotics. *Semiotic Encyclopedia Online*. Retrieved September 16, 2011, from http://www.semioticon.com/seo/S/social_semiotics.html
Houser, N., et al. (1998). *The Essential Peirce: Selected Philosophical Writings* (Vol. 2). Bloomington: Indiana University Press.
Kant, I. (1781/2003). *Critique of Pure Reason*, the Project Gutenberg e-text produced by Aldarondo, C. A. (J. M. D. Meiklejohn, Trans.). Retrieved November 18, 2011, from http://www.gutenberg.org/cache/epub/4280/pg4280.html
Kress, G. (1997). *Before Writing: Rethinking the Paths to Literacy*. London: Routledge.
Kress, G. (2003). *Literacy in the New Media Age*. London: Routledge.
Kress, G., & van Leeuwen, T. (2006). *Reading Images: The Grammar of Visual Design*. London: Routledge.
Kuhn, T. S. (1996). *The Structure of Scientific Revolutions*. Chicago: University of Chicago Press.
Locke, J. (1690). *An Essay Concerning Human Understanding*. Retrieved November 22, 2011, from http://www.ilt.columbia.edu/publications/Projects/digitexts/locke/understanding/chapter0421.html
Maran, T. (2006). Where do your borders lie? Reflections on the semiotical ethics of nature. In C. Gersdort & S. Mayer (Eds.), *Nature in Literary and Cultural Studies. Transatlantic Conversations on Ecocriticism* (pp. 455–476). Amsterdam/New York: Rodopi.
Markus, R. A. (1957). St. Augustine on signs. *Phronesis*, *2*(1), 60–83.
Peirce, C. S. (1868). On a new list of categories. *Proceedings of the American Academy of Arts and Sciences*, *7*, 287–298. Retrieved November 22, 2011, from http://www.peirce.org/writings/p32.html
Peirce, C. S. (1878). How to make our ideas clear. *Popular Science Monthly*, 286–302.
Peirce, C. S. (1904). Ideas, stray and stolen, about scientific writing. In *The Essential Peirce. Selected Philosophical Writings* (Vol. 2, pp. 325–330). Bloomington: Indiana University Press.
Peirce, C. S. (1966). *Charles S. Peirce: Selected Writings* (P. P. Wiener, Ed.). New York: Dover.
Peirce, C. S. (1997). *Pragmatism as a Principle and Method of Right Thinking: The 1903 Harvard Lectures on Pragmatism* (P. A. Turrisi, Ed.). New York: SUNY Press.
Peirce, C. S. (2000). *Writings of Charles S. Peirce: A Chronological Edition* (N. Houser, et al., Ed., Vol. 6). Bloomington: Indiana University Press.
Petrilli, S., & Deely, J. (2010). *Sign Crossroads in Global Perspective: Semioethics and Responsibility*. New Brunswick/London: Transaction.
Pikkarainen, E. (2010). The semiotics of education: A new vision in an old landscape. *Educational Philosophy and Theory*. Retrieved November 22, 2011, from http://onlinelibrary.wiley.com/journal/10.1111/(ISSN)1469-5812/earlyview
Plato (390BCE). The myth of the cave. In *The Republic*. Retrieved September 16, 2011, from http://people.bridgewater.edu/~jjosefso/The%20Myth%20of%20the%20Cave.htm
Poinsot, J. (1632). Tractatus de signis: The semiotic of John Poinsot. In *Artis Logicae Prima et Secunda Pars* (1631,1632). Arranged in bilingual format by John Deely in consultation with Ralph A. Powell. Berkeley: University of California Press, 1985.
Popper, K. (1959). *The Logic of Scientific Discovery*. London: Hutchinson.

Rutten, K., Mottart, A., & Soetaert, R. (2010). The rhetorical construction of the nation in education. The case of Flanders. *Journal of Curriculum Studies*, *42*(6), 775–790.

Sebeok, T. A. (1992). 'Tell me, where is fancy bred?': The biosemiotic self. In T. A. Sebeok & J. Umiker-Sebeok (Eds.), *Biosemiotics: The Semiotic Web* (pp. 333–343). Berlin: Mouton de Gruyter.

Soto, D. (1529, 1554). *Summulae* (1st ed. Burgos; 3rd. rev. ed., Salamanca; Facsimile of 3rd ed). Hildesheim, NY: Georg Olms Verlag.

Stables, A. (2008). Semiosis, Dewey and difference: Implications for pragmatic philosophy of education. *Contemporary Pragmatism*, *5*(1), 147–162.

Stjernfelt, F. (2007). *Diagrammatology: An Investigation on the Borderlines of Phenomenology, Ontology and Semiotics*. Dordrecht: Springer.

Wittgenstein, L. (1967). *Philosophical Investigations*. Oxford: Blackwell.

1.2 Saussure and the Continental Tradition

Barthes, R. (1972). *Mythologies* (A. Lavers, Trans.). London: Paladin.

Barthes, R. (1977). The death of the author. In *Image, Music, Text* (S. Heath, Trans., pp. 142–148). London: Fontana.

Bouissac, P. (2004). Saussure's legacy in semiotics. In C. Sanders (Ed.), *The Cambridge Companion to Saussure* (pp. 240–260). Cambridge: Cambridge University Press.

Chomsky, N. (1955). *The Logical Structure of Linguistic Theory*. New York: Plenum.

Chomsky, N. (1972). *Language and Mind*. New York: Harcourt Brace Jovanovich.

Cixous, H. (1998). *Stigmata: Escaping Texts*. New York: Routledge.

Culler, J. (1977). *Saussure*. London: Fontana.

Deely, J. (1990). *Basics of Semiotics*. Bloomington: Indiana University Press.

Derrida, J. (1978). *Writing and Difference* (A. Bass, Trans.). Chicago: University of Chicago Press.

Derrida, J. (1987). *The Post Card: From Socrates to Freud and Beyond* (A. Bass, Trans.). Chicago: University of Chicago Press.

Derrida, J. (1993). *Aporias* (T. Dutoit, Trans.). Palo Alto, CA: Stanford University Press.

Derrida, J., & Attridge, D. (1992). *Acts of Literature*. New York: Routledge.

Falk, J. S. (2004). Saussure and American linguistics. In C. Sanders (Ed.), *The Cambridge Companion to Saussure* (pp. 107–123). Cambridge: Cambridge University Press.

Greimas, A. J. (1989). *The Social Sciences. A Semiotic View* (F. Collins & P. Perron, Trans.). Minneapolis: University of Minnesota Press.

Hutchings, S. C. (2004). The russian critique of Saussure. In C. Sanders (Ed.), *The Cambridge Companion to Saussure* (pp. 139–156). Cambridge: Cambridge University Press.

Jakobson, R. (1971–1985). *Selected Writings* (S. Rudy, Ed., Vols. 1–6). The Hague/Paris: Mouton.

Kristeva, J., & Moi, T. (1986). *The Kristeva Reader*. New York: Columbia University Press.

Lacan, J. (2006). *Écrits* (B. Fink, Trans.). New York: Norton.

Levinas, E. (1967). *Totality and Infinity: An Essay on Exteriority* (A. Lingis, Trans.). Pittsburgh: Dusquesne University Press.

Lévi-Strauss, C. (1969). *The Elementary Structures of Kinship*. London: Taylor and Francis.

Lyotard, J.-F. (1988). *The Differend: Phrases in Dispute* (G. V. D. Abbeele, Trans.). Minnesota: University of Minnesota Press.

Merleau-Ponty, M. (1964). *The Visible and the Invisible* (A. Lingis, Trans.). Evanston: Northwestern University Press.

Mounin, G. (1970). *Introduction à la Semiologie*. Paris: Minuit.

Ogden, C. K., & Richads, I. A. (1923). *The Meaning of Meaning*. New York: Harcourt Brace and World.

Popper, K. (1959). *The Logic of Scientific Discovery*. London: Hutchinson.

Proust, M. (2003). *In Search of Lost Time*. London: Penguin.

REFERENCES

Rousseau, J. J. (1762). *Émile* (B. Foxley, Trans.). Retrieved November 28, 2011, from http://www.gutenberg.org/ebooks/5427
Sartre, J.-P. (2000). *Nausea* (R. Baldick, Trans.). London: Penguin.
Saussure, F. de (1974). *Course in General Liguistics* (C. Bally & A. Sechehaye, Eds., W. Baskin, Trans.). London: Fontana.
Smollett, T. (1759). *The Life and Opinions of Tristram Shandy, Gentleman.* Retrieved November 28, 2011, from http://www.gutenberg.org/ebooks/1079
Ungar, S. & McGraw, B. R. (Eds.). (1989). *Signs in Culture: Roland Barthes Today.* Iowa: University of Iowa Press.
Voloshinov, V. (1973). *Marxism and the Philosophy of Language.* Cambridge, MA: Harvard University Press.
Wittgenstein, L. (1967). *Philosophical Investigations.* Oxford: Blackwell.

1.3 Wittgenstein and the Language Game as Bridging Concept

Ayer, A. (1959). *Logical Positivism.* New York: Free Press.
Blake, N., Smeyers, P., Smith, R., & Standish, P. (1998). *Thinking Again: Education After Postmodernism.* Westport, CT: Greenwood Press.
Conant, J. (2002). The method of the tractatus. In E. H. Reck (Ed.), *From Frege to Wittgenstein: Perspectives on Early Analytic Philosophy.* Oxford: Oxford University Press.
Deleuze, G., & Guattari, F. (1996). *What is Philosophy?* New York: Columbia.
Derrida, J. (1988). Afterword, *Limited Inc.* Evanston: Northwestern University Press.
Diamond, C. (1991). *The Realistic Spirit: Wittgenstein, Philosophy, and the Mind.* Bradford: Bradford Books.
Kuhn, T. (1962). *The Structure of Scientific Revolutions.* Chicago: University of Chicago Press.
Lyotard, J.-F. (1988). *The Differend: Phrases in Dispute* (G. V. D. Abbeele, Trans.). Minnesota: University of Minnesota Press.
Monk, R. (1991). *Ludwig Wittgenstein: The Duty of Genius.* New York: Vintage.
Lyotard, J.-F. (1986). *The Postmodern Condition: A Report on Knowledge.* Manchester: Manchester University Press.
Ostrow, M. B. (2002). *Wittgenstein's Tractatus, a Dialectical Interpretation.* Cambridge: Cambridge University Press.
Pincock, C. (2003). *Wittgenstein's Tractatus, a Dialectical Interpretation.* Review of Ostrow, M. B. *Notre Dame Philosophical Reviews.* Retrieved November 29, 2011, from http://ndpr.nd.edu/review.cfm?id=1174
Reid, L. (1998). Wittgenstein's ladder: The tractatus and nonsense. *Philosophical Investigations, 21*(2), 97–151.
Richter, D. J. (2004). Ludwig Wittgenstein (1889–1951). *Internet Encyclopedia of Philosophy.* Retrieved October 17, 2010, from http://www.iep.utm.edu/wittgens/#H7
Wittgenstein, L. (2001). *Tractatus Logico-Philosophicus.* London: Routledge.
Wittgenstein, L. (1967). *Philosophical Investigations.* Oxford: Blackwell.

1.4 Semiosis as fundamental process: three further sets of considerations

Bai, H., & Cohen, A. (2007). Breathing qi, following dao: Transforming this violence-ridden world. In C. Eppert & H. Wang (Eds.), *Cross-cultural Studies in Curriculum: Eastern Thought and Educational Insights* (pp. 35–54). Mahweh, NJ: Lawrence Earlbaum.
Daniels, H. (2010). *Vygotsky and Pedagogy.* London: Routledge.
Dawkins, R. (1976). *The Selfish Gene.* Oxford: Oxford University Press.

Deely, J. (1990). *Basics of Semiotics*. Bloomington: Indiana University Press.

Derrida, J. (1992). *Acts of Literature*. New York: Routledge.

Geroch, R. (1981). *General Relativity from A to B*. Chicago: University of Chicago Press.

Hartshorne, C. (1991). *The Philosophy of Charles Hartshorne*. La Salle, IL: Open Court.

Maran, T. (2006). Where do your borders lie? Reflections on the semiotical ethics of nature. In C. Gersdort & S. Mayer (Eds.), *Nature in Literary and Cultural Studies. Transatlantic Conversations on Ecocriticism*.

McDowell, J. (1996). *Mind and World*. Cambridge, MA: Harvard University Press.

Pattee, H. H. (1982). Cell psychology: An evolutionary approach to the symbol-matter problem. *Cognition and Brain Theory, 5*, 325–341.

Pattee, H. H. (1995). Evolving self-reference: Matter, symbols and semantic closure. *Communication and Cognition – Artificial Intelligence, 12*, 9–28.

Rae, A. I. M. (2005). *Quantum Physics: A Beginner's Guide*. London: Oneworld.

Rescher, N. (2008). Process philosophy. *Stanford Encyclopedia of Philosophy*. Retrieved November 30, 2011, from http://plato.stanford.edu/entries/process-philosophy/

Sebeok, T. A. (1992). 'Tell me, where is fancy bred?': The biosemiotic self. In T. A. Sebeok & J. Umiker-Sebeok (Eds.), *Biosemiotics: The Semiotic Web* (pp. 333–343). Berlin: Mouton de Gruyter.

Sharov, A. (1998). *What is Biosemiotics?* Retrieved August 18, 2010, from http://home.comcast.net/~sharov/biosem/geninfo.html

Smith, R. D. (2011, April). Re-reading Plato: The slow cure for knowledge. *Annual Conference of the Philosophy of Education Society of Great Britain*. Oxford.

Stables, A. (2005). *Living and Learning as Semiotic Engagement*. Lewiston, NY/Lampeter: Mellen Press.

Stjernfelt, F. (2007). *Diagrammatology: An Investigation on the Borderlines of Phenomenology, Ontology and Semiotics*. Dordrecht: Springer.

Uexküll, J. von (1957). A stroll through the worlds of animals and men. In C. H. Schiller (Ed. and Trans.). *Instinctive Behavior: The Development of a Modern Concept* (pp. 5–80). New York: International Universities Press.

Whitehead, A. N. (1929a). *Process and Reality: An Essay in Cosmology*. New York: Macmillan.

Whitehead, A. N. (1929b). *The Aims of Education and Other Essays*. New York: Free Press.

Whitehead, A. N., & Russell, B. (1910, 1912, 1913). *Principia Mathematica* (3 Vols.). Cambridge: Cambridge University Press.

Wittgenstein, L. (2001). *Tractatus Logico-Philosophicus*. London: Routledge.

Wittgenstein, L. (1967). *Philosophical Investigations*. Oxford: Blackwell.

CHAPTER 2

Moving in Time: Consciousness and Reason

2.1: Physical Transcendent Presence: The Now and Then Dimensions

Dewey, J. (1896). The reflex arc concept in psychology. *Psychological Review, 3*, 357–370. Retrieved November 14, 2006, from http://spartan.ac.brocku.ca/~lward/Dewey/Dewey_1896.html

Finkielkraut, A. (2000). *In the Name of Humanity* (J. Friedlander, Trans.). New York: Columbia University Press.

Giddens, A. (1991). *Modernity and Self-Identity in the Late Modern Age*. Palo Alto, CA: Stanford University Press.

Habermas, J. (1984/1987). *Theory of Communicative Action*. Cambridge: Polity.

Harré, R. (1983). *Personal Being: A Theory for Individual Psychology*. Oxford: Blackwell.

REFERENCES

Harré, R. (1998). *The Singular Self.* London: Sage.
Hume, D. (1748). *Enquiry Concerning Human Understanding.* Retrieved November 1, 2011, from http://www.earlymoderntexts.com
Hung, R. (2009, December 3–6). Caring about strangers: A lingsian reading of Kafka's metamorphosis. *38th Annual Conference of the Philosophy of Education Society of Australasia.* Hawaii, USA. Retrieved November 1, 2011, from www2.hawaii.edu/~pesaconf/zpdfs/34hung.pdf
Kukathas, C. (1989). *Hayek and Modern Liberalism.* Oxford: Oxford University Press.
Lingis, A. (1994). *The Community of Those Who have Nothing in Common.* Bloomington: Indiana University Press.
Lyotard, J.-F. (1986). *The Postmodern Condition: A Report on Knowledge.* Manchester: Manchester University Press.
Lyotard, J.-F. (1996). *The Differend: Phrases in Dispute.* Minnesota: University of Minnesota Press.
Rorty, R. (1993). Human rights, rationality and sentimentality. In S. Shite & S. Hurley (Eds.), *On Human Rights: The Oxford Amnesty Lectures 1993* (pp. 111–134). New York: Basic.
Russell, J. (2009). Review of stables, A. *Childhood and the Philosophy of Education: An Anti-Aristotelian Perspective, Environmental Education Research, 15*(5), 621–624.
Stables, A. (2005). *Living and Learning as Semiotic Engagement: A New Theory of Education.* Lewiston, NY/ Lampeter: Mellen Press.
Stables, A. (2008a). Can humanism be an environmentalism? *The Trumpeter: Journal of Ecosophy, 24*(3), 86–95. Published online at http://trumpeter.athabscau.ca
Stables, A. (2008b). *Childhood and the Philosophy of Education: An anti-Aristotelian Perspective.* London: Continuum.
Stables, A. (2005). *Living and Learning as Semiotic Engagement: A New Theory of Education.* Lewiston, NY/ Lampeter: Mellen Press.
Young, R. (1992). *Critical Theory and Classroom Talk.* Clevedon: Multilingual Matters.
Wittgenstein, L. (1967). *Philosophical Investigations.* Oxford: Blackwell.

2.2 Semiosis and (the myth of?) Reason

Descartes, R. (2010). *Dexcartes' Meditations* (D. B. Manley & C. S. Taylor, Eds.). Retrieved November 3, 2011, from http://www.wright.edu/cola/descartes/
Everett, D. L. (2008). *Don't Sleep, There are Snakes: Life and Language in the Amazonian Jungle.* London: Profile.
Frankena, W. K. (1973). Education. In *Dictionary of the History of Ideas: Studies of Selected Pivotal Ideas* (P. P. Wiener, Ed., Vol. 2). New York: Charles Scribner's Sons.
Moore, G. E. (1925). A defence of common sense. In *Contemporary British Philosophy* (J. H. Muirhead, Ed.). London: Allen and Unwin.
Nagel, T. (1986). *The View from Nowhere.* Oxford: Oxford University Press.
Peters, R. S. (1967). *Concept of Education.* London: Routledge and Kegan Paul.
Popper, K. (1959). *The Logic of Scientific Discovery.* London: Hutchinson.
Rorty, R. (1981). *Philosophy and the Mirror of Nature.* Princeton, NJ: Princeton University Press.
Stables, A. (2006). Review of The Aims of Education Revisited (J. White, Ed.). *Journal of Curriculum Studies.*
Wittgenstein, L. (2001). *Tractatus Logico-Philosophicus.* London: Routledge.

CHAPTER 3

Thens Within Now

3.1 Humanity as Aspiration

Derrida, J. (1978). Structure, sign, and play in the discourse of the human sciences. *Writing and Difference* (A. Bass, Trans., pp. 278–294). London: Routledge.

Dewey, J. (1916). *Democracy and Education.* Retrieved November 5, 2011, from www.ilt.columbia.edu/publications/dewey.html

Guenther, L. (2009). Who follows whom? Derrida, animals and women. *Derrida Today, 2*(2), 151–165.

Maran, T. (2006). Where do your borders lie? Reflections on the semiotical ethics of nature. In C. Gersdorf & S. Mayer (Eds.), *Beyond Wild Nature: Transatlantic Perspectives on Ecocriticism* (in the series 'Nature, Culture and Literature'). Amsterdam: Rodopi.

Mintz, S. (2004). *Huck's Raft: A History of American Childhood.* Cambridge, MA: Harvard University Press.

More, M. (1990). *Transhumanism: Towards a Futurist Philosophy.* Retrieved November 5, 2011, from http://www.maxmore.com/transhum.htm

Pattee, H. H. (1995). Evolving self-reference: Matter, symbols, and semantic closure. *Communication and Cognition - Artificial Intelligence, 12,* 9–28.

Stables, A. (2005). *Living and Learning as Semiotic Engagement.* Lewiston, NY/Lampeter: Mellen.

Stables, A. (2008). *Childhood and the Philosophy of Education: An anti-Aristotelian Perspective.* London: Continuum.

Than, K. (2010). Neanderthals, humans interbred – first solid DNA evidence. *National Geographic Daily News.* Retrieved November 4, 2011, from http://news.nationalgeographic.com

3.2 From Literacy to Semiosy: Learning as Semiosic Development

Austin, J. L. (1962). *How To Do Things With Words.* Cambridge, MA: Harvard University Press.

Bauman, Z. (2000). *Liquid Modernity.* Cambridge: Polity.

Beck, U. (1992). *Risk Society: Towards a New Modernity.* London: Sage.

Biesta, G. (2006). *Beyond Learning: Democratic Education for a Human Future.* Herndon, VA: Paradigm.

Bowers, C. A. (1974). *Cultural Literacy for Freedom: An Existential Perspective on Teaching, Curriculum and School Policy.* Eugene, OR: Elan.

Freire, P. (1972). *Pedagogy of the Oppressed.* London: Penguin.

Carnap, R. (1959). The elimination of metaphysics through logical analysis of language. In A. J. Ayer (Ed.), *Logical Positivism* (pp. 60–81). Glencoe, Ill.: The Free Press.

Derrida, J. (1976). *Of Grammatology.* Baltimore: Johns Hopkins University Press.

Giddens, A. (1991). *Modernity and Self-Identity in the Late Modern Age.* Palo Alto, CA: Stanford University Press.

Gough, S., & Stables, A. (2012 – in press). Interpretation as adaptation: Education for survival in uncertain times. *Curriculum Inquiry.*

Gunaratana, B. (2011). Mindfulness. In *A Guide to Buddhism*. Shambhala Publications. Retrieved November 8, 2011, from http://www.shambhala.com/html/learn/features/buddhism/basics/mindfulness.cfm

Harré, R. (1998). *The Singular Self*. London: Sage.

Harré, R. (1983). *Personal Being: A Theory for Individual Psychology*. Oxford: Blackwell.

Hirsch, J. D. (1987). *Cultural Literacy: What Every American Needs to Know*. Boston: Houghton Mifflin.

Lyotard, J.-F. (1986). *The Postmodern Condition: A Report on Knowledge*. Manchester: Manchester University Press.

Pollard, A., & Filer, A. (1999). *The Social World of Pupil Career: Strategic Biographies through Primary School*. London: Continuum.

Postman, N. (1994). *The Disappearance of Childhood*. New York: Vintage.

Rich, E. (2011a.). Exploring the relationship between pedagogy and physical cultural studies: The case of new health imperatives in schools. *Sociology of Sport Journal, 28*, 64–84.

Rich, E. (2011b). 'I see her being obesed!': Public pedagogy, reality media and the obesity crisis. '*Health': An Interdisciplinary Journal for the Social Study of Health, Illness and Medicine, 15*(1), 3–121.

Ross, M., Radnor, H., Mitchell, S., & Brierton, C. (1993). *Assessing Achievement in the Arts*. Buckingham: Open University Press.

Saussure, F. de (1916/1983). *Course in General Linguistics* (C. Bally & A. Sechehaye, Eds., R. Harris, Trans.). La Salle, IL: Open Court.

Rutten, K., Mottart, A., & Soetaert, R. (2010). The rhetorical construction of the nation in education. The case of Flanders. *Journal of Curriculum Studies, 42*(6), 775–790.

Stables, A. (1998). Environmental literacy: Functional, cultural, critical. The case of the SCAA guidelines. *Environmental Education Research, 4*(2), 155–164.

Stables, A. (2003a). *Education for Diversity*. Aldershot: Ashgate.

Stables, A. (2003b). School as imagined community in discursive space: A perspective on the school effectiveness debate. *British Educational Research Journal, 29*(6), 895–902.

Stables, A., Jones, S., & Morgan, C. (1999). Educating for significant events: The application of Harré's social reality matrix across the lower secondary school curriculum. *Journal of Curriculum Studies, 31*(4), 449–461.

Tassie, N. (2010). An exploration of meanings attributed to a dyslexic diagnosis. *Critical Social Thinking: Policy and Practice, 2*, 109–124. Retrieved November 8, 2011, from http://www.ucc.ie/en/appsoc/research/cstj/CSTJournalVolume22010/Theme3Disability/Nicola-Tassie.pdf

Vygotsky, L. (1962). *Thought and Language*. Cambridge, MA: MIT Press.

Vygotsky, L. (1978). *Mind in Society: The Development of Higher Psychological Processes*. Cambridge, MA: Harvard University Press.

Wiener, N. (1948). *Cybernetics: Or Control and Communication in the Animal and the Machin*. Paris: Hermann & Cie / Cambridge, MA: MIT Press.

Williams, J. D., & Snipper, G. C. (1990). *Literacy and Bilingualism*. New York: Longman.

3.3 What do schools do?

Arendt, H. (1958). *The Human Condition*. Chicago: University of Chicago Press.

Ball, S. J. (2003). *Class Strategies and the Education Market: The Middle Classes and Social Advantage*. London: Routledge.

Barnes, D., & Sheeran, Y. (1991). *School Writing*. Buckingham: Open University Press.

Barrow, R. (2005). On the duty of not taking offence. *Journal of Moral Education, 34*(3), 265–275.

Biesta, G. (2006). *Beyond Learning: Democratic Education for a Human Future.* Herndon, VA: Paradigm.

Bourdieu, P. (1986). The forms of capital (R. Nice, Trans.). In E. Richardson (Ed.), *Handbook of Theory of Research for the Sociology of Education* (pp. 241–258). San Fransisco: Greenwood.

Cavell, S. (1992). *The Senses of Walden.* Chicago: Chicago University Press.

CDC (Centers for Disease Control and Prevention). (undated). *Handwashing: Clean Hands Save Lives.* Retrieved November 9, 2011, from http://www.cdc.gov/handwashing

Cohen, J. (2009, April 27). Do surgical masks stop Swine Flu? Probably not. *Slate.* Retrieved November 9, 2011, from www.slate.com/articles

Hegel, G. W. F. (1977). *Phenomenology of Spirit* (A. V. Miller, Trans.). Oxford: Clarendon.

Hodgson, N. (2010). What does it mean to be an educated person? *Journal of Philosophy of Education, 44*(1), 109–123.

Kristeva, J. (1982). *The Powers of Horror: An Essay on Abjection* (L. S. Roudiez, Trans.). New York: Columbia University Press.

Magnusson, S. (2010). *Life of Pee: The Story of How Urine Got Everywhere.* London: Aurum.

Murakami, K., Stables, A., & McIntosh, S. (2012). *Conceptions of Effort Among Year 8 Students, their Teachers and Parents within a School in Somerset.* Report to the British Academy.

Saito, N., & Standish, P. (2010). Crossing borders within: Stanley Cavell and the politics of interpretation. *Educational Theory, 60*(4), 419–433.

Stables, A. (2005). *Living and Learning as Semiotic Engagement: A New Theory of Education.* Lewiston, NY/Lampeter: Mellen Press.

Tubbs, N. (undated). Hegel and the philosophy of education. In *Encyclopedia of Philosophy of Education.* Retrieved November 9, 2011, from http://www.ffst.hr/ENCYCLOPEDIA

Wentzel, K. R., & Caldwell, K. (1997). Friendships, peer acceptance and group membership: Relations to academic achievement in middle school. *Child Development, 68*(6), 1198–1209.

Whitehead, A. N. (1916). *The Aims of Education.* Retrieved November 9, 2011, from https://webspace.utexas.edu/hcleaver/www/330T/350kPEEwhiteheadaimstable.pdf

Willis, P. (1978). *Learning to Labour.* Aldershot: Ashgate.

Wittgenstein, L. (1975). *On Certainty* (G. E. M. Anscombe & G. H. von Wright, Eds., D. Paul & G. E. M. Anscombe, Trans.). Oxford: Blackwell.

Wood, A. W. (1998). Hegel on education. In A. O. Rorty (Ed.), *Philosophers on Education: New Historical Perspectives* (pp. 300–317). London: Routledge.

Young, M. (2009). What are schools for? In H. Daniels, H. Lauder & J. Porter (Eds.), *Knowledge, Values and Educational Policy.* London: Routledge.

CHAPTER 4

Be(com)ing Responsible: Humans, Others and Ethics

4.1 Towards Human Response-Ability

Anderson, B. (1983). *Imagined Communities: Reflections on the Origin and Spread of Nationalism.* London: Verso.

Deely, J. (1990). *Basics of Semiotics.* Bloomington: Indiana University Press. Retrieved February 26, 2009, from http://carbon.cudenver.edu/~mryder/deely/basics

Deleuze, G., & Guattari, F. (1987). *A Thousand Plateaus: Capitalism and Schizophrenia.* Minneapolis: University of Minnesota Press.

Dewey, J. (1916). *Democracy and Education.* Toronto: Macmillan.

REFERENCES

Dewey, J. (1925). *Experience and Nature.* La Salle, Ill.: Open Court.
Finkielkraut, A. (2000). *In the Name of Humanity* (J. Friedlander, Trans.). New York: Columbia University Press.
Hobbes, T. (2009). *Leviathan, Project Gutenberg e-book.* Retrieved November 10, 2011, from www.gutenberg.org
Houser, N., et al. (1998). *The Essential Peirce: Selected Philosophical Writings* (Vol. 2). Bloomington: Indiana University Press.
Kant, I. (1998). *Groundwork of the Metaphysics of Morals* (P. Guyer, Ed.). Lantham, MD: Rowman and Littlefield.
Kant, I. (2000). *Critique of Pure Reason.* Cambridge: Cambridge University Press.
Levinas, E. (1967). *Totality and Infinity: An Essay on Exteriority* (A. Lingis, Trans.). Pittsburgh: Dusquesne University Press.
Locke, J. (first published 1692). *Some Thoughts Concerning Education.* (Modern History Sourcebook). Retrieved June 20, 2008, from www.fordham.edu/halsall/mod/1692locke-education.html
Maran, T. (2006). Where do your borders lie? Reflections on the semiotical ethics of nature. In C. Gersdorf & S. Mayer (Eds.), *Beyond Wild Nature: Transatlantic Perspectives on Ecocriticism* (in the series 'Nature, Culture and Literature'). Amsterdam: Rodopi.
McDowell, J. (1996). *Mind and World.* Cambridge, MA: Harvard University Press.
Rawls, J. (1993). *Political Liberalism.* New York: Columbia University Press.
Rousseau, J.-J. (1991). *Émile, Or On Education.* London: Penguin.
Scharp, K. & Brandom, R. B. (Eds.). (2007). *In the Space of Reasons: Selected Essays of Wilfrid Sellars.* Cambridge, MA: Harvard University Press.
Sebeok, T. A. (2001). *Global Semiotics.* Bloomington, IN: Indiana University Press.
Stables, A. (2008). Semiosis, Dewey and difference: Implications for pragmatic philosophy of education. *Contemporary Pragmatism, 5*(1), 147–162.
Stables, A. (2003). School as imagined community in discursive space: A perspective on the school effectiveness debate. *British Educational Research Journal, 29*(6), 895–902.
Stables, A. (2004). Responsibility beyond rationality: The case for rhizomatic consequentialism. *International Journal of Children's Spirituality, 9*(2), 219–225.
Stables, A. (2008). *Childhood and the Philosophy of Education: An Anti-Aristotelian Perspective.* London: Continuum.
Storme, T., & Vlieghe, J. (2011). The experience of childhood and the learning society: Allowing the child to be philosophical and philosophy to be childish. *Journal of Philosophy of Education, 45*(2), 183–198.

4.2 Post-Humanist Ethics: Response-ability beyond the Human

Berger, P. L., & Luckmann, T. (1966). *The Social Construction of Reality: A Treatise in the Sociology of Knowledge.* Garden City, NY: Anchor.
Biesta, G. (2006). *Beyond Learning. Democratic Education for a Human Future.* Boulder, CO: Paradigm.
Bonnett, M. (2004). *Retrieving Nature: Education for a Post-humanist Age.* Oxford: Blackwell.
Bostrom, N. (2005). In defence of posthuman dignity. *Bioethics, 19*(3), 202–214.
Cooper, D. E., & James, S. P. (2005). *Buddhism, Virtue and Environment.* Aldershot: Ashgate.
Deely, J. (1990). *Basics of Semiotics.* Bloomington: Indiana University Press.
Derrida, J. (1995). *The Gift of Death* (D. Wills, Trans.). Chicago: University of Chicago Press.
Durkheim, E. (1973). *Moral Education: A Study in the Theory and Application of the Sociology of Education.* New York: Free Press.

Finkielkraut, A. (2000). *In the Name of Humanity* (J. Friedlander, Trans). New York: Columbia University Press.

Hayles, N. K. (1999). *Now We Became Posthuman: Virtual Bodies in Cybernetics, Literature and Informatics.* Chicago: University of Chicago Press.

Hobbes, T. (1651). *Leviathan.* Retrieved November 16, 2011, from http://oregonstate.edu/instruct/phl302/texts/hobbes/leviathan-c.html

Horsthemke, K. (2010). *The Moral Status and Rights of Animals.* London: Porcupine.

Huckle, J. (2010). ESD and the current crisis of capitalism: Teaching beyond green new deals. *Journal of Education for Sustainable Development, 4*(1), 135–142.

Jansson, A.-M., Hammer, M., Folke, C., & Costanza, R. (Eds.). (1994). *Investing in Natural Capital: The Ecological Economics Approach to Sustainability.* Washington, DC: Island.

Levinas, E. (1967). *Totality and Infinity: An Essay on Exteriority* (A. Lingis, Trans.). Pittsburgh: Dusquesne University Press.

Locke, J. (1690). *Two Treatises of Government.* Retrieved November 16, 2011, from http://oregonstate.edu/instruct/phl302/texts/locke/locke2/locke2nd-a.html

Locke, J. (1692). *Some Thoughts Concerning Education.* Retrieved November 16, 2011, from http://www.bartleby.com/37/1/1.html

Næss, A. (1973). The shallow and the deep, Long-Range ecology movement. *Inquiry, 16,* 95–100.

Petrilli, S. (2010). *Sign Crossroads in Global Perspective: Semioethics and Responsibility.* New Brunswick/London: Transaction.

Roden, D. (undated). *Posthumanism and Instrumental Eliminativism.* Retrieved November 15, 2011, from
http://open.academia.edu/DavidRoden/Papers/399801/Posthumanism_and_Instrumental_Eliminativism

Rousseau, J.-J. (1762). *The Social Contract* (G. D. H. Cole, Trans.). Retrieved November 16, 2011, from http://www.constitution.org/jjr/socon.htm

Stables, A. (2008). Semiosis, Dewey and difference: Implications for pragmatic philosophy of education. *Contemporary Pragmatism, 5*(1), 147–162.

Stables, A. (2010). The song of the earth: A pragmatic rejoinder. *Educational Philosophy and Theory, 42*(7), 796–807.

Stables, A., & Scott, W. (2001). Post-Humanist liberal pragmatism? Environmental education out of modernity. *Journal of Philosophy of Education, 35*(2), 269–280.

Stibbe, A. (2005). Ecology and the magic of economics. *Language and Ecology, 1,* 4. www.ecoling.net/journal.html

Vygotsky, L. S. (1978). *Mind in Society: The Development of Higher Psychological Processes.* Cambridge, MA: Harvard University Press.

CHAPTER 5

Promoting Human Progress

5.1 Relative Safety? Differing Conceptions of the Good

Aristotle (350 BCE). *Nicomachean Ethics* (W. D. Ross, Trans.). *The Internet Classics Archive.* Retrieved November 17, 2011, from http://classics.mit.edu/Aristotle/nicomachaen.html

Habermas, J. (1984/1987). *Theory of Communicative Action* (Vols. 1, 2, T. McCarthy, Trans.). Cambridge: Polity.

REFERENCES

Harré, R. (1984). *Personal Being: A Theory for Individual Psychology.* Cambridge, MA: Harvard University Press.
Hume, D. (2009). *An Enquiry Concerning Human Understanding.* Retrieved November 17, 2011, from http://ebooks.adelaide.edu.au/h/hume/david/h92e/
Kant, I. (1998). *Groundwork of the Metaphysics of Morals* (P. Guyer, Ed.). Lantham, MD: Rowman and Littlefield.
Locke, J. (1692). *Some Thoughts Concerning Education.* Retrieved November 16, 2011, from http://www.bartleby.com/37/1/1.html
Lyotard, J.-F. (1984). *The Postmodern Condition: A Report on Knowledge* (G. Bennington & B. Massumi, Trans.). Minneapolis: University of Minnesota Press.
Lyotard, J.-F. (1988). *The Differend: Phrases in Dispute* (G. Van den Abbeele, Trans.). Minneapolis: University of Minnesota Press.
Miller, A. B. (1974). Aristotle on habit (εθō) and character (ηθō): Implications for the rhetoric. *Speech Monographs, 41*(4), 309–316.
Nietzsche, L. (2005). *Thus Spoke Zarathustra* (G. Parkes, Trans.). Oxford: Oxford World's Classics.
Rawls, J. (1993). *Political Liberalism.* New York: Columbia University Press.
Rorty, R. (1989). *Contingency, Irony, and Solidarity.* Cambridge: Cambridge University Press.
Saito, N. (2011). Quiet Desperation, secret melancholy: Polemos and passion in citizenship education. *Ethics and Education, 6*(1), 3–14, .3.
Sartre, J.-P. (1993). *Being and Nothingness* (H. E. Barnes, Trans.). New York: Washington Square.
Siegel, H. (1987). *Relativism Refuted: A Critique of Contemporary Epistemological Relativism.* Dordrecht: D. Reidel.
Stables, A. (1996). *Subjects of Choice.* London: Cassell.
Straughan, R. (1988). *Can We Teach Children to be Good? Basic Issues in Moral, Personal and Social Education.* Buckingham: Open University Press.
Wikeley, F., & Stables, A. (1999). Changes in school students' approaches to subject option choices: A study of pupils in the West of England in 1984 and 1996. *Educational Research, 41*(3), 287–299.
Wittgenstein, L. (1967). *Philosophical Investigations.* Oxford: Blackwell.

5.2 On Human Progress: knowledge, numbers and time

Biesta, G. (2006). *Beyond Learning. Democratic Education for a Human Future.* Boulder, CO: Paradigm.
Bourdieu, P. (1986). The forms of capital (R. Nice, Trans.). In E. Richardson (Ed.), *Handbook of Theory of Research for the Sociology of Education* (pp. 241–258). San Fransisco: Greenwood.
Gooding, D. (2006). From phenomenology to field theory: Faraday's visual reasoning. *Perspectives on Science, 14*(1), 40–65.
Kant, I. (1781/2003). *Critique of Pure Reason.* The Project Gutenberg e-text produced by Aldarondo, C. A. (J. M. D. Meiklejohn, Trans.). Retrieved November 18, 2011, from http://www.gutenberg.org/cache/epub/4280/pg4280.html
Plato (360BCE). *The Republic* (B. Jowett, Trans.). Available online at *The Internet Classics Archive.* Retrieved November 18, 2011, from www.classics.mit.edu/Plato/republic.html
Stables, A. (2010). Making meaning and using natural resources: Education and sustainability. *Journal of Philosophy of Education, 44*(1), 137–152.
Stables, A. (2005). *Living and Learning as Semiotic Engagement: A New Theory of Education.* Lewiston, NY/ Lampeter: Mellen Press.
Stables, A. (2009). Should the debate about compulsory education be re-opened? (with response from Paul Smeyers). In *2009 Philosophy of Education* (p. 153). Urbana, IL: Philosophy of Education Society, U.S.

Lightning Source UK Ltd.
Milton Keynes UK
UKOW04f2101201013

219408UK00005B/161/P

9 789460 919954